T0389587

Games and Education

Gaming Ecologies and Pedagogies Series

The titles published in this series are listed at *brill.com/geps*

Games and Education

Designs in and for Learning

Edited by

Hans Christian Arnseth, Thorkild Hanghøj,
Thomas Duus Henriksen, Morten Misfeldt,
Robert Ramberg and Staffan Selander

Foreword by

James Paul Gee

BRILL

SENSE

LEIDEN | BOSTON

All chapters in this book have undergone peer review.

Library of Congress Cataloging-in-Publication Data

Names: Arnseth, Hans-Christian, editor.
Title: Games and education : designs in and for learning / edited by Hans
  Christian Arnseth, Thorkild Hanghoj, Thomas Duus Henriksen, Morten
  Misfeldt, Robert Ramberg, and Staffan Selander.
Description: Boston : Brill Sense, [2019] | Series: Gaming ecologies and
  pedagogies series | Includes bibliographical references and index. |
Identifiers: LCCN 2018039949 (print) | LCCN 2018047184 (ebook) | ISBN
  9789004388826 (E-Book) | ISBN 9789004388802 (pbk. : alk. paper) | ISBN
  9789004388819 (hardback : alk. paper)
Subjects: LCSH: Video games in education. | Educational change.
Classification: LCC LB1028.75 (ebook) | LCC LB1028.75 .G35 2018 (print) | DDC
  794.8--dc23
LC record available at https://lccn.loc.gov/2018039949

ISSN 2589-9880
ISBN 978-90-04-38880-2 (paperback)
ISBN 978-90-04-38881-9 (hardback)
ISBN 978-90-04-38882-6 (e-book)

CONTENTS

JAMES PAUL GEE

FOREWORD

Like other creatures on earth, we humans are *types* of beings. We act, think, learn, and flourish better in some ways than in others (Sapolsky, 2017). Humans are great at face recognition; it is one of our super-powers. Calculating large sums in our heads is not, for most of us, a power at all, let alone a super one. And we humans simply cannot fly unaided, no matter what anyone demands of us.

Other animals cannot create institutions that force them into ways of being that go against their "nature". If cats could pass laws outlawing meat eating—and they proceeded to do so—they would all starve. They are not "made" (in terms of their internal structures) for a vegetarian diet. Humans, however, can and do pass laws and design institutions that demand that humans do, be, and become what they cannot. Traditional schools are one good example.

Based on research from a variety of different areas, here is how the human mind actually works (Gee, 2017): Humans have embodied experiences in the world. If they care enough (emotionally) about these experiences, they store them in their long-term memories (LTMs). They connect and integrate the elements of their memories into a large resource base. Then they use this resource base—mixing and matching elements of their memories—to do the following (Seligman, Railton, Baumeister, & Sripada, 2016):

1. *Anticipate.* In contexts of acting in the world, humans use past experiences to anticipate what might happen in the near future and get ready to respond to it.
2. *Plan.* Humans use their past experiences to plan for future action by role-playing scenarios in their mind so they can "think" before they "act" and make good choices.
3. *Imagination.* Humans use their past experiences (mixed and remixed) to imagine, hope, and create.
4. *Sense Making.* Humans use their past experiences to make sense of what has happened, is happening, or might happen to themselves and to the world around them.

Here are two things humans are quite poor at: recall and truth. Humans change their memories as they use them to engage in the four tasks above. When they use memories, they mix, match, construct, and reconstruct elements of these memories. Since they change their memories through use, humans are, for instance, very bad at giving eye-witness testimony, as a great deal of research clearly shows

(Loftus, 1976). In the sense of being a veridical record of the past, humans do not actually have memory. In humans, memory is future oriented, not past oriented.

The human mind is made in such a way that only a very small part of the processing the brain does—and the decisions it makes (and why) about how to feel, what to think and believe, and how to act—are open to consciousness and reflection (Gazzaniga, 1988). Thus, our unaided views about ourselves and others are often wrong. However, it turns out that, in any case, humans are tropic to sense making—to believing that things make sense, happen for a (good) reason, and are meaningful—and not to unvarnished truth or "facts" out of the context of meaning, sense-making, mattering, and hope.

Now what do we *get* in traditional schooling? Facts and recall. What do humans *need*: to learn how to use to use our experiences in the world (and media) to make good choices and good futures; to anticipate, plan, imagine, and make sense in ways that allow us to flourish with each other in a flourishing world (Schwartz & Arena, 2013). School is a vegetarian diet for carnivores.

Now, unlike other animals, humans can greatly expand what they can experience in the world by using tools (that allow them to see things they cannot see unaided) and media (that allow them to experience things they cannot do in real life). These is exactly what science and art are for, though rarely is science used in school this way. Rather than being a new way of seeing and experiencing the world, science in school is too often the facts and just the facts. And, at least in the United States, we don't much bother with art any more at all in school. Furthermore, since humans, are tropic to meaning and not truth, the truths of science and art must be placed into patterns of meaning and hope.

Humans learn from experience and use that experience for the tasks we have discussed. However, humans do not learn well from just any old experience (Gee, 2013). They learn best when they are in an experience where they have an action to take or a problem to solve; where they care affectively (emotionally) about the outcome (this usually means that they feel something important to them is "at stake"); and where someone or something helps them to know when and how to pay attention in the experience (which is too replete with details, especially for "newbies") to explore and try things and to accomplish their goals (and persist past failure). This last feature (managing attention) means that people need good "teachers" whether these are people or smart tools.

Now, what has this all to do with video games? Video games are a technology that can offer us just the sorts of experiences that are best suited for human learning and development. They focus on problem solving. They help players persist past failure. They create caring (mattering, making something "at stake"). They order problems in good ways (level design) and mentor players (through good game design) to manage their attention; use feedback fruitfully; and learn to solve problems often in multiple ways. They offer players tools that allow them to see and experience the world in new ways (for example, the portal gun in *Portal* allows players to see new affordances for action even in the real world).

Game play in good games precisely makes players use past experiences (in and out of the game) to anticipate, test, choose, create, imagine, and plan, just as human experiences are meant to be used by humans as they are and not as school imagines them. In the end, they learn to be better problem solvers and better choosers, just what we need in a world faced with many complex systems running out of control thanks, in large part, to human stupidity on the part of people nearly all of whom have gone to school (Gee, 2013).

Games, however, will not do good all these things by themselves. Like any powerful technology they can be used for good, bad, or trivia. Like other technologies, games supplement and enhance capacities that are already in the setting into which they are placed (like, for example, the ability to see failure as a form or learning), otherwise we need to curate these capacities, not just trust they will arise (Toyama, 2015).

Games, even in the entertainment industry, reach their true learning heights, when players move beyond unreflective play to think like designers and join with others in affinity spaces (Gee, 2017) to discuss strategy; to create new tools to enhance playing and understanding a game; and to create new levels or even new games ("modding"). This "transfer" (moving between the game and a critical, reflective, design-centric social group) does not happen all by itself. It happens socially and with mentoring.

The chapters in this book are among the earliest explorations of this new technology for "teaching" humans (in and out of school) as they actually are, as they live in the world, and as they will need to be to change the world.

REFERENCES

Gazzaniga, M. S. (1988). *Mind matters: How mind and brain interact to create our conscious lives.* Boston: Houghton Mifflin.

Gee, J. P. (2013). *The anti-education era: Creating smarter students through digital media.* New York: Palgrave/Macmillan.

Gee, J. P. (2017). *Teaching, Learning, Literacy in Our High-Risk High-Tech World: A Framework for Becoming Human.* New York: Teachers College Press.

Loftus, E. F. (1976). *Memory: Surprising new insights into how we remember and how we forget.* Lanham, MD: Rowman & Littlefield.

Sapolsky, R. M. (2017). *Behave: The biology of humans at our best and worst.* New York: Penguin.

Schwartz, D. L. & Arena D. (2013). *Measuring what matters most: Choice-based assessments for the digital age.* Cambridge, MA: MIT Press.

Seligman, E. P. M., Railton, P., Baumeister, R. F., & Sripada, C. (2016). *Homo prospectus.* New York: Oxford University Press.

Toyama, K. (2015). *Geek heresy: Rescuing social change from the cult of technology.* New York: Public Affairs.

James Paul Gee
Mary Lou Fulton Presidential Professor of Literacy Studies
Regents' Professor
Arizona State University

PREFACE

This anthology is the result of a joint PhD-course on games and learning. This course was a collaboration between the University of Oslo in Norway, Stockholm University in Sweden and Aalborg University in Denmark. During the course PhD-students and senior researchers from these universities took part in three seminars across universities. For each meeting we also invited international and local experts to give talks. At the time of this PhD-course the use of games in education still was a hot topic in the educational sciences. Now, trends have perhaps shifted more towards facilitating 21st century skills in makerspaces and through coding. Nevertheless, we believe the contributions in this book represents nuanced and context sensitive approaches to studying games in education, and the contributions do not fall prey to the temptation to represent games as an easy solution to make learning more engaging and relevant to students. Even though the road towards publication has been long and winding and despite the complexities involved when we need to coordinate activities with so many editors, we are really happy about the result. We believe this showcases high quality research on games in education in the Scandinavian countries.

When we met and started talking during seminars, we got the sense that there were some similarities across the Scandinavian countries and we started to discuss whether we could find any particular Scandinavian approach or perspective on education. As we started to reflect more on these issues we could perhaps agree that there were some interesting historical similarities in how we organize education and how education is seen as an important factor in civic society and in building human character. However, we also found that the theories and methodologies we employed were very international and the topics and questions we pursued in our research also resonated with more global concerns to do with how games can be used to facilitate teaching and learning. We hope that international readers find this mix of international concerns and approaches and particularities of educational practices in Scandinavia interesting.

What unites the contributions of this research anthology is an interest in how we can facilitate participatory approaches to design and learning with digital games across a range of settings and subjects. Involving teachers and students in research partnerships is also a crucial aspect of designing new learning environments, and in making sure they are sufficiently grounded in the realities of the classroom. Contributors to the volume share an interest in conceptualizing learning as changing participation in educational practices, and we are all concerned with how learning ecologies are designed and supported. Participation is also a crucial aspect of our methodologies. In both designs for learning and designs in learning researchers, designers, teachers and students are involved.

ACKNOWLEDGEMENTS

Thanks to our two highly qualified editors of this series, Sandra Schamroth Abrams and Hannah R. Gerber, for their thoughtful and encouraging feedback on the manuscript. It has been quite a journey to create this book and we would not have gotten here without your help. Also thanks to our anonymous reviewers for all their critical and constructive comments, who helped to improve the chapters. A special thanks to Pernille Toftgaard Christensen for her assistance with proofreading and formatting. We would also like to thank all the participants at the three NORDGOLD (Nordic Network on Game-Oriented Learning Designs) PhD seminars held in Copenhagen, Oslo and Stockholm for their excellent presentations, which sparked the initial idea for this book.

FIGURES AND TABLES

FIGURES

TABLES

NOTES ON CONTRIBUTORS

EDITORS

Hans Christian Arnseth is Professor of learning and digital technologies at the University of Oslo. Currently he is head of research at the Department of Education. In his research he studies the various ways digital technologies transform learning, cognition and identity across formal and informal contexts. Professor Arnseth has substantial experience in leading research projects, and recently he also directed a national research school in the Educational sciences. Currently he is involved in a MCA-RISE project called Makerspaces in the Early Years. He has published widely in leading international journals on the topics of learning and identity, simulations and game-based learning and computer supported collaborative learning. In his research he specializes in sociocultural approaches to learning and meaning making and in using ethnographic and interaction analytic methods to study learning and cognition in context.

Thorkild Hanghøj is an Associate Professor in game-based learning at Aalborg University, where he Co-Directs the Center for Applied Game Research (CEAGAR). His research focuses on the educational use and design of games with special emphasis on game-related literacy practices and the role of the teacher in facilitating games. He has developed a theory of scenario-based education, which he has used to describe and understand the interplay of knowledge practices in educational gaming across in and out of school domains. His research has been published in international journals such as *L1*, *Designs for Learning*, and *British Journal of Educational Technology*. Recently, he has published the research anthology *Hvad er scenariedidaktik?* [*What is scenario-based education?*], which is co-edited with Jeppe Bundsgaard, Morten Misfeldt, Simon Skov Fougt and Vibeke Hetmar. Moreover, he is managing the GBL21 project (gbl21.aau.dk), which explores and measures how design thinking and game-based learning can develop students' 21st century skills in Danish, Mathematics and Science across twenty secondary schools.

Thomas Duus Henriksen is an Associate Professor in Internal Communication and Organisational Processes at Aalborg University. His research focuses on how organisational processes and development is mediated through the use of tools, learning games, and other artefacts that affect how an organisation functions, and has been published in Development and Learning in Organizations. He has published several models on learning games and simulations in adult education and organisational development, and emphasised how game immersive processes have an inhibiting effect on adult learning. In recent research, Henriksen has been preoccupied with how manufacturing companies work with leadership dilemmas, and its facilitation.

Morten Misfeldt is a Professor in Mathematics Education and Technology at Aalborg University. Misfeldt's research revolves around the influence of digital technology on mathematical practice in research, teaching and learning, including how games and simulations can foster learning, and how computational thinking can be adopted as a learning objective in mathematics. Recently Misfeldt has been focusing on how digitalisation influences mathematics teachers work which is an area that combines mathematics education research with both learning analytics and organisational learning. His research has been published in leading international journals in the disciplines Mathematics Education, Semiotics, Philosophy of Mathematics and Technology Enhanced Learning. He recently co-edited the research anthology *Hvad er scenariedidaktik?* [*What is scenario-based education?*], with Thorkild Hanghøj, Jeppe Bundsgaard, Simon Skov Fougt and Vibeke Hetmar.

Robert Ramberg earned his PhD in cognitive psychology at the department of psychology, Stockholm University and holds a position as Professor at the department of computer- and systems sciences, Stockholm University (Technology enhanced learning and collaboration). Ramberg also holds a position as research director at the Swedish air force simulation center (FLSC), Swedish Defense Research Agency. He has been the chairman of the center for cognitive science and information technology in Stockholm (a collaboration between three larger universities: Stockholm university, the Royal Institute of Technology and the Karolinska institute), and served on the board of the Swedish Cognitive Science Society. His research has been published in international journals such as *International Journal of Technology and Design Education*, *International Journal of CoCreation in Design and the Arts*, *Designs for Learning*, and *Computers & Education*. Broadly conceptualized, his research focuses the design and evaluation of representations and representational artefacts to support learning, training and collaboration. Of particular interest to his research are socio-cultural perspectives on learning and cognition and how theories must be adapted when designing and evaluating technology enhanced learning and training environments. And more specifically how artifacts of various kinds (information technology and other tools) mediate human action, collaboration and learning.

Staffan Selander is PhD and Senior Professor in Didactic Science at the Department of Computer and Systems Sciences, Stockholm University. A major part of Selander's research during the last 10 years has focused on designs for learning, knowledge representations and digital learning environments, including games for learning. He has been leading several external, international research projects, financed by The Swedish Foundation for Humanities and Social Sciences (Riksbankens Jubileumsfond), The Swedish Research Council (Vetenskapsrådet), the KK-foundation, and has also been engaged in smaller developmental projects financed by e.g. The Swedish National Agency for Education/Skolverket, and the Education Departments at Stockholm City and Nacka Community. Selander has tutored over 40 doctoral students and 20 licentiat students, and has also been part of developing a Scandinavian collaborative work on designs for learning and game-based learning, including the open-access e-journal *Designs for Learning* (of which he also is Chief Editor) and the bi-annual Scandinavian conference Designs for learning.

CONTRIBUTORS

Jeppe Bundsgaard is a PhD and Professor in Subject Didactics and ICT with a special focus on the Danish subject at the Danish School of Education, Aarhus University. He has participated in a number of projects that developed and tested innovative digital learning designs in real life settings, and he has developed instruments to study the role of teaching and learning material in context. He has developed a curriculum theory called Prototypical Situation Oriented Curriculum Logic, laying out principles for development of 21st Century teaching and learning standards. The focus in his current research is on developing scenario based standardized assessments that are capable of measuring 21st Century Skills like collaboration, critical thinking and information literacy. In many of his research projects Jeppe Bundsgaard has developed web-based software to be used in the research (e.g. systems for structured observation, assessment tools, evaluation of students' well-being etc.). He has published widely in books and journals nationally and internationally. He recently co-edited the research anthology *Hvad er scenariedidaktik?* [*What is scenario-based education?*], with Thorkild Hanghøj, Morten Misfeldt, Simon Skov Fougt and Vibeke Hetmar.

Caroline Cruaud has a Ph.D. from the Department of Education of the University of Oslo (Norway) on the topic of gamification of education. With a background in foreign language learning and teaching, she is researching playful learning and the use of digital tools in education. In her Ph.D. thesis she developed a framework based on play theories and the concept of frame, to design and analyse play situations in a classroom context. Her research interests also cover game-based learning, design-based research, and the process of designing tools for learning.

Filipa de Sousa is a psychologist for over 18 years, having graduated at the Faculty of Psychology and Educational Sciences, University of Lisbon, in 1996. During her entire career she has been working with the use of narratives for emotional development among the youth. Over the years she coordinated several international projects on Global Education and developed many projects concerning education through dialogue. She is currently a PhD candidate at the University of Oslo and researches the role of dialogism in technological-enhanced education. She is especially interested in Game-based Learning and the use of the interactive narratives presented by commercial videogames to teach about moral, ethics and citizenship.

Victor Lim Fei is Assistant Professor at the English Language and Literature Academic Group, National Institute of Education, Nanyang Technological University, Singapore.

Victor researches on multimodality in education, multiliteracies, and digital literacy. In particular, he has published and been cited on his work in multimodal discourse analysis, designs for learning through classroom orchestration, and multimodal literacy. Victor was previously Lead Specialist and Deputy Director, Technologies for Learning, at the Singapore Ministry of Education, where he has experience in translational research, policy formulation, and programme development, with a focus on innovations with educational technology to improve teaching and learning.

Uno Fors graduated as DDS at Karolinska Institutet (KI) 1980 and earned his PhD in Medical informatics at Karolinska Institutet 1990, where he later on became Professor in Educational Simulation in 2007. Fors was head of department of Learning, Informatics, Management and Ethics at KI between 2002–2010. In 2010, Fors moved to Stockholm University where he became professor in IT and Learning (from 2010) and head of department for Computer and Systems Sciences since 2015. Fors' main research area has always been Technology Enhanced Learning, where he has been working in a variety if areas, including Digital assessment, Visualisation and Simulation for Learning. However, during the last 30 years, Fors' main focus has been in Virtual cases for Learning and Assessment, and has been developing and studying such applications in several domains, including healthcare, medicine, teacher education, law and social work.

Simon Skov Fougt earned his PhD from the Faculty of Arts at the University of Aarhus and is now an Associate Professor in Danish (L1) at the Faculty of Education at University College Copenhagen. Fougt's research focuses on Teacher Professional Development and ICT. He developed the theory on Teacher's Scenario Competence conceptualising the complexity for teachers and students in project-based teaching. He has defined the concept of teacher scenario competences as a circular process consisting of dependence between planning and execution competences—from notions of scenario and situation to the execution, evaluation, and revision of scenario and situation. Recently, he has published the research anthology *Hvad er scenariedidaktik?* [*What is scenario-based education?*], which is co-edited with Thorkild Hanghøj, Jeppe Bundsgaard, Morten Misfeldt, and Vibeke Hetmar.

James Paul Gee is the Mary Lou Fulton Presidential Professor of Literacy Studies and a Regents' Professor at Arizona State University. He is an elected member of the National Academy of Education. His most recent books are: *The Anti-Education Era: Creating Smarter Students through Digital Learning* (2013); *Unified Discourse Analysis: Language, Reality, Virtual Worlds, and Video Games* (2014); *Literacy and Education* (2014); *The Essential James Gee: An Introduction to Discourse Analysis* (2015); *Teaching, Learning, Literacy in Our High-Risk High-Tech World: A Framework for Becoming Human* (2017); and *Introducing Discourse: From Grammar to Society* (2017). Professor Gee has published widely in journals in linguistics, psychology, the social sciences, and education.

Carsten Jessen is emeritus at Centre for Teaching Development and Digital Media, Aarhus University and chairman of the Danish section of International Play Association. His research has focused on play, computer games and children's culture for several decades, where he was employed at University of Southern Denmark, the Danish University of Education and the Technical University of Denmark, and he has published papers on play, computer games and learning since the 1990's. He has especially been interested in developing a new research field, playware, that combines play and game research with technical research, and in collaboration with robot researchers he founded Center for Playware at the Technical University of Denmark.

Jari Due Jessen is PhD in play, technology, learning and robotics from Center for Playware at the Technical University of Denmark. In his PhD thesis he developed the concept play dynamics as a theoretical perspective that aims to bridge the gap between theory of play and games and practical design. His research is now focused on the use of technology in preschools, and he is currently Concept and Design Lead at the Danish company KUBO Robotics.

Lise Busk Kofoed is Professor in interdisciplinary learning and teaching strategies. Primary research interests are within the fields of technological and organizational changes and innovation with special focus on learning processes in interdisciplinary environments. Particularly interested in Problem Based Learning processes using new digital media and how it will influence the design of new PBL based learning activities e.g. blended learning, flipped classroom, and the use of purposive game development in a virtual PBL context (Center for Applied Game Research). Methodologically working with user driven innovation, and action research using mixed methods and a special interest in combining qualitative oriented video ethnographic methods and quantitative data collection studies. Have been involved in research projects dealing with the integration of technical, organizational as well as the human factors in innovation and change processes.

Johanne Öberg is a PhD student at the Department of Computer and Systems Sciences at Stockholm University since 2014, with student participation as the main interest. Her research is situated in a school context with focus on learners view and aims at facilitating pupil participation using Technology Enhanced Learning.

Kristine Øygardslia is a postdoctoral researcher at the Norwegian University of Science and Technology. With a background in serious game design, she has a passion for researching how games can make the world a better place. Her current research interests include game design as a learning activity in classrooms and computer games for promoting integration.

Lars Reng is a Teaching Associate Professor with a primary research interest within the fields of motivation, learning, programming, media development, new media technology, and designing new educations and courses to enhance learning of technical topics e.g. programing and software development. Through an applied research approach he has developed and managed new digital game development courses for more than 1000 pupils and students at a broad array of educations. Lars is also co-founder and co-directing the Center for Applied Game Research (CEAGAR), and the Samsung Media Innovation Lab for Education (SMILE).

Henrik Shoenau-Fog is an Associate Professor at Aalborg University, Copenhagen where he is researching motivational factors and assessment of engagement in games, learning and interactive media. He is also working with interactive adaptive real-time storyworlds, purposive games and games for learning while teaching and supervising projects related to games, interactive storytelling, emergent narratives, animation and media technologies. He is furthermore using game-enhanced learning models and game design and development to motivate for learning in the classroom. Moreover, he is also co-directing the Samsung Media Innovation Lab for Education (SMILE) and the Center for Applied Game Research (CEAGAR), which aims to promote interdisciplinary applied game research.

Kenneth Silseth is Associate Professor at Department of Education, University of Oslo. He specializes in sociocultural and dialogic approaches to young people's learning, meaning making and identity processes. Among his research interests are classroom interaction, technology-enhanced learning, everyday experiences as resources for learning in school, and learning identity. Silseth has published articles on topics such as game-based learning, contextualizing instruction, social media, and digital storytelling, in journals such as *International Journal of Computer-Supported Collaborative*, *Instructional Science*, and *Learning, Culture and Social Interaction*.

Olga Timcenko is an Associate Professor in Media Technology at Aalborg University. Her research interest is investigating how technology can help processes of active and blended learning at university level. The inspiration for this work comes from her previous experience as one of developers of LEGO Mindstorms robots, where she witnessed how a carefully designed technological artefact can inspire especially group learning and empower players to acquire knowledge previously considered to belong to university level curriculum (robot programming). She has participated in several EU research projects, and currently is active in European Art-Science-Technology network EASTN-DC. She published papers in fields of robotics, children and technology, and mathematics and programming education, and she holds three international patents.

Charlotte Lærke Weitze, PhD, is an Assistant Professor in technology and learning design at learnT—Centre for learning technology at the Technical University of Denmark. Since 2009 Charlotte has been researching on how students (K2-K12) can learn by creating digital learning games teaching specific subject matters, while at the same time developing their computational thinking skills. In order to create efficient and motivating learning processes involving technology another focus has been the development and measurement of student and teacher motivation and engagement in learning situations. Charlotte is furthermore educated pianist.

Mats Wiklund has a PhD in computer and systems sciences at Stockholm University where he teaches computer games related courses. Current research areas focus on game related communication, learning and behavioural issues, both within games and through other channels regarding games. Of special interest is the use of entertainment games as part of the teacher's toolbox when designing learning environments that span across the (somewhat porous) boundary between games and classroom.

HANS CHRISTIAN ARNSETH, THORKILD HANGHØJ,
THOMAS DUUS HENRIKSEN, MORTEN MISFELDT,
ROBERT RAMBERG AND STAFFAN SELANDER

INTRODUCTION

Scandinavian Perspectives

INTRODUCTION

This book brings together contributions from Scandinavian researchers interested in digital games, learning and learning designs, and how dialogue and deliberation work as key aspects in supporting and facilitating learning in a variety of settings. The Scandinavian countries of Denmark, Sweden and Norway have traditionally emphasised a broad, egalitarian and sustainable education for all citizens, delivered through a publicly funded comprehensive school system. In these countries, education is traditionally perceived as a way of providing equal opportunities for all, and as a means for sustaining and securing the welfare state. In a globalised economy where differences in wealth are increasing, the Scandinavian countries are still characterised by a political will to provide services for everyone through state funded public institutions. Historically, dialogue and deliberation have also been significant to foster participation in a democratic society.

After the Second World War, education was an important instrument for creating and sustaining the social democratic state, and comprehensive school systems took on an integral role in achieving social goals, such as equal opportunities for all and reducing differences in society (Telhaug et al., 2006). Still, school policies were often determined by the state in a top down fashion, and schools were seen as an instrument for the state. In the 1970s and 1980s there was a stronger emphasis on individual emancipation influenced by new radical movements. Local policymakers and teachers received more control of their pedagogy (Telhaug et al., 2006). In late modernity, we find a stronger emphasis on output measures; the state governs through assessing results and outcomes. However, the Nordic model still emphasises teacher autonomy and we still find an emphasis on "Bildung"; that developing whole persons as autonomous and responsible citizens is an important aim. Notions of deliberation and dialogue have therefore been important parts of pedagogy in Scandinavia, and fostering creativity and agency in students have been, and still are, important aims for education.

What unites the contributions of this research anthology is an interest in how we can facilitate participatory approaches to design and learning with digital games across a range of settings and subjects. Involving teachers and students in research partnerships is also a crucial aspect of designing new learning environments, and in making sure they are sufficiently grounded in the realities of the classroom. Contributors to the volume share an interest in conceptualising learning as changing participation in educational practices, and we are all concerned with how learning ecologies are designed and supported. Participation is also a crucial aspect of our methodologies. In both designs for learning and designs in learning researchers, designers, teachers and students are involved.

Designs in learning refers to how learners' trajectories, or learning paths, are constituted in social interaction, and how this develops and can be supported over time. *Designs for learning* concerns the shaping of the conditions and tools for learning. The chapters in the book are organised according to this distinction. The main aim of each is to provide concepts, models and empirical research on game-oriented learning, and, through a participatory lens, address issues of designs in and for learning. This is all part of a strategy of innovating pedagogy with digital games.

In this introductory chapter, we will first briefly describe the social context of game-based learning, both internationally and in the Scandinavian countries. In this way, we want to show that there is not one specifically Scandinavian approach to games and learning, but that Scandinavian researchers working within the field have taken inspiration from existing research traditions. This means that the Scandinavian perspectives on games and learning presented in this book should be seen as a part of an ongoing dialogue, with key issues and methodologies concerning the role of education in late modernity, and perspectives on design, participation, scenarios, organisations and broader aspects of game culture. Finally, we will describe in more detail the notions of designs in and designs for learning and briefly describe the various contributions to this edited book.

SOCIAL CONTEXT OF GAME-ORIENTED LEARNING

Our postindustrial or late modern world can be characterised in many ways. We can understand modern society through the change from a rather stable, to a "liquid" modernity (Bauman, 2015). This change concerns international economic and technological interdependence, migration, open information sources and a culture of information sharing, crowd sourcing, and new ways of analysing big data, but also epistemological globalisation. In terms of cognitive orientation, we can talk about "hyper attention" (Hayles, 2007), and in terms of children's learning we can notice a change from the "unique" and "competent" child to the "superchild", who is trained early on to collaborate, make decisions, and shape their own future (Lindstrand et al., 2016).

Against this background, the conceptualisation of game-based learning has changed a lot during the last decades; from "edutainment" and "learning games" via "serious games" to "expressive and persuasive games". We also find an emerging interest in researching learning within games as virtual worlds, and also in studying games as part of broader ecologies, comprising both online and offline interactions. These developments are connected to a change in approaches to learning, from more behaviouristic models of games and game design to broader socially oriented approaches to learning and design. At least four different aspects are worth noticing: (1) we start to see a mix between the use of commercial games and games designed for learning (Johansson et al., 2014); (2) the advanced graphical interface of commercial games meets a much simpler one in expressive and persuasive games, where individuals express their attitude and affinity towards some important political or cultural issue (Mitgutsch, 2011); (3) in learning settings, the pedagogical and didactical arrangement uses both advanced games (like *World of Warcraft*), or educational versions of commercial games (such as *Minecraft*) and game-elements (as in some Apps, e.g. Devlin, 2011); and (4) a move beyond a narrow focus on games as closed worlds to a broader perspective on how educational scenarios involve an interplay of in and out-of-school domains (Hanghøj et al., 2017).

These four aspects point to a richness and variety in "games", much the same as when we use the concept "book". Games, as books, cannot therefore be conceptualised as either "good" or "bad" for learning purposes. It is time to think anew, to shape concepts and metaphors that function as guidelines for our understanding of games for learning in our contemporary society. In terms of education and learning, we need to focus on a reconceptualisation of pedagogy and didactics as "designs for/ in learning" (Kress & Selander, 2010; Selander & Kress, 2012; Selander, 2015), where the learner's design of their learning environment is highlighted as much as the educational system's design for learning.

DESIGNS IN AND FOR LEARNING

Designs for learning is an approach which focuses on several layers of learning in different kinds of formal or nonformal settings (from schools to museums and game-oriented learning designs)—and future oriented learning (Bergström, 2012; Egenfeldt et al., 2011; Selander & Kress, 2010).

The concept entails, in our view, both designs *for* learning, which highlights the shaping of conditions and tools for learning (like buildings, schedules, resources and assessment systems), and designs *in* learning, which focuses on the way the learner organises their learning environment and learning paths (also see Kjällander, 2011; Åkerfeldt & Selander, 2011; Åkerfeldt, 2014).

The concepts of designs for learning combines educational research approaches with multimodal approaches (Kress, 2003, 2010; van Leeuwen, 2004) and design approaches (design research, design-based research etc.; see for example Barab & Squire, 2004; Dorst, 2015; Squire, 2011). The use of the notion of "design" in a learning context was perhaps first formulated by the New London Group in order to emphasise the active role of students and teachers in meaning-making processes (1996). At the same time, in a Scandinavian context, there is a strong link between both the continental, didactic traditions and development in design, design thinking

3

and design-based-research. Some important differences might also be noted, such as a stronger emphasis on knowledge traditions, knowledge representations, and resources as tools for thinking, rather than just communicative devices (Leijon & Lindstrand, 2012; Selander, in press). This means that the role of *representations* of knowledge in different media are highlighted, as are the *transformative* processes in learning, and it means that design is not only a question of form and function, but first and foremost a question of *framing* and *participation*.

INTERACTION DESIGN AND PARTICIPATORY DESIGN METHODOLOGY

Scandinavia has a strong tradition within the field of Human Computer Interaction, building on the so-called "Scandinavian approach" within systems development (Bødker et al., 1987; Ehn, 1988). Key to this tradition is the concept of *participation*, i.e. involving future users throughout the design process. Concepts of democracy, values of design and imagined futures, as well as how conflicts and contradictions are regarded as resources for design, have been pointed out as characteristic of Scandinavian approaches to participatory design (Gregory, 2003). Interaction design as an academic field is internationally well-represented by Scandinavian researchers investigating the digital material and its characteristics (Löwgren, 2009; Wiberg, 2014), as well as processes involved in the creation of design representations and the role that representational tools and action (designers' design-oriented actions) play in processes of sketching (Karlgren & Ramberg, 2012; Arvola & Artman, 2007).

Building on research into how designers sketch and create representations, and an acknowledged difficulty in the teaching and learning of interaction design in an academic context (Karlgren et al., 2015), have resulted in the development of a game-oriented and didactic format so-called interactionaries (Artman et al., 2015; Ramberg et al., 2013; Karlgren et al., 2015). Research into how interaction design students sketch when using different materials to represent, visualise, and communicate design ideas have led to adaptations of the original format of interactionaries to fit in education (Ramberg, et al., 2013; Karlgren et al., 2015).

Interaction design and the design of digital technology naturally becomes crucial to several fields of research and practice, where digital technology is developed to facilitate and support various processes and activities. Interaction design for learning, and more specifically mobile learning, counts as one example in which participatory design methodology (e.g. Co-design) is utilised in collaboratively designing mobile learning tools and activities together with teachers and pupils (Eliasson et al., 2011). This concerns designing tools and activities to support the learning of different subjects, such as mathematics and biology. To engage future users not only concerns collaboratively designing physical tools, artefacts and learning activities, but also the methodology and techniques. Examples of interaction design methodologies and techniques concern documenting and developing design patterns for how information technology can be used in teaching and learning (e.g. Knutsson & Ramberg, 2018; Mor & Winters, 2008).

SCENARIO-BASED EDUCATION

Within recent years, there have also been several attempts to combine the strong Scandinavian tradition for project-based education with various types of scenario-based teaching tools, such as simulations, virtual worlds, role-play, storytelling, and digital games. All of these tools can be used to create engaging interactional frames that support students' exploratory learning and meaning-making processes. A number of Danish research projects have looked into different types of scenario-based learning: e.g. students "being" scientists and forensic experts in order to explore a murder case in the ICT-supported role-playing game *Homicide* (Magnussen, 2009); as board game designers in maths, using the digital tool Geogebra (Misfeldt, 2013); using the online system *The Editorial Office* to collaboratively write a newspaper, or learning citizenship through *The Power Game*, which is an ICT-supported debate game on parliamentary elections (Hanghøj, 2008). These approaches can all be understood through the theoretical framework of *scenario-based education* (Hanghøj et al., 2017; Hanghøj et al., this book). Building on the inquiry-based learning theory of Dewey and the notions of *educational scenarios* and *scenario competence*, this perspective seeks to understand and design learning environments where students have to imagine, enact, and reflect on possible outcomes of situated challenges. These will often involve the production of relevant resources, such as newspaper articles or game designs. In this way, the aim of the scenario-based education perspective is both to understand and enhance meaningful translations of knowledge practices across in and out-of-school domains with specific validity criteria for what counts and does not count as legitimate knowledge.

THE SCANDINAVIAN APPROACH TO ORGANISATIONAL GAMING

During the past 20 years, the use of games in organisational processes has grown increasingly common (Henriksen & Löfvall, 2012). Games are being used to facilitate a variety of processes, including organisational development and learning, as well as innovative product creation. To the adult learner, games offer an opportunity to develop operational understandings of otherwise static theories (Henriksen, 2010).

When using games for teaching organisational change or leadership styles, they play a pivotal role in the process. However, they are always deployed as part of a didactically designed process, which combines the game-based experience with theoretical understandings, reflective processes, and group discussions on how to make use of new insights (Henriksen, 2014). In the Scandinavian approach to organisational gaming, the group plays centre stage, in terms of both playing and learning. When playing, participants collaborate to explore the game's presentation of a practice, formulate hypotheses on how various options have certain effects, and formulate strategies. The group encourages reflection and constantly prompts the participants to discuss and reflect on why they want to follow a particular line of action.

The Scandinavian approach emphasises the participatory element of bringing in several people into the learning process, thus striving towards democratic values of involvement and inclusion. This is often done by playing games in collaborative groups, which either competes against other groups, or simply against the machine. To better promote group-based learning processes, board games and other analogue materials are often blended into the otherwise digital game-based learning. To Scandinavian designers, tangible materials promote social processes, thereby acting as objects for discussion, which allow the process to unfold among the participants, rather than between a group of participants and a game. This embraces the idea of collaborative construction, which emphasises adult learning, not as a matter of conveying knowledge from the game to the participants, but as a matter of participating and being involved in epistemic practices. Finally, participant knowledge is often allowed to play a key role in the learning process (Henriksen & Børgesen, 2016). As players collaboratively explore the game-embedded knowledge, its ideas and models are discussed in light of their experiences. The group-based structure acts as a platform for bringing in participant knowledge, thereby allowing the game-based process to be enriched. From this approach, the game might be seen as an enzyme for learning, but is in no way considered the only resource (Børgesen, Nielsen, & Henriksen, in press). Instead, the approach embraces a constructivist understanding by recognising facilitators, participant knowledge, and group processes as equally important sources from which to learn.

THE ROLE OF THE GROWING GAME MARKET

Even though it makes sense to identify different research traditions, it is also important to understand how the growing game market is changing the cultural view of gaming. Since the first computer game companies appeared in the late 1970s, the global game industry has grown at an explosive rate into a huge entertainment business with a total value of more than $100 billion. Today's gaming landscape involves numerous technological platforms and a broad variety of genres aimed at many different groups across the globe. During the last decade, there has also been a cultural change toward a broader understanding and also acceptance of gaming as a part of everyday culture and within educational contexts.

One of the most important technological developments driving the broad cultural acceptance of games has been the explosion of the game app market, including Scandinavian titles such as *Subway Surfer* and *Candy Crush*. Through game apps, casual and social games have become an omnipresent part of everyday life, especially through smart phones, which can be carried and accessed everywhere we go. The widespread distribution of "mini games" has also contributed to a significant change in player demographics. In contrast to the pioneering years in the 1980s and 1990s, which was dominated by male teenagers, the average game player in the US is now approximately 35 years old, with almost an equal amount of men and women playing games (ESA, 2015). The move from "closed" games to apps and game-inspired learning environments seems to be a growing part of our daily life, as well as gaming as a general term to understand not only traditional play, but rather as a much broader understanding of changes in how we learn in different situations.

A second driver for the changed cultural perception of games is the recognition of players as potential game designers and co-creators of game worlds. This is apparent in the numerous available tools for game development—e.g. Scratch, Unity, RPG Maker, Game Salad etc.—and in different types of grassroots movements and educational activities, which promote students as coders and game developers. Another major example of the player-as-creator is the Swedish sandbox game *Minecraft*, which started out as an indie game project in 2009. Within a few years, the user driven development of the open-ended game world created a huge fan base fuelled by a desire to create their own maps, which often related to various forms of pop culture. The strong interest in the game is reflected in the millions of "Let's Play" videos uploaded to YouTube, which are used by players to document and present their in-game *Minecraft* activities. Moreover, there is a global community of educators, which have become attracted to the game as it can be redesigned to fit many different types of learning objectives, for example learning mathematics, social science or collaboration skills. The importance of the game as a new and open model for playing, learning, interaction and production was only emphasised when the industry giant Microsoft bought the game in 2014 for the staggering amount of $2.5 billion, with the aim of pushing the game more towards schools.

The widespread distribution and positive cultural perception of digital games has been emphasised by several researchers, with Gee's identification of 36 learning principles embedded in "good game design" standing out as one of the most important publications (Gee, 2003). Following Gee's work, numerous books on the topic have followed (e.g. Shaffer, 2006; Squire, 2011; Steinkuehler, Squire, & Barab, 2012), as well as dedicated journals and conferences, which have explored and discussed the value of games and learning. Today, the discussion is not so much the ideological question of whether games should have a place in formal education. Rather, it has moved to a more pragmatic focus on classical didactic questions, such as:

- Which game should be selected?
- What are the requirements (time, money, space, technology, curricular aims) for teaching with a specific game?
- What competencies and experiences do students and teachers need in order to play the game?
- What learning activities can be built around the game?
- How does the game experience align with specific learning aims?
- What pedagogical approaches should be chosen in order to teach with the game?
- How can the learning outcomes be discussed and assessed?

A SHORT INTRODUCTION TO CHAPTERS AND THEMES OF THE BOOK

The book consists of two parts, which follow the distinction between Designs in learning and Designs for learning mentioned earlier. Part 1, *Designs in learning*, focuses on how the learner organises their learning environment and how participation changes as part of evolving educational practices.

In the chapter "Digital Games and Simulations for Learning", Staffan Selander, Victor Lim Fei, Mats Wiklund, and Uno Fors argue that, even though they are not new phenomena, the use of games and simulations for learning has gathered increasing interest in recent years. With digital ubiquity, games and simulations are more attractive than ever. The authors state that there is a pressing need to develop new learning designs with games and simulations, designs that address the students' development of 21st century skills and knowledge. This chapter discusses how the design-perspective on learning works in relation to the use of games and simulations in education.

In their text "Unpacking the Domains and Practices of Game-Oriented Learning", Thorkild Hanghøj, Morten Misfeldt, Jeppe Bundsgaard and Simon Skov Fougt say that researchers should broaden their approach by seeing games as part of an interplay of practices across formal and informal learning ecologies. They present scenario-based education as an example of game-oriented learning that provides such an extended approach. To illustrate they present two case studies, each exploring the translation processes and framings involved in game-oriented learning designs. The examples show some of the complexities involved in trying to bridge informal and formal worlds and experiences. It is not simply a matter of importing an object into a school context. The translations of game-oriented learning involve reconfigurations of both the pedagogical and the personal domain. They conclude that the assumed "authentic" or "realistic" potentials of game and simulation-oriented designs should not be taken for granted, and their empirical examples demonstrate the need for redesign to fit classroom concerns.

In "Game-based Learning in the Dialogical Classroom", Filipa de Sousa focuses on game-based learning and the way a commercial videogame was used to foster collaborative reasoning about morality and ethics in citizenship education. A high school class was video recorded during one month and the data was analysed to investigate how students collaboratively reasoned in the GBL situation. Data from interviews were also considered. The study found that reasoning was mediated both by the videogame and the dialogical interactions facilitated by the teacher. Students appropriated both bottom-up and top-down reasoning processes to anchor practical and conceptual knowledge. De Sousa proposes a model that describes the anchoring process as an important tool to promote the understanding of content and meta-reflection on game-oriented learning across contexts.

"Designing for Increased Participation by using Game-Informed Learning and Role-Play" is a chapter where Johanna Öberg reports on a study of a game-informed learning design for promoting active participation and critical thinking among students. The learning activity used role-play in the form of co-researching to give the pupils a different role. The pupils got to decide their own research question and which methods they wanted to employ in order to investigate it. Observations indicate that there were several factors that affect the pupils' engagement. One was the ability to be in control, like the player is in control of the character and its decisions. Another was the surroundings, which is similar to how the game environment changes depending on the character's current mission. By participating as co-researchers, pupils gained experience in finding and expressing opinions, analysing results, and engaging in decision-making.

In her chapter "Stories about History: Exploring Central Elements when Students Design Game Narratives", Kristine Øygardslia explains how narrative is a central feature of successful game-oriented learning. The chapter reports on a study of the characteristics on the narratives within games designed by students in a classroom setting, and how this was related to educational objectives. The data consists of the games students created and video recordings of their design work. Øygardslia argue that narrative is crucial for developing and maintaining students' learning and engagement when they design computer games. The following characteristics were identified in how the students worked on game narratives: (1) content learning while shaping the game narrative; (2) exploration of alternative versions of history, often testing the limits of what is legitimate to include in a school setting; (3) emphasis of story when presenting and evaluating each other's games; (4) working on narrative skills; and (5) challenging stereotypes.

Part 2, *Designs for learning*, focuses on the shaping of the conditions and tools for learning. Jari Jessen and Carsten Jessen present a theory of what they term "play dynamics" in their chapter "A Theory of Play Dynamics". The purpose of play dynamics is to push the user into a state of play, which is a special way of being in the world. The authors present examples of play dynamics in both digital and non-digital gaming activities. They argue that the notion of play dynamics brings a better understanding of why certain games work better than others and what it is that makes them function.

In the chapter "Games as Tools for Dialogic Teaching and Learning", Hans Christian Arnseth, Thorkild Hanghøj and Kenneth Silseth draw together some of the recent findings from their research on the use of computer games in classrooms. The importance of the teacher's role is discussed in particular detail. They introduce a dialogical model for analysing and implementing computer games within education. This model, which is based on dialogic theory, is not a means to an end for the rational planning of instruction. It recognises the complexities of classroom practices, and attributes great agency to teachers and students in learning with games in the classroom. An important argument for introducing games is that they can be used to create new experiential spaces and learning opportunities, which may sometimes be disruptive to the established knowledge criteria of the classroom.

Charlotte Lærke Weitze reports on a design-based research project that experimented with a gamified learning design, enabling adult learners to design digital games while implementing learning goals from their curriculum. Her chapter is titled "Learning and Design Processes in a Gamified Learning Design". The aim was to develop a reusable learning design for upper secondary teachers and students who are game design novices. The gamified learning design supported the innovative learning processes for the students, and the teacher participated as an inspirational guide for them as they designed curriculum-based learning games. Weitze describes the learning design, how the teachers contributed to the students' cognitively complex learning processes, and how various processes for designing and learning supported this design. She concludes that students experienced deep and motivating learning, and that teachers experienced this design as problem-based and engaging.

Caroline Cruaud is concerned with gamification and second language learning. In her chapter with the title "Designing with Teachers", she argues that it is vital to look at the role of teacher before and during the implementation of a gamified educational resource. Design-based research on gamification and game-based learning tends to focus exclusively on students and very little has been said about teachers (Kenny & McDaniel, 2011). Cruad contrasts two teachers' experiences with the implementation of a gamified app in regard to their participation in the design process. Interviews with teachers and video data from the classroom have been analysed to find out how the teachers experienced the implementation, and in what way their involvement in the project is reflected in their respective experience and in the account of their experience. The analysis revealed that the two teachers had very different experiences. While the first teacher developed familiarity with and ownership to the application, the second felt lost and stopped using it. The study is interesting in that it opens up new questions on a teacher's role in the integration of games and gamified applications in the classroom.

"Group Processes in Learning Games for Adults" is a chapter written by Thomas Duus Henriksen. He states that very little research has been done to better understand how group-based structuration affects game-oriented learning. Despite this, adult participants in learning games are more often than not organised in a group structure, e.g. as small groups competing against each other. On several occasions, games have been seen structured as cooperative or semicooperative, thereby allowing the dynamics of mutual competition to be replaced, at least partly, by cooperative group mechanics. When played in groups, the sheer volume of activity is evidence of the level of engagement, but while the game and the group might serve as a frame for this engagement, a multitude of other, simultaneous activities are unfolding at the same time. To better understand these, Duus Henriksen claims it is necessary to explore the various processes that emerge while playing a business game.

In the chapter "Motivated Learning through Production-Oriented Game Development", the researchers Henrik Schoenau-Fog, Lise Busk Kofoed, Lars Reng and Olga Timcenko point out that the concept of game-oriented learning, when using educational or commercial games in the classroom, has been proven to have many possibilities for supporting the motivation to learn, and for better learning outcomes.

However, there might also be great potential in having children and young people develop games themselves. The skills and effort needed to design and program even simple games have for decades been a barrier for many educators. Still, in the last few years new, simpler development tools and software have made it significantly easier to engage in game design. Recent evolutions in media hardware, such as virtual and augmented reality devices, wearables, tablets and smartphones, have created a rapid growth in the possibilities, impact, and future careers for those who learn to master the development of games and other interactive media solutions. Setting up a framework where education can simulate *real* productions of meaningful artefacts allows for educating and investigating a series of important areas, which are often very hard to make in formal settings.

REFERENCES

Åkerfeldt, A. (2014). *Didaktisk design med digitala resurser. En studie av kunskapsrepresentationer i en digitaliserad skola* (dissertation). Stockholm University, Stockholm.

Åkerfeldt, A., & Selander, S. (2011). Exploring educational video game design: Meaning potentials and implications for learning. In P. Felicia (Ed.), *Handbook of research on improving learning and motivation through educational games: Multidisciplinary approaches* (pp. 1004–1018). Hershey, PA: IGI Global. doi:10.4018/978-1-60960-495-0.ch046

Artman, H., House, D., & Hultén, M. (2015). Designed by engineers: An analysis of interactionaries with engineering students. *Designs for Learning, 7*(2), 28–56.

Arvola, M., & Artman, H. (2007). Enactments in interaction design: How designers make sketches behave. *Artifact, 1*(2), 106–119.

Barab, S., & Squire, K. (2004). Design-based research: Putting a stake in the ground. *The Journal of the Learning Sciences, 13*(1), 1–14.

Bauman, Z. (2015). *Liquid modernity*. Cambridge, MA: Polity Press.

Bergström, P. (2012). *Designing for the unknown: Digital design for process-based assessments in technology-rich learning environments* (PhD dissertation). Umeå universitet, Umeå.

Berkun, S. (2001). *Interactionary 2000*. Retrieved June 21, 2016, from http://scottberkun.com/essays/interactionary-and-design-sports/interactionary-2000/

Bødker, S., Ehn, P., Kammersgaard, J., Kyng, M., & Sundblad, Y. (1987). A Utopian experience. In G. Bjerknes, P. Ehn, & M. Kyng (Eds.), *Computers and democracy: A Scandinavian challenge*. Aldershot: Avebury.

Børgesen, K., Nielsen, R. K., & Henriksen, T. D. (2016). Exploiting formal, non-formal and informal learning when using business games in leadership education. *Development and Learning in Organization, 30*(6), 16–19.

Collins, A., & Halverson, R. (2009). *Rethinking education in the age of technology*. New York, NY: Teachers College Press.

Devlin, K. (2011). *Mathematics education for a new era: Video games as a medium for learning*. Boca Raton, FL: CRC Press.

Dorst, K. (2015). *Frame innovation: Create new thinking by design*. Cambridge, MA: The MIT Press.

Egenfeldt–Nielsen, S., Meyer, B., & Sørensen, B. H. (2011). *Serious games in education: A global perspective*. Aarhus: Aarhus University Press.

Ehn, P. (1988). *Work-oriented design of computer artifacts*. Hillsdale, NJ: Lawrence Erlbaum Associates.

Eliasson, J., Cerratto-Pargman, T., Nouri, J., Spikol, D., & Ramberg, R. (2011). Mobile devices as support rather than distraction of mobile learners: Evaluating guidelines for design. *The International Journal of Mobile and Blended Learning, 3*(2), 1–15.

Gregory, J. (2003). Scandinavian approaches to participatory design. *International Journal of Engineering Education, 19*(1), 62–74.

Hanghøj, T. (2008). *Playful knowledge: An explorative study of educational gaming* (PhD dissertation). University of Southern Denmark, Odense.

Hanghøj, T., Bundsgaard, J., Misfeldt, M., Fought, S. S., & Hetmar, V. (2017). *Hvad er scenariedidaktik?* [What is scenario-based education?]. Århus: Århus Universitetsforlag.

Hayles, N. K. (2007). Hyper and deep attention: The generation divide in cognitive modes. *Profession, 13*, 187–199.

Henriksen, T. D. (2010). *A little more conversation, a little less action, please*. Saarbrücken: Lambert Academic Publishing.

Henriksen, T. D. (2014). Challenges to designing game-based business. In S. A. Meijer & R. Smeds (Eds.), *Frontiers in gaming simuation, 44th International Simulation and Gaming Association Conference* (Stockholm, Sweden) (pp. 247–252). Switzerland: Springer International Publishing.

Henriksen, T. D., & Børgesen, K. (2016). Can good leadership be learned through business games? *Human Resources Development International, 19*(5), 388–405.

Henriksen, T. D., & Löfvall, S. (2012). Experiences and opportunities for enhancing business education with games: A review on current and past experiences with learning games at business schools. In C. Nygaard, N. Courtney, & E. Leigh (Eds.), *Transforming university teaching into learning via simulations and games*. Faringdon: Libri Publishing.

Karlgren, K., & Ramberg, R. (2012). Collaborative interaction design: Running into gaps of framing problems and the use of design patterns. *Special Issue on Quality of Collaboration in Design: CoDesign. International Journal of CoCreation in Design and the Arts, 8*(4), 231–246.

Karlgren, K., Ramberg, R., & Artman, H. (2015). Designing interaction: How do interaction design students address aspects of interaction. *International Journal of Technology and Design Education, 26*(3), 439–459.

Kjällander, S. (2011). *Design for learning in an extended digital environment: Case studies of social interaction in the social science classroom* (Dissertation). Stockholm University, Stockholm.

Knutsson, O., & Ramberg, R. (2018). Teachers' collaborative pattern language design. *Designs for Learning, 10*(1), 1–17.

Kress, G. (2003). *Literacy in the new media age*. London: Routledge.

Kress, G. (2010). *Multimodality: A social semiotic approach to contemporary communication*. London: Routledge.

Kress, G., & Selander, S. (2012). Multimodal design, learning and cultures of recognition. *The Internet and Higher Education, 15*(4), 265–268.

Leijon, M., & Lindstrand, F. (2012). Socialsemiotik och design. Två multimodala teorier om lärande, representation och teckenskapande. *Pedagogisk forskning i Sverige, 17*(3–4), 171–192.

Lindstrand, F., Insulander, E., & Selander, S. (2016). Mike the knight in the neo-liberal era: A multimodal approach to children's multi-media entertainment. *Journal of Language and Politics, 15*(3), 337–351.

Löwgren, J. (2009). Toward an articulation of interaction aesthetics. *New Review of Hypermedia and Multimedia, 15*(2), 129–146.

Magnussen, R. (2009). Representational inquiry competences in science games. In S. G. A. Rodrigues (Ed.), *Multiple literacy and science education: ICTs in formal and informal learning environments*. Hershey, PA: IGI Global.

Misfeldt, M. (2013). *Instrumental genesis in geogebra based board game design*. In Proceedings for CERME 8, the 8th European Conference of Mathematics Education CERME, Antalia, Turkey.

Mitgutsch, K. (2011). Serious learning in serious games: Learning in, through, and beyond serious games. In M. Ma, A. Oikonomou, & L. C. Jain (Eds.), *Serious games and edutainment applications*. London: Springer.

Mor, Y., & Winters, N. (2008). Participatory design in open education: A workshop model for developing a pattern language. *Journal of Interactive Media in Education, 2008*(1), 12. Retrieved from http://jime.open.ac.uk/2008/13/

Ramberg, R., Artman, H., & Karlgren, K. (2013). Designing learning opportunities in interaction design: Interactionaries as a means to study and teach student design processes. *Designs for Learning, 6*(1–2), 30.

Selander, S. (2015). Conceptualization of multimodal and distributed designs for learning. In B. Gros, Kinshuk, & M. Maina (Eds.), *The futures of ubiquitous learning: Learning designs for emerging pedagogies* (pp. 97–113). Berlin: Springer.

Selander, S. (2017). *Didaktiken efter Vygotskij. Design för lärande.* Stockholm: Liber.

Selander, S., & Kress, G. (2010). *Design för lärande—ett multimodalt perspektiv.* Stockholm: Norstedts.

Squire, K. (2011). *Video games and learning: Teaching participatory culture in the digital age.* New York, NY: Teacher's College Press.

Telhaug, A. O., Mediås, O. A., & Aasen, P. (2006). The nordic model in education: Education as part of the political system in the last 50 years. *Scandinavian Journal of Educational Research, 50*(3), 245–283.

The New London Group. (1996). A pedagogy of multiliteracies: Designing social futures. *Harvard Educational Review, 66*(1), 60–92.

van Leeuwen, T. (2005). *Introducing social semiotics.* London: Routledge.

van Leeuwen, T. (2011). *The language of colour: An introduction.* Abingdon: Routledge.

Wiberg, M. (2014) Methodology for materiality: Interaction design research through a material lens. *Personal and Ubiquitous Computing, 18*(3), 625–636.

PART 1
DESIGNS IN LEARNING

STAFFAN SELANDER, VICTOR LIM FEI,
MATS WIKLUND AND UNO FORS

1. DIGITAL GAMES AND SIMULATIONS FOR LEARNING

ABSTRACT

Digital games and simulations for learning are not new phenomena. However, with the advancements in technology, they have gathered increasing interest over recent years. With digital ubiquity, games and simulations offer a compelling case for use in schools. As such, it is useful to understand the value and issues related to the use of digital games and simulations for learning as well as to develop a new frame for thinking on how to design learning in educational settings, harnessing the affordances of technology through the effective use of digital games and simulations.

Keywords: game design, designs in learning, designs for learning, scenario pedagogy

INTRODUCTION

Education is no longer just about imparting knowledge to students, it is a design science, claims Laurillard (2012). In this light, we need new ways of understanding how to design for meaningful learning across contexts in the 21st Century by harnessing the new tools that technology affords us. Digital games and simulations offer exciting possibilities to deepen learning and provide opportunities for the development of 21st Century Competencies in students.

Games and simulations have been used for training for many decades. Early examples of game-based learning and simulation include the RAND corporation's logistics simulator modelling activities of the US Air Force supply system, where players acted as inventory managers (Jackson, 1959), and the first business simulation game used in college education as early as 1957 (Watson, 1981). Aviation, space and nuclear power plant industry, as well as military and medical training, have so far been among those who have benefited the most (Paige et al., 2009). The effective use of simulations includes virtual engineering laboratories and virtual chemistry labs as well as simulated archaeological excavations (Sundkvist, 2005) and geology fieldwork simulations (Edelbring et al., 2004).

In recent years, there has been an increased use of (social) simulation based on case studies in teacher training, law education and business training (Allodi et al., 2012; Boyne, 2012; Fors & Skoglund, 2013; DeLacey & Leonard, 2002).

In many of these examples, Virtual characters or Virtual Humans (VHs) have been used as agents to interact with the learners. Learners ask questions, discuss, and engage with the simulated characters. Through these simulated scenarios, learners develop critical reasoning and decision making. In particular, within healthcare education, Virtual Patients, (VPs), have been used as engaging and effective training tools (Botezatu et al., 2010). With the rapid development of technology, the simulations for learning have grown to include the use of Virtual Reality (VR) as well.

Virtual case systems with virtual humans can, like in medical training, present possibilities for learners to select and order lab tests, imaging analysis, documents as well as access web-based materials for information to solve the cases. Most virtual case systems also offer automated feedback to the learner, who may then learn from their mistakes and improve his reasoning as well as formulate strategies to solve similar cases in the future. Studies on the reception of feedback from virtual agents have reported positive impact (Ekblad et al., 2013).

Duke (1974) had suggested games to be used in formal education for student's learning. Some 30 years later, Woods (2004) continues to argue that gaming remains "a future's language" and saw immense possibilities in its application and impact to teaching and learning. More recently, there has also been an increased use of game (both digital and non-digital) scenarios in pedagogical settings (Misfeldt, 2015), where games and game-scenarios are a part of the design for learning. The enduring value of games and simulations for training and learning presents a cogent argument for further research and a more nuanced understanding of how they can be used productively to deepen learning and develop 21st Century Competencies in our students, in this day and age.

LEARNING THROUGH GAMES AND SIMULATIONS

Students in the 21st Century have been described as 'digital natives', exposed to interactive digital media from young, and savvy with the use of technology (Prensky, 2001). This claim has been popularised but has also been challenged by others. For example, Bennett and Maton (2010) note that while there are many young people that are adept with technology; there are also others that do not have the level of access and technology skills. Even though not very young person may have a personal computing device, access to technology within the school environment as well as in the shared spaces, such as the public libraries, are common. This brings about a certain digital ubiquity all over the world (Tamara, 2017). Given the digital ubiquity and the profile of our students today, it is useful for educators to harness the affordances of digital games and simulations to "engage with the young on the grounds of their experience" (Kress, 2003, p. 175).

The 21st Century Competencies (21CC)—or 21st Century Skills—describe the competencies needed for students to be future-ready and thrive in todays' world. While there is no firm consensus of what these specific 21CC are, interpretation often include elements such as media literacy and multimodal literacy (O'Halloran & Lim, 2012), communication and collaboration skills, as well as critical and creative thinking (Care, Griffin, & Wilson, 2011). Technology, in the use of games and simulations, presents new possibilities for teachers to design meaningful learning experiences for their students and provides opportunities for the development of 21CC (Lim & Hung, 2016). The use of digital games for the development of 21CC has been gaining growing reception over the years. Digital games, in the category of role-playing games, strategy games, and sandbox games, have been used to teach students about responsible decision making, trade-offs, as well as values such as fair play, resilience, and integrity.

Research on digital games as educational tools has pointed out several aspects where games fit well into key patterns of successful learning. One aspect of this is when the player has to perform specific tasks to get to the next step or the next level in the game. As Papert (1998, p. 88) famously observes, "what is best about the best games is that they draw kids into some very hard learning … kids prefer things that are hard, as long as they are also interesting". Apparently impossible tasks seem to be one of the strongest factors promoting player collaboration (Hämäläinen et al., 2006, p. 59).

Digital games also provide opportunities for learners to learn from the in-game experience and critically reflect on their learning with the help of the out-of-game teacher's facilitation (Hanghøj & Brundt, 2010). Dong and Oei (2013, p. 29) argue that "collaborative games provide excellent opportunities for students to reflect on their learning processes". Coupled with facilitation by the teacher, learners can be guided, through questions, to reflect on their actions in the game and how these reflected certain values and attitudes.

Digital games seem to support engagement and interest (Rigby & Ryan, 2011). Gee (2003)—who focuses on what playing videogames can teach us about learning—lists a number of important learning principles, such as practice, achievement, ongoing learning and probing. In a formal learning context, it seems to be important for teachers to be able to facilitate learning experience also by giving meaningful feedback, facilitating the students' reflections, and consolidation of learning from the game-play. As Lim, Woo, and Lee (2016, p. 4) note, "to ensure a transfer of skills outside the digital-game environment, the games must be coupled with effective pedagogy. Pre- and post-game discussions are necessary to tie the learning in games to other contexts".

Like all educational tools, the use of games and simulations are most effective when they are embedded in curricula and well-integrated into educational practices to serve specific learning outcomes. Hays (2005, p. 23) found that an instructional game would be most effective when designed to meet specific instructional objectives and used as intended. As such, the ways in which the games are used and facilitated by the teacher, that is the pedagogy, is key. Edelbring et al. (2012) shows that a thorough course integration of a digital game (case simulation) was necessary for learners' perceived benefit.

LEARNING OUTCOMES

In this section, we discuss issues related to digital games and simulations for learning, in terms of the learning outcomes. The reader might be aware that so far, not many studies have been able to demonstrate that digital games and simulation have a strong causal relationship with learning outcomes, except in a few specific areas. For example, a meta-analysis by Girard et al. (2013) reports that only three of 11 games could demonstrate good learning outcomes. In addition, Cook and Triola (2009) argue that most studies on the application of simulations for learning, such as the use of Virtual Patient in healthcare education, did not show statistically significant evidence for improved learning outcomes. Other studies have found mixed learning effects from the use of digital games and simulations in learning. For example, Guillén-Nieto and Aleson-Carbonell (2012) report a small learning effect on intercultural awareness and a medium learning effect on intercultural knowledge, but large learning effects on intercultural communicative competence. Studies have also examined whether virtual cases would lead to an improved confidence among the users to solve problems (Pantziaras et al., 2014). Nonetheless, it has also been noted that confidence as a measure of improvements can be contested (Davis et al., 2006; Fernandez et al., 2004).

Many studies show that the learners believe that they learned better and/or that the users report being motivated by the interactive systems. There have also been studies that highlight evidential learning gains when digital games and simulations are used well, that is when coupled with effective pedagogy. For instance, Barab et al. (2009) investigate the use of a 3D-based game for science learning. In this study, undergraduate students were assigned randomly to four different learning methods: (a) expository textbook, (b) simplistic framing condition, (c) immersive world condition, and (d) a single-user immersive world condition. The results showed that the immersive-world approach and immersive-world single user conditions led to significantly better performance than the electronic textbook group on standardized items. The immersive-world group performed significantly better than either the expository textbook or the descriptive framing condition on a performance-based transfer task. The immersive-world group also performed significantly better than the expository textbook condition on standardized test items. The findings from that study suggested that immersive game-based learning environments could provide a powerful form of curriculum for teaching and learning science.

In this light, it is important to consider, not only the intended learning objectives articulated by the designers of the games, but also the incidental learning that could occur through the game. This incidental learning is beyond the intent of the game developers, but inherently within the design of the game itself, as well as the context, such as the educational environment. An example of this is when surgeons play a computer game to train their dexterity and reflexes before entering the operating theatre. In such a case, the game may not be designed for this purpose but its functional affordances allow surgeons to use it to practise and enhance their skills.

Another form of incidental learning can be exemplified by the game *Darfur is Dying*. It is intended to encourage empathy for children in the 3rd world country, but may instead end up lulling the 1st world players into a larger-than-life perspective of the plight of the people in 3rd world countries. It also constructs an unhealthy paradigm of 'us' and the 'others'. These ideas, while not intended by the game developers, nonetheless, present ethical issues, which must be addressed. Hence, it is of importance for evaluators to understand the different types of learning that can take place within the construction and playing of a game.

Another aspect of learning with games concerns the reward system. If rewards are built into the game to keep the player playing, then the levelling up of qualification might be deceptive. In this case, the levelling up is not a result of greater skills, but a part of the game architecture. Linderoth (2012) describes cases where the underlying design of some games reward the amount of time spent playing, rather than tasks hard to complete. This can be done explicitly, or implicitly by requiring the player to perform repetitive tasks, or rewarding them for doing so. Such a game design may give a sense of achievement and progress even if only a repetitive and non-challenging task is performed by the player. Linderoth (2012, p. 59) argues that games can create an "illusion of learning" by proving a sense of progress without "demanding that we develop the kind of skills that many other domains require". Another effect of the rewards in digital games is the drive, and distraction, where students are led to focus on winning instead of learning. Coining the term 'Gamer Mode', Frank (2012) observes students detaching themselves from the underlying domain in focus from a learning perspective and instead exploit the game functionality in order to win at all cost.

There is also much debate on whether games can meaningfully fulfil specific objectives of learning. It is crucial to put the serious game or simulation into a curricular context as just adding the possibility to run a simulation into an existing course neither mean that students will spend time on it, nor learn from it, if the teacher does not tell the students what to do with the simulation and how they should benefit from its use (Edelbring et al., 2012). In the entire curricula structure, it is probably still unrealistic to expect a game to be designed for the specific learning goals. For instance, Robertson and Good (2005) describe the Game Maker Workshop, where children create their own games using the Neverwinter Nights toolset, and discuss the educational implications observed from the study. However, one could question what is learnt in the Game Marker Workshop and how that may relate to the curricular outcomes. In creating their own games, children may acquire multimodal literacy and technical skills, but this may not relate directly to the outcomes from the curriculum, such as mastery of specific subject content.

While recognising the value of learning through games and simulations, questions have also been raised to invite a deeper exploration of the complex issues involved in the use of digital games and simulations as learning resources in the classroom. Fundamentally, as Gunter, Kenny and Vick (2006) observe, when it comes to the use of games and simulations for learning, the "designer's focus is necessary but insufficient. In addition to the designer's focus, a didactic focus is required for serious games design" (see also, Åkerfeldt & Selander, 2011). Other theoretical approaches to facilitate the use of games and simulations for learning include thinking in terms of designs for learning (Selander, 2008a, 2008b) as well as the use of design patterns to develop teaching practices (Ramberg et al., 2013).

While a clear pedagogic aim is required to make explicit the relationship between what is learnt in the digital gaming environment in relation to the learning goals, it has been observed that gaming could have transferrable learning effects, both in the formal and informal learning spaces, that is, inside as well as outside the school context (Gee, 2004; Ito, 2010). As such, given the increasing blurring of boundary between formal and informal learning, educators need to develop fresh insights on the design of learning activities wherever they take place (Collins & Halverson, 2009).

CASE STUDY IN BOTKYRKA

An education project based on computer games was initiated in 2003 in the Swedish municipality of Botkyrka, as a way of reaching upper-secondary students with low probability of undertaking their (non-compulsory) education (Wiklund & Ekenberg, 2009). Key features of the project were that digital games would be used as the main teaching tool in the classroom, and that only commercial, off-the-shelf computer games would be used. A total of 21 students participated, and the game-based approach was used for all classes except physical training. The learning environment consisted of a combination of in-game playing activities and teacher-induced activities such as group discussions and paper-writing assignments, linking gameplay to various study fields.

This game-centered learning environment replaced traditional rostrum teaching as the main classroom activity. This was only marginally complemented with traditional instruction at large intervals. The students were free to suggest the game titles to be used. As the students were free to play games of their own liking, each student's learning environment was heavily influenced by their favourite game genre. A common teaching approach was to use the in-game activities as starting points for various discussions and assignments. The multidisciplinary nature of the game-based setting was also demonstrated. As one student playing a historical strategy game remarked:

> When you ask the teacher what some tricky medieval English word means, he tells you the Swedish word for that. Then you do not know what that means, either. Then he explains it, and you know a new Swedish word too. (ibid., p. 50)

Digital games allow for different types of knowledge representations. Students' increased motivation also meant a more engaged learning experience. The in-game activities were used as starting points for exploration of the knowledge landscape. An advantage with game-based learning in the form used in the project was also reported when it came to handling students with special needs. One of the teachers pointed out that:

> It's easier to go back and forth between a more advanced and a more basic level here, than it is [when we] are addressing students in the traditional way as a group in a classroom. I can give the students more individual treatment. (ibid., p. 49)

During their participation in the project, the students were interviewed about their traditional media consumption habits. The results showed an unsurprising decrease in the number of hours spent watching television, but an increase in number of books read. This is contrary to what is often taken for granted regarding youth being engaged heavily in gaming activities (Wiklund, 2007). The increasing (printed) book reading trend was particularly clear regarding non-fictional prose—from 1.2 books/year at the beginning of the study to 4 books/year at the end of the study (ibid.).

An interesting pattern also appeared in the students' perceptions of what can be learnt in an environment with game play and with facilitation from the teachers, compared by game-play alone. In general, the teacher/game combination was perceived by the students to have a higher potential for learning (ibid.) The results from the project show that unmodified entertainment computer games can be effective as learning tools in the classroom if accompanied by the teachers' efforts to include in-game experiences in the learning environment (Wiklund & Ekenberg, 2009).

DESIGNS FOR LEARNERS, DESIGNS IN LEARNING

A design-oriented perspective on learning has been developed in the Scandinavian countries (see e.g. Andreasen et al., 2008; Bergström, 2012; Björklund Boistrup, 2010; Egenfeldt et al., 2011; Kjällander, 2011, Lindstrand et al., 2016; Nødtvedt Knudsen, 2017; Nouri, 2014; Selander & Svärdemo Åberg, 2008; Selander, 2008, 2017; Åkerfeldt, 2014; Østern & Strømme, 2014). It is a development of a socio-cultural perspective, especially focussing on aspects such as engagement, agency and collaborative learning, technology enhanced learning, knowledge representations, multimodality and re-design, framing, cultures of recognition and signs of learning. Inspiration was also drawn from both a strong Scandinavian tradition concerning democratic traditions and evening-schools (informal education for everyone— "folkbildning"), including problem-oriented learning and project-learning, and from a Scandinavian, collaborative design tradition, where designers work with those who will use the new products.

The focus on the design-perspective on learning also includes the design for learning (such as technology and resources, learning spaces, time allocation, collaborative information seeking and the role of the teacher), and the design in learning (with such aspects as engagement, a feeling of control, meaningful learning and the construction of individual learning paths; see further (Kjällander, 2011; Nouri, 2014; Selander, 2017; Selander & Kress, 2010; Åkerfeldt & Selander, 2011).

From the learner's point of view, games and simulations support individual ways of learning, which calls for a new way of organizing learning in a distributed learning environment. Games and simulations also support learning as interactive design, i.e. the individual way to interact with other persons and/or with the digital artefact.

When games and simulations are used, this also affects the ways we (multimodally) represent knowledge and competence. This aspect relates to a wider understanding of text, also including visual representations of different kinds (cf Danielsson & Selander, 2016). A greater demand to implement games and simulations in learning activities will be followed by a demand to understand multimodal knowledge representations anew, which include the *actions* of the player/user (instead of the traditional "reader") and new cultures of recognition and new assessment practices (cf. Bergström, 2012; Kress & Selander, 2012).

CONCLUSION

This chapter raises issues on the use of digital games and simulations for learning. Today, there are many new games of different kinds, including the expanding field of augmented reality (whereof Pokémon Go is but one example; also see Collins & Halverson, 2009; Mitgutsch, 2013; Steinkuehler et al., 2012). With the rapid changes brought about by disruptive technologies, we live in a world with greater complexities, and hence, we need to develop theoretical tools, understandings and practices to meet new demands and navigate the new world order (cf. Morin, 1999, 2008). While learning gains from the use of digital games and simulations for teaching, in general, can sometimes be elusive and often dependent on a range of factors, especially, teachers' competence, it is recognised that the appropriate use of technology, in this case, digital games and simulations, can deepen the learning of traditional literacy, numeracy and the mastery of subject knowledge. The use of technology also provides opportunities for the development of 21st Century Skills (Lim & Hung, 2016). From our own experience, and backed up by several other authors, games and simulations can be important tools for learning. Digital games and simulation also show potential for increasing student motivation, and thus learning outcomes. However, there needs to be a clear aim when using games and simulations, as well as clear and concrete ideas on how to implement then into the curriculum and lesson effectively.

The use of digital games and simulations for teaching and learning invites further theorisations both in the field of game development, pedagogy, knowledge representations and research on how to measure outcomes (cf Shaffer, 2009). A related question is what kind of knowledge representations we accept and value as knowledge and learning in the school context (Kress, 2010; Kress & Selander, 2012). As Kress and Selander (2012) note, the integration of games and simulations in assessment practices also requires a meta-reflection of contemporary (school-) "cultures of recognition". In particular, a focus on the design-perspective on learning developed in Scandinavian countries offers an approach on the effective and meaningful use of digital games and simulations for learning. While possibly ambitious, this is an exciting and meaningful endeavour to more optimally harness the affordances of new technologies in the form of digital games and simulations to design for effective learning experiences for our students.

REFERENCES

Åkerfeldt, A. (2014). *Didaktisk design med digitala resurser. En studie av kunskapsrepresentationer i en digitaliserad skola* [Didactic design with digital resources. A study of knowledge representations in a digitized school] (dissertation). Stockholm University, Stockholm.

Åkerfeldt, A., & Selander, S. (2011). Exploring educational video game design: Meaning potentials and implications for learning. In P. Felicia (Ed.), *Handbook of research on improving learning and motivation through educational games: Multidisciplinary approaches*. Hershey, PA: IGI Global.

Allodi, M. W., Linikko, J., & Fors, U. (2012, November). *Simulation of establishing an individual education plan for a virtual pupil*. EAPRIL Conference, Jyväskylä, Finland.

Barab, S. A., Scott, B., Siyahhan, S., Goldstone, R., Ingram-Goble, A., Zuiker, S. J., & Warren, S. (2009). Transformational play as a curricular scaffold: Using videogames to support science education. *Journal of Science Education and Technology, 18*(4), 305–320. doi:10.1007/s10956-009-9171-5

Bennett, S., & Maton, K. (2010). Beyond the 'digital natives' debate: Towards a more nuanced understanding of students' technology experiences. *Journal of Computer Assisted Learning, 26*(5), 321–331.

Botezatu, M., Hult, H., Kassaye Tessma, M., & Fors, U. (2010). Virtual patient simulation for learning and assessment: Superior results in comparison with regular course exams. *Medical Teacher, 32*(10), 845–850.

Care, E., Griffin, P., & Wilson, M. (2018). *Assessment and teaching of 21st century skills: Research and approaches*. Cham: Springer.

Cook, D. A., & Triola, M. M. (2009). Virtual patients: A critical literature review and proposed next steps. *Medical Education, 43*(4), 303–311.

Danielsson, K., & Selander, S. (2016). Reading multimodal texts for learning: A model for cultivating multimodal literacy. *Designs for Learning, 8*(1), 25–36.

Davis, D. A., Mazmanian, P. E., Fordis, M., Van Harrison, R., Thorpe, K. E., & Perrier, L. (2006). Accuracy of physician self-assessment compared with observed measures of competence. *JAMA, 296*(9), 1094–1102.

DeLacey, B. J., & Leonard, D. A. (2002). Case study on technology and distance education at the Harvard business school. *Educational Technology and Society, 5*(2), 1–22.

Dong, G., & Oei, H. (2013). Digital game based learning. In C. H. Mun (Ed.), *i in practice, educational technology division, ministry of education, Singapore* (Vol. 1, pp. 29–33). Retrieved November 26, 2013, from https://ictconnection.moe.edu.sg/publications/i-in-practice/volumes

Duke, R. (1974). *Gaming: The future's language*. New York, NY: Sage Publications.

Edelbring, S., Broström, O., Henriksson, P., Vassiliou, D., Spaak, J., Dahlgren, L. O., Fors, U., & Zary, N. (2012). Course integration of virtual patients: Follow-up seminars and perceived benefit. *Medical Education, 46*(4), 417–425.

Edelbring, S., Fors, U., & Sæther, B. (2004). SvalSim: Field work simulation system for problem-oriented learning in petroleum geology. *CAL-Laborate, 12*, 9–11.

Ekblad, S., Mollica, R. F., Fors, U., Pantziaras, I., & Lavelle, J. (2013). Educational potential of a virtual patient system for caring for traumatized patients in primary care. *BMC Medical Education, 13*, 110. doi:10.1186/1472-6920-13-110

Fernandez, A., Schillinger, D., Grumbach, K., Rosenthal, A., Stewart, A. L., Wang, F., & Pérez-Stable, E. J. (2004). Physician language ability and cultural competence: An exploratory study of communication with Spanish-speaking patients. *Journal of General Internal Medicine, 19*, 167–174.

Fors, U., & Skoglund, Å. (2013). A pilot study of virtual cases in law education. *European Journal of Law and Technology, 4*(3). Retrieved from http://ejlt.org/article/view/252/413

Frank, A. (2012). Gaming the game: A study of the gamer mode in educational wargaming. *Simulation & Gaming, 43*, 118–132. Retrieved April 4, 2013, from http://sag.sagepub.com/content/43/1/118.full.pdf+html

Gee, J. P. (2003). High score education: Games, not school, are teaching kids to think. *Wired Magazine, 11*(5). Retrieved February 5, 2013, from http://www.wired.com/wired/archive/11.05/view.html?pg=1

Gee, J. P. (2004). *What video games have to teach us about learning and literacy*. New York, NY: Palgrave Macmillan.

Girard, C., Ecalle, J., & Magnan, A. (2013, June). Serious games as new educational tools: How effective are they? A meta-analysis of recent studies. *Journal of Computer Assisted Learning, 29*(3), 207–219.

Guillén-Nieto, V., & Aleson-Carbonell, M. (2012, January). Serious games and learning effectiveness: The case of it's a deal! *Computers & Education, 58*(1), 435–448.

Gunter, G., Kenny, R. & Vick, E. (2006). A case for a formal design paradigm for serious games. *The Journal of the International Digital Media and Arts Association, 3*(1), 93–105.

Ito, M. (2010). *Hanging out, messing around and geeking out: Kids living and learning with new media*. Cambridge, MA: MIT Press.

Jackson, J. R. (1959). Learning from experience in business decision games. *California Management Review, 1*(2), 92–107.

Kjällander, S. (2011). *Designs for learning in an extended digital environment: Case studies of social interaction in the social science classroom* (dissertation). Stockholm University, Stockholm.

Kress, G. (2003). *Literacy in the new media age*. London: Routledge.

Kress, G. (2010). *Multimodality: A social semiotic approach to contemporary communication*. London: Routledge.

Kress, G., & Selander, S. (2012). Multimodal design, learning and cultures of recognition. *The Internet and Higher Education, 15*(4), 265–268.

Laurillard, D. (2012). *Teaching as a design science: Building pedagogical patterns for learning and technology*. London: Routledge.

Lim, F. V., & Hung, D. (2016). Teachers as learning designers: What technology has to do with learning. *Educational Technology, 56*(4), 26–29.

Lim, F. V., Woo, H. M., & Lee, M. Y. (2016). *Serious games to develop social and emotional learning in students* (pp. 3–12). Joint Conference on Serious Games (JCSG), 2016 Proceedings, Springer Lecture Notes in Computer Science (LNCS), Brisbane, Australia.

Linderoth, J. (2012). Why gamers don't learn more: An ecological approach to games as learning environments. *Journal of Gaming and Virtual Worlds, 4*(1), 45–62.

Lindstrand, F., Insulander, E., & Selander, S. (2016). Mike the knight in the neo-liberal era: A multimodal approach to children's multi-media entertainment. *Journal of Language and Politics, 15*(3), 337–351.

Misfeldt, M. (2015). Scenario Based Education as framework for understanding student's engagement and learning in a project management simulation game. *Electronic Journal of E-Learning, 13*(3), 181–191.

Mitgutsch, K. (2013). *Context matters! Exploring and reframing games and play in context*. Wien: New Academic Press.

Morin, E. (1999). *Les sept savoirs nécessaires à l'éducation du futur*. Paris: Seuil.

Morin, E. (2008). *On complexity*. Cresskill, NJ: Hampton Press.

Nødtvedt Knudsen, K. (2017). *#iLive—konturer af en performative dramadidaktik i en digital samtid* [#iLive—outline of a performative dramadidactic approach in a digitized time] (Dissertation). NTNU, Trondheim.

Nouri, J. (2014). *Orchestrating scaffolded outdoor mobile learning activities* (Dissertation). Stockholm University, Stockholm.

O'Halloran, K. L., & Lim, F. V. (2011). Dimensions of multimodal literacy. *Viden om Læsning, 10*, 14–21.

Paige, J. T., Kozmenko, V., Yang, T., Paragi Gururaja, R., Hilton, C. W., Cohn, I., & Chauvin, S. W. (2009). High-fidelity, simulation-based, interdisciplinary operating room team training at the point of care. *Surgery, 145*(2), 138–146.

Pantziaras, I., Fors, U., & Ekblad, S. (2014). Innovative training with virtual patients in transcultural psychiatry: The impact on physicians' confidence. *PLOS ONE, 10*(3), e0119754.

Papert, S. (1998, June). Does easy do it? Children, games and learning. *Game Developer Magazine*, 88. Retrieved February 5, 2013, from http://www.papert.org/articles/Doeseasydoit.html

Prensky, M. (2001). Digital natives, digital immigrants. *On the Horizon, 9*(5), 1–6. Retrieved August 9, 2013, from http://www.marcprensky.com/writing/Prensky%20-%20Digital%20Natives,%20 Digital%20Immigrants%20-%20Part1.pdf

Ramberg, R., Artman, H., & Karlgren, K. (2013). Designing learning opportunities in interaction design: Interactionaries as a means to study and teach student design processes. *Designs for Learning, 6*(1–2), 30–50.

Rigby, S., & Ryan, M. (2011). *Glued to games: How video games draw us in and hold us spellbound.* Santa Barbara, CA: Praeger.

Robertson, J., & Good, J. (2005). Story creation in virtual game worlds. *Communications of the ACM, 48*(1), 61–65.

Selander, S. (2008a). Designs for learning: A theoretical perspective. *Designs for Learning, 1*(1), 10–22.

Selander, S. (2008b). Designs for learning and the formation and transformation of knowledge in an era of globalization. *Studies in Philosophy of Education, 27*, 267–281.

Selander, S. (2008c). Designs for learning and ludic engagement. *Digital Creativity, 19*(3), 199–208.

Selander, S. (2017). *Didakiken efter Vygotskij—Design för lärande* [Education after Vygotskij—Designs for learning]. Stockholm: Liber.

Selander, S., & Kress, G. (2010). *Design för lärande—ett multimodalt perspektiv* [Designs for learning—A multimodal perspective]. Stockholm: Norstedts.

Shaffer, D. W. (2009). Epistemic network analysis: A prototype for 21st century assessment of learning. *Foundations & Findings, 1*(2), 1–22.

Steinkuehler, C., Squire, K., & Barab, S. (Eds.). (2012). *Games, learning, and society: Learning and meaning in the digital age.* Cambridge: Cambridge University Press.

Tamara, L. S. (2017). Data literacy for social studies: Examining the role of data visualizations in K–12 textbooks. *Theory & Research in Social Education, 46*(2), 194–231.

Watson, H. J. (1981). *Computer simulation in business.* New York, NY: John Wiley & Sons.

Wiklund, M. (2007). *Computer game use and communication habit changes* (pp. 31–38). In Proceedings of CGAMES 2007, 10th International Conference on Computer Games: AI, Animation, Mobile, Educational and Serious Games, University of Wolverhampton, School of Computing and Information Technology, Wolverhampton.

Wiklund, M., & Ekenberg, L. (2009). Going to school in world of warcraft: Observations from a trial programme using off-the-shelf computer games as learning tools in secondary education. *Designs for learning, 2*(1), 36–55.

Woods, S. (2004). Loading the dice: The challenge of serious videogames. *Game Studies: The International Journal of Computer Game Research, 4*(1). Retrieved August 9, 2013, from http://www.gamestudies.org/0401/woods/

THORKILD HANGHØJ, MORTEN MISFELDT,
JEPPE BUNDSGAARD AND SIMON SKOV FOUGT

2. UNPACKING THE DOMAINS AND PRACTICES OF GAME-ORIENTED LEARNING

ABSTRACT

Using games for learning tends to blur boundaries across across in- and out-of-school domains. In this way, it becomes difficult to describe and understand the meaning-making processes involved in game-oriented learning. In this chapter, we present the analytical framework of scenario-based education, which can be used to explore the translation processes and framings in relation to using game-oriented learning designs. The framework is used to analyse two empirical cases. The first case concerns the use of two different types of computer games (the serious game *Global Conflicts: Latin America* and the horror game *Penumbra*) in formal education and focuses on the relation between schooling and everyday life. The second case concerns the development and use of a specially designed practice simulation that invites school children into a universe as professional journalists and newspaper editors and hence builds on a designed relation between schooling and professional domains. Based on these examples, we discuss how the aims and practices of game-oriented learning designs must be translated, communicated, negotiated, integrated, and thus reframed by teachers and students in order to produce relevant and valid forms of educational knowledge.

Keywords: scenario-based education, domains, framing, translations, commercial games, serious games, practice simulations

INTRODUCTION

Theories on play and games tend to describe games as bounded and neatly delineated phenomena such as "magic circles" (Huizinga, 1950), "world-building activities" (Goffman, 1961), "multimodal texts" (Burn et al., 2006), or "rule-based systems" (Salen & Zimmerman, 2003). However, as Gee (2011) argues, it is important for educational game researchers to look beyond the isolated game design and take a broader perspective on the learning ecology, which emerges when teachers and students enact specific game environments. Thus, if we wish to understand game-oriented learning, we cannot simply reduce the phenomenon to questions of game design, as learning always involves negotiation and meaning-making processes between the involved participants. To complicate things further, the educational use of games both reflects and tends to move beyond the existing knowledge practices in schools, as games allow participants to not only explore specific game worlds, but also bring in their own game experiences or their everyday experiences of the worlds and practices that specific games try to simulate.

This raises a key question, which we address in this chapter: How can we describe and understand game-oriented learning environments as an interplay of practices across in- and out-of-school domains? In order to answer this question, we view game-oriented learning as an example of *scenario-based education* (Hanghøj, 2013; Hanghøj et al., 2017). This means that we conceptualize game-oriented learning as game participants' active processes of imagining, enacting, and reflecting on particular courses of action and possible outcomes of situated game scenarios. The theory of scenario-based education further assumes that simulations or games used for education always enact *several domains of practice*, which both involve the domain-specific practices of the school context and refer to practices outside the educational setting. This means that game-oriented learning reflects multiple ways in which the participants are able to frame and become framed by their game experiences. In this way, our aim is to present scenario-based education as an analytical framework, which can be used to describe and understand the translation processes of game-oriented learning that may both create clashes as well as congruence between frames across in- and out-of-school domains.

In this chapter, we will present two case studies that each explore the translation processes and framings in relation to game-oriented learning designs. The first case concerns the use of two different types of computer games in formal education and focuses on the relation between schooling and everyday life. The second case concerns the development and use of a specially designed practice simulation that invites school children into a universe as professional journalists and newspaper editors and hence, builds on a designed relation between schooling and professional domains.

EDUCATIONAL SCENARIOS

The notion of scenario has multiple meanings (Hanghøj, 2008; Hanghøj et al., 2017). A scenario both refers to a *process* (e.g. teachers and students' envisioned courses of action) and an *object* (e.g. the course of actions embedded in a lesson plan or in a design for learning). In an educational context, we can speak of *educational scenarios*, which refer to teaching-learning sequences that allow learners to explore more or less explicit scenarios. Scenario-based learning activities may be supported through various types of game-oriented learning designs, such as storylines, role-play, drama, what-if scenarios, simulations, and computer games.

Furthermore, we argue that scenario-based learning can be conceptualized using Dewey's pragmatist philosophy of learning, which emphasizes transactions between experience and reflection (Dewey, 1916). Consequently, educational scenarios may promote learning through *scenario-based inquiry*, which allows learners to solve problems by conducting a "dramatic rehearsal" of various possible outcomes and to make decisions by weighing imagined as well as experienced consequences (Dewey, 1922, p. 190).

Finally, the term scenario also encompasses *scenario competence*, which involves the ability to imagine, enact, and reflect upon choices and their possible outcomes across game- and non-game domains. Thus, teachers may be more or less scenario competent in terms of planning and realizing game-oriented learning environments, just as students may be more or less scenario competent when exploring specific games and engaging in encompassed knowledge practices.

Our interest in understanding and exploring how scenarios can be used in educational contexts stems from our involvement in studies that explore several different approaches to game-oriented learning. These studies include the use of debate games in social studies and mother tongue education (Hanghøj, 2008); computer games in social studies and mother tongue education (Bourgonjon & Hanghøj, 2011; Hanghøj, 2011; Hanghøj & Hautopp, 2016); board game design in mathematics education (Bundsgaard, Misfeldt, & Hetmar, 2011; Misfeldt, 2013); a web-based learning game for teaching skills in planning and complexity for pre-service education in the construction sector (Misfeldt, 2010); and practice scaffolding interactive platforms in mother tongue education (Bundsgaard, 2009; Fougt, 2009).

Combined, these studies cover a broad range of game-oriented learning designs aimed at different school subjects and types and levels of education ranging from primary school to higher education. A common feature is that the designs facilitate teaching through game-related and scenario-based models of action, which position learners as imaginative producers of new knowledge through active experiments and reflections. However, the scope and breadth of the studies also point to the necessity for developing a common analytical framework for describing and understanding how game-oriented learning is enacted in practice. In order to present such a framework, two interrelated questions are addressed:

1. What domains and which translations of knowledge practices are involved in game-oriented teaching and learning?
2. How are teachers' and students' experiences framed through particular game-oriented educational scenarios?

Two case studies are used to address these questions. The first case concerns the translation of knowledge practices between the domain of schooling and the everyday life domain. The second case involves the translation of knowledge practices between the domain of schooling and the professional domain.

THEORETICAL FRAMEWORK

This section defines domains and framings as key concepts in our analytical framework for conceptualizing and understanding the practice of teaching and learning through educational scenarios.

Domains and Educational Scenarios

Educational scenarios are always enacted within and in relation to particular domains, which can be understood as "structured, patterned contexts", in which specific practices unfold (Barton & Hamilton, 2000, p. 11). As we argue elsewhere (Hanghøj et al., 2017), scenario-based education involves the interplay of meaning across four domains, which each refer to specific groups of practices:

- *Pedagogical domain*: institutionalized pedagogical practices that are recognized as "school only", e.g. by being based on an asymmetric relationship between the teacher and their students and modes of communication embedded in local classroom cultures.
- *Disciplinary domain*: specialized knowledge practices within disciplines such as mathematics, history, science, and mother tongue education.
- *Scenario domain*: knowledge practices that are enacted through specific scenarios, which may involve simulations of professional practices (e.g. journalism, engineering, and medicine) or exploration of other types of imaginary worlds (e.g. literary fictions or commercial computer games).
- *Everyday domain*: everyday, non-specialized knowledge practices such as friendships, family, sports, and media use.

The empirical focus of this chapter is formal education, which means that the educational use of game-oriented scenarios represents a common ground in relation to the other four domains. Figure 2.1 illustrates how the educational use of game-oriented scenarios relates to the four domains.

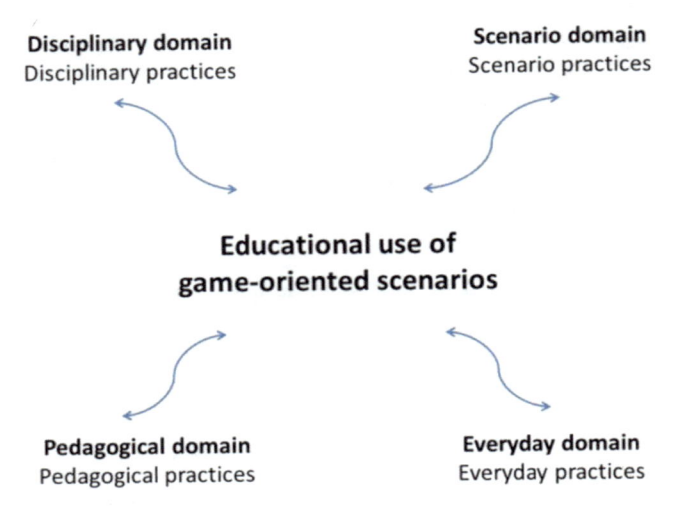

Disciplinary domain
Disciplinary practices

Scenario domain
Scenario practices

Educational use of game-oriented scenarios

Pedagogical domain
Pedagogical practices

Everyday domain
Everyday practices

Figure 2.1. The four domains of scenario-based education

Drawing clear boundaries between the four domains is difficult, as the boundaries are often blurred—e.g. doing homework may take place within the physical domain of a student's home, but the practice of doing homework still refers to the disciplinary and pedagogical domains of the school context. This blurring and crossing of practices across domains becomes even more relevant to consider due to the widespread use of digital media (Mills, 2010) and to the importance of "not-school" learning spaces (Sefton-Green, 2013). Even though the categories are not rigidly distinct from one another, maintaining the overall domain categories is useful for describing and understanding how educational scenarios are performed in practice.

Integrating non-school domains into school contexts is by no means a new practice and has often been described as a tension between progressive and traditional forms of education (Dewey, 1938; Shaffer, 2004). However, this chapter does not focus on the philosophical aims and values of various types of education, but rather on describing and understanding the contingent translation processes that occur when trying to integrate different knowledge practices across school and non-school domains (Hanghøj, 2011). As a result, we assume that different domains always involve particular knowledge practices with corresponding validity criteria for what counts and what does not count as legitimate knowledge (Barth, 2002).

Furthermore, we assume that scenario-based teaching and learning that include non-school domains always involve reductions or simplifications of non-school knowledge practices. As will be shown, students' experiences as gamers or as journalists in a school context are significantly different from the out-of-school practices involved in playing games and writing journalism. We wish to ask the following questions: How do teachers and students experience non-school domains within educational contexts? And, what forms of knowledge are created when students take on the identities and practices of non-school domains?

Framing Educational Scenarios

In order to answer these questions, we need to address how particular scenarios *frame* and become *framed* by social actors within educational contexts; in other words, we must address how the meanings of particular scenarios and domains are created through teachers' and students' sociocognitive negotiation of different interpretive frames (Goffman, 1974; Fine, 1983; Hanghøj, 2008). One of the most commonly recurring forms of framing within educational domains is formed around teacher-centered initiation-response-evaluation (IRE) dialog structures (Sinclair & Coulthard, 1975), in which a teacher initiates dialog, students respond, and the teacher conducts an evaluation. Many people view this form of communication as simply being synonymous with schooling or "school-only" (Purcell-Gates, Duke, & Martineau, 2007), as it only occurs in schools. Thus, IRE is "… almost universally accepted as 'the essential teaching exchange'" (Wegerif, 2004, p. 4). To some degree, the IRE structure of communication is a staged scenario, with teachers and students playing different roles in an orchestrated dialog. This form of communication, however, is rarely *experienced* as a scenario and is instead framed as a naturalized or *tacit* pedagogical practice within the domain of schooling. By contrast, scenario-based teaching with games or simulations aims to be experienced as *explicit scenarios* that break with the framing of the IRE structure.

In educational research, the notions of frame and framing have been used prescriptively to identify educational aims such as the acquisition of "epistemic frames" in relation to professional practices (Shaffer, 2006) and the rhetorical framing of language within mother tongue education (Andrews, 2011). In this chapter, we propose a more *descriptive* use of frame theory in order to understand how teachers and students experience the interplay of the domains and knowledge practices in relation to specific educational scenarios. Applying the descriptive use of frame theory to the example of a student taking part in a debate game on parliamentary elections reveals that the student continually shifts between the following overall framings in relation to the four domains (Hanghøj, 2008):

- The frame of *being a student* and taking part in classroom dialogue (the pedagogical domain)
- The frame of *being a person* with individual beliefs and ideological values (the everyday domain)
- The frame of *adopting the assigned role* as a politician representing an ideological and political function/position (the disciplinary domain)
- The frame of the *performance as a player* (the scenario domain).

Thus, educational scenarios enable a variety of possible framings, which require mutual negotiation between the intentions of students, teachers, and learning resources in relation to the knowledge practices of different domains. Obviously, describing how individual teachers and students experience particular situations is complex, as interpretive frames and framings often constitute *tacit* aspects of human experience. As a result, frames sometimes only become visible when there is a conflict or clash of frames (Goffman, 1974). At the same time, underplaying the importance of framing in scenario-based teaching and learning is problematic, especially in relation to the mix of school and non-school domains, which involve a complicated interplay of different framings—e.g. between the experience of being a student, a person, a role, and a player—that may be experienced as more or less meaningful.

From a realist point of view, it is tempting to assume that educational scenarios represent a continuum of learning trajectories that gradually introduce students to intended out-of-school ways of thinking, knowing, and being. However, as the case studies presented below indicate, educational scenarios often involve conflicting and sometimes contradictory frames, which may be difficult to predict. Thus, there is no guarantee that educational scenarios or any other type of teaching necessarily lead to more engaging, authentic, or realistic learning experiences (Petraglia, 1998). In order to address this complexity, we believe that the notion of frames forms a highly relevant part of a framework for understanding educational scenarios for at least two reasons. First, frame analysis pays close attention to the ways in which the tacit dimensions of different knowledge practices become visible when teachers and students break or re-frame their experiences in relation to different domains. Second, frame analysis can be used to describe and understand teachers' and students' explicit social negotiation of the meaning and validity of the different knowledge practices involved, when using scenarios for educational purposes.

BRIDGING SCHOOLING AND EVERYDAY LIFE

The first aspect of educational scenarios described here concerns relations between students' experience of "doing school" and their everyday worlds as children outside school contexts. As Bruner notes, one of the most important points to learn in school is assimilating the culture of schooling: "The chief subject matter of school, viewed culturally, is school itself. That is how most students experience it, and it determines what meaning they make out of it" (1996, p. 28). Following this claim, the analytical framework of scenario-based education can be used to explore the ways in which students do identity work to become more or less legitimate members of school domains.

The relationship between students' school practices and their everyday life practices outside school contexts has often been described as the difference between learning processes that take place in formal and informal learning contexts (Scribner & Cole, 1973; Sefton-Green, 2013). Hence, it is often argued that formal school activities may benefit from the inclusion of learning experiences, literacies, and knowledge practices that mainly exist outside the school context. In recent years, attempts to integrate phenomena outside of school into educational scenarios have increasingly focused on the use of online digital media in and outside school contexts (Mills, 2010; The New London Group, 1996). Thus, it is assumed that school curricula and teaching practices need to change and reflect the ways in which digital technologies promote valuable forms of knowledge production, communication, and participation.

In order to illustrate this complexity, we use the research and practices of Digital Game-Based Learning as an example. Several researchers within the field of games and learning have made strong claims regarding the potential of games and game elements to reform the pedagogical practices of teaching, learning, and schooling (Gee, 2003; Shaffer, 2006; Squire, 2011). These sweeping claims, however, are only backed by limited empirical research in everyday school contexts and have been criticized for creating problematic dichotomies between the "boring" reality of schooling and the "engaging" learning processes taking place when children play games (Buckingham, 2007; Pelletier, 2010). Consequently, there is an important demand for more empirical research on how play and game phenomena can—and cannot—be meaningfully included within the context of formal schooling.

Case: Framing Computer Games in Educational Contexts

To illustrate the complex meaning-making processes involved in using computer game scenarios for educational purposes, we compare two studies of game-based learning. The first example concerns a study in Danish, Norwegian, and English 8th and 9th grade classrooms on the use of *Global Conflicts: Latin America* (GC: LA), a learning game designed to meet cross-curricular aims in secondary and upper secondary education (Hanghøj, 2011). The second example, taken from a study of a Danish secondary teacher's game literacy practices, focuses on the educational use of Penumbra, a commercial computer horror game, in an 8th grade classroom (Bourgonjon & Hanghøj, 2011). Comparing these two examples (see Figure 2.2) allows us to describe how game-based learning can entail widely different framings related to the possibility space of particular game genres, teachers' design of educational scenarios, and students' game experiences of educational gaming.

Figure 2.2. Screendumps from Global Conflicts: Latin America and Penumbra

With regard to game design, the two computer games represent two exceedingly distinct genres designed for quite different purposes. GC: LA is an educational adventure game that invites players to take on the role of a journalist who must navigate a conflict-ridden environment (e.g. border crossings between the U.S. and Mexico) to collect various types of information to confront the villain (e.g. a corrupt mayor) at the end of the game. The game session is either followed by an assignment, which requires the students to write a critical chapter, or a class group discussion, which requires students to engage in a discussion regarding what they experienced and the topic of the game. The game is accompanied by a relatively comprehensive set of teaching materials that guides the teacher in presenting the game to the students and matching the curricular objectives. As a result, GC: LA is primarily an educational game with relatively limited game worlds designed to be played within the scope of a few lessons.

In contrast, Penumbra is a commercial horror computer game in which players must locate and use an assortment of objects, such as keys and weapons, to solve various puzzles and fight monsters. The game scenario is based on a compelling, suspense-driven narrative that takes place in a highly immersive atmosphere in an abandoned mine filled with dark locations and creepy sound effects. The absence of learning objectives and a highly difficult game play that may easily leave players stuck for hours trying to solve a puzzle clearly suggest that Penumbra was not designed for educational purposes.

The next aspect of our comparison concerns the educational scenarios, which teachers plan, enact, and evaluate when teaching using the two games. Classroom studies of ten GC: LA game sessions documented how most of the participating teachers found themselves "looking over the shoulders" of their students without interrupting their game play (Hanghøj & Brund, 2011). This indicates that the majority of the teachers was relatively passive during the game sessions and only gave limited instructions on how to play the game or on the educational purpose of playing the game. Partly, the teachers' passive approach may have stemmed from their overall lack of gaming experience and the actual design of the game, which required students to read large amounts of text. The post-game interviews made it clear that several of the teachers believed that the game would intuitively appeal to the students, especially the boys, who the teachers felt should be allowed to explore the game independently. In this way, several of the teachers felt less obliged to plan detailed educational scenarios for enacting and assessing the outcome of the game sessions.

In comparison, the Danish secondary teacher who taught with Penumbra chose a rather detailed approach when planning, enacting, and evaluating his educational game scenario (Bourgonjon & Hanghøj, 2011). Due to the complexity of the horror game world and the lack of inherent learning objectives, the teacher had to make several educational decisions in order to translate the knowledge practices of the game into a meaningful learning resource to be used within the disciplinary domain of Danish as a school subject. More specifically, he used the game demo (approximately an hour of free game play) with his 8th grade class as a part of a teaching-learning sequence on genre writing and linguistic awareness, which focused on defining the characteristics of horror genre across games, films, and books. By letting the students play Penumbra, the teacher aimed to let the students become "immersed" in the narrative experience of the horror genre. Next, the students were asked to write a horror scene from the game using their own words. In order to fully immerse the students in the horror game, the teacher asked them to play the game demo in small groups using laptops in the school's dark basement. By choosing this setting, the teacher deliberately opted out of the everyday physical learning environment of the classroom and the computer lab in favor of staging an unfamiliar, but more relevant place in terms of supporting the experience of the horror scenario.

The final aspect of our comparison concerns the framing of the students' experience across the two game examples. The GC: LA study shows how the game received a rather mixed reception by the participating students (Hanghøj, 2011). To the majority of the boys, the adventure game clearly failed to live up to their expectations of a 3D computer game due to, for example, the limited possibilities for interaction, lack of explicit violence, and no risk of dying. When watching the game trailer, some boys initially compared the game to the violent sandbox game Grand Theft Auto, but their excitement was soon replaced by lack of interest and disruptive forms of play. Following this clash of expectations, some of the boys explicitly framed the game as a "school game" and failed to create meaningful translations of their game experiences into disciplinary concepts and the written assignment. At the same time, other students clearly became engaged in the game and managed to translate their game experiences into lengthy journalistic feature articles. In particular, one of the girls surprised her teacher by coming up with a well-written feature told from a first-person point of view that positively exceeded her classmates' expectations of what was allowed to be written in the genre of journalism. As these examples indicate, there were significant differences in how the students perceived the game design of GC: LA as being meaningful or not.

Returning to the Penumbra example, the teacher's framing of the educational scenario around the game clearly influenced the students' game-based writing experience. Drawing on their game experience, the students were asked to write a short horror scene from the game. This task required the students to translate their game experience into the fictional genre of horror writing, which related to their knowledge of the discipline and their everyday knowledge of the horror genre. To prevent the students' fictional texts from being reduced purely to school texts (i.e. texts that only exist and only have relevance within a school context), the teacher asked each of the student groups to select their "best horror sentence" to be compared and discussed in class. After writing these sentences on the board, the teacher then orchestrated a discussion on how the sentences could or could not be viewed as good horror sentences and how they differed from other related genres, such as the splatter, noir, or thriller genres. In this way, the students were asked to write and present sentences that should convince not only the teacher, but also their classmates of the quality of their "horror literacy". According to the teacher, the students were both quite engaged when they played the game in small groups in the basement and when they discussed the quality of their horror sentences in class.

In summary, we have compared two examples of game-based writing experiences, which involve dissimilar game genres, distinct educational scenarios, and contrasting framings of the participating students. We have shown some of the complex knowledge translations and framings involved when integrating students' game practices and everyday experiences with the pedagogical and disciplinary practices of the school. The findings indicate that educational scenarios designed to bridge and integrate the domains of "gaming" and "schooling" imply contingent outcomes and learning experiences that can be difficult to predict. The example of GC: LA shows how following the commonsensical assumption that computer games appeal more to boys, who can find out what to do on their own, is problematic. As the teachers only briefly addressed the dynamics of the game world and their relation to the disciplinary domain of social studies, the students were often left on their own for either discarding or accepting the game as a school game. Similarly, the educational use of commercial computer games such as Penumbra can create immersive learning experiences, but this approach requires that teachers have sufficient game literacy and disciplinary knowledge to develop meaningful educational scenarios. Consequently, the educational use of commercial games may potentially provide more demanding and more engaging learning experiences than learning games.

Together, the two examples show how attempts to bring students' everyday game experiences into the domain of schooling are not simply a matter of importing knowledge from one domain to the other. By using the analytical framework of scenario-based education, it becomes clear that the translations and framings of game-based learning involve reconfiguration of all the involved domains—especially in relation to the framing of the "student" (the pedagogical domain) and the framing of the "player" (the everyday life domain). Moreover, the examples show that teachers tend to choose widely different pedagogical approaches—e.g. as passive observers or as active re-designers of game-based learning processes—when translating the knowledge practices of computer games into educational scenarios.

SCHOOLING AND PROFESSIONAL PRACTICE

The second aspect of scenario-based education this chapter deals with concerns the relationship between professional practice and schooling. Pedagogues such as Dewey (1916) and Freinet (1941, 1969) promoted the simulation of professional practice in school settings, and Kent (1990), for example, promoted realistic problem solving in the more recent movement for entrepreneurship education. In this way, it is assumed that learning activities that resemble professional work practices can motivate and increase meaningfulness, as well as engage students in active dialog (Freinet, 1969; cf. Acker, 2007) and create "thick authenticity" (Shaffer, 2006).

Simulating a professional practice in a school setting is by no means an easy task. Being a journalist or an architect is a demanding profession that involves complex practices. A scenario consisting of simply saying to students, "Now you're journalists", is unlikely to make the students frame their activities in relation to a deep understanding of the professional domain of journalism. The students—and probably their teacher—would typically identify journalism with writing and lay outing articles, and perhaps interviewing, for example, politicians. The students would not know, however, all of the other parts of the professional practice, such as the process of selecting or identifying stories, focusing and selecting an angle, preparing for an interview, doing research, making appointments with editors and photographers, aligning with genre conventions, and meeting deadlines in a timely manner.

Thus, most aspects of a professional practice remain invisible or tacit to non-professionals, which make simulating the practices of journalists difficult. Consequently, students and teachers need support for *framing* their understanding of the scenario that they work with towards the professional domain of journalism. This kind of support can be carried out by making, for instance, processes, interactions, and rules more manifest. Furthermore, structuring the work process, collaboration, and the acquisition of relevant knowledge can also support the students' journalistic practices. All these functions can be integrated into a coherent computer-based design for learning, which is called a Practice Scaffolding Interactive Platform (PracSIP) (Bundsgaard, 2009; Bundsgaard, 2018).

Case: Translating Journalism into Classroom Contexts

The Editorial Office is an example of a PracSIP that supports students' production of a newspaper by addressing the well-known challenges of project-based teaching, which can be summed up as the challenges involved in structuring the work process and organizing collaboration and learning content while working on a project (cf. Barron et al., 1998; Bundsgaard, 2009). Figure 2.3 shows how *The Editorial Office* scaffolds students' journalistic work process.

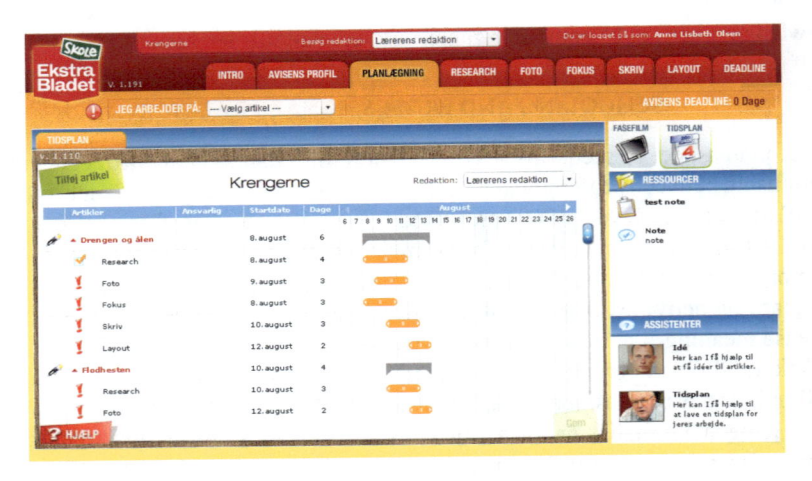

Figure 2.3. The "planner" tool in The Editorial Office

The Editorial Office manifests journalism processes by guiding students through seven phases from idea to print.[1] A planning tool helps students on the editorial teams organize their collaboration by making a simple Gantt chart to support which articles to write, the delegation of subtasks, and the setting of deadlines. During the work process, the students must continuously update the status of the subtasks they are each responsible for, thus providing the editorial team and the teacher with an overview of the process. To support students' acquisition of content knowledge about journalism practices and the newspaper's main subject (e.g. developing ideas, searching the internet, preparing an interview, choosing an angle, and writing in a given journalistic genre), *The Editorial Office* integrates more than 40 interactive assistants who guide students through a reflective process relevant to their current task, which involves introducing students to core terms, instructing students in professional and academic work processes, and collecting relevant student answers in a report to be used in later work (cf. Bundsgaard, 2009; Fougt, 2009).

One major finding stands out from studies of students who used *The Editorial Office* (Fougt, 2009; Henderson, 2008). This PracSIP primarily works as a scaffold for the students and their teacher by structuring and organizing their work, offering content-related support along the way, and helping students produce high-quality newspapers, with respect to the newspapers' content, look, and feel, compared to student-produced newspapers made without the aid of tools like *The Editorial Office*. The studies further suggest that PracSIPs have considerable potential for supporting the management of work and collaboration process while also supporting the acquisition of content, thereby engaging students in a meaningful practice (Henderson, 2008, p. 103).

In traditional forms of teaching, primarily referred to as the pedagogical domain in our model, the teacher alone mediates the tools, processes, and concepts that may be connected to a professional practice, but the focus is typically on academic content, and the teacher does not address professional practices. With such teaching practices, students may be working with, for example, newspaper genres, but without access, or maybe even attention to the practices of journalism. In other words, the domain of schooling has detached and assimilated a selected subset of artifacts from the professional domain. In a teaching practice using a PracSIP, the students receive support to help them understand and simulate a professional practice by accessing manifestations of the professional practice that the PracSIP provides, thus giving the students highly tangible support to frame their experience as a journalist practice. Even though the professional practice is more manifest in a PracSIP approach, the students do not actually participate in the practice of journalism. Instead, they participate in a *boundary practice* (Henderson, 2008, p. 34f; cf. Wenger, 1998) between the ordinary domains of the school context and the professional domain with the practices of journalism they are simulating. They have a more explicit relationship with the simulated practice, but it is still foreign or unfamiliar. This means that teachers and students can be observed negotiating how to frame their practice while interacting with the PracSIP.

Observations of two 8th grade classes at the same school showed significant variation in how students and teachers accepted and took part in the scenario of journalism practice (Henderson, 2008). The students expressed, for example, two opposing framings of working with *The Editorial Office*: some students framed working with *The Editorial Office* as part of a journalism practice, while other students did not. In the following quote from a group interview on what the students thought about *The Editorial Office*, one student speaks about the role of the teacher:

Interviewer: What did you think about Gry [the teacher] during this project?

Student 1: Eager, again… She was eager for us to learn something about this. She likes journalism I suppose, and she likes it … that we're a real editorial office. She likes it … that we pictured ourselves like a real newspaper production process. She was very proud, not like different. Yes, she was more proud of us

> this time than the last time [we produced a newspaper]… last time was just like a little …

Student 2:   The keyword is just PROUD.

Student 1:   "Proud teacher!" [talks like she is quoting a headline]

(Henderson, 2008, p. 12)

In another study of *The Editorial Office* by Bundsgaard (2009), the teachers and students were more hesitant about framing their experience as being part of a journalism practice:

Interviewer: Did you feel like journalists in this project?

Student 3:   I didn't … I didn't entirely feel like a journalist, but like …
I don't know … not quite. But a little… (Bundsgaard, 2009, p. 9)

As this example indicates, not all students enacted their parts in the role-play about making a newspaper. When students who are used to class teaching primarily based on an IRE-dominated conversation structure (cf. Sinclair & Coulthardt, 1975) suddenly must work and learn in a scenario-based teaching practice, they may experience difficulties adapting to a new practice and tend to play "their traditional roles" (Stigler & Hierbert, 1999, p. 99). On the other hand, the studies also showed that when one of the two teachers introduced and willingly played her role as chief editor, it encouraged the students to fulfill their assigned roles.

To some degree, the tensions between different framings may be explained by a clash between everyday school practices and the simulated practices of the professional domain. Some of the students clearly resisted working like journalists as a relevant practice in a school context. In an interview with a group of students, who had been preparing an interview using an interactive assistant, one student stated, "the activity did not produce any learning about the school subject" (Fougt, 2009, p. 71). The interview further clarified how learning about the school subject for these students meant learning about grammar, punctuation, and spelling. When asked about the subject content introduced through the PracSIP (e.g. learning questioning techniques), the students hesitated to accept it as learning properly about a subject. Other students emphasized less narrow aspects of their learning outcomes:

Interviewer: So, you think, broadly speaking … that you've learned something about Danish and you've learned something about project …?

Student 1:   Yes … I've learned very much about the project and collaborating … and I've learned that you always need to have a plan, so you know what to do … everyone … (Henderson, 2008, p. 16)

This student accepted complex collaboration, process management, and communication practices as relevant and legitimate to the academic content, which justified her framing of her experience as journalism in practice, even though it took place in a school context.

In summary, the students and their teachers found it challenging to work, think, and act like journalists. Generally speaking, the students and teachers were accustomed to more traditional teaching practices, which may explain why many of them found it difficult to simulate professional practices and why some of the students did not experience the activity as "doing school" (Gee, 2003) the right way. By drawing in journalism as an out-of-school knowledge practice (cf. Figure 2.1), the framing of the educational scenario made it unclear and difficult for the students to understand their writing activities as a part of the disciplinary domain of Danish as a school subject. In this way, the case shows how educational scenarios require that both teachers and students adapt to new roles of participation to undergo meaningful learning experiences. As the examples indicate, teachers may benefit from accepting new roles as managers, guides, or co-players in an educational scenario that supports students' use of different resources and from discussing students' work and experiences with such resources.

The students, on the other hand, may benefit from accepting new roles as self-managing and collaborating professionals that produce valuable products. Thus, the educational use of professional scenarios only makes sense if both teachers and students can identify and follow the relevant validity criteria (Barth, 2002) for professional knowledge practices within school domains. This requires teachers and students to view academic content not only as facts and basic procedural knowledge, but also as knowing how to collaborate, produce, and communicate critically about the production of written and multimodal products (Bundsgaard & Fougt, 2017).

DISCUSSION

The two different types of cases, computer games versus simulation, showed how translations and framings of practices across domains may take on quite different forms, depending on the contexts of specific educational scenarios. Thus, the first case showed how attempts to integrate the students' everyday game knowledge into the pedagogical and disciplinary domains of schooling may easily run counter to teachers' prior expectations—e.g. that all boys like to play computer games and that they should be able to play the game without guidance. The case further emphasized the crucial role of the teacher in being able to design educational scenarios, which clearly identify and communicate the goals and dynamics of specific games in relation to selected pedagogical and disciplinary activities. The second case, which describes the educational use of an interactive platform for scaffolding writing within the domain of professional journalism, showed how teachers and students need to accept new roles, as well as new validity criteria for subject-related content, in order for educational scenarios to become meaningful.

Taken together, the two types of cases argue that the idea of integrating untransformed, game-oriented learning designs directly into schooling is problematic, as it does not account for differing knowledge practices and potential clashes between different framings. In this way, assumed "authentic" or "realistic" potentials of practice simulations and game-oriented scenarios should not be taken for granted but subjected to empirical analysis. The use of game-oriented scenarios in schools will always frame and be framed in relation to teachers and students' mixed experience of the enacted practices and how they translate across domains in relation to different knowledge practices and validity criteria.

As the cases show, the use of game-oriented educational scenarios can lead teachers to become passive observers of their students, who, in turn, may lose sight of the disciplinary aims. In this way, the learning potential of game-oriented scenarios is challenged by the high complexity of game scenarios, which may obscure teachers' curricular and pedagogical aims or transform those aims into unquestioned assumptions. Thus, the targeting of non-school domains may easily lead to confusion or frame clashes concerning aims, activities, and validity criteria. In this way, the cases show how the aims and practices of game-oriented learning designs must be translated, communicated, negotiated, integrated, and thus *reframed* by teachers and students in ways that produce relevant and valid forms of educational knowledge.

CONCLUSION

Game-oriented teaching and learning directly and explicitly enacts the imaginative aspect of students' scenario-based inquiry. The complexity of cross-domain framings that emerges when enacting educational scenarios, however, arguably both represents the most significant challenge and the most rewarding opportunity of using game-oriented learning designs. Hence, it is crucial for teachers to be able to not only design, communicate, enact, and assess educational scenarios, but also to address the implied knowledge practices of the involved domains and how this relates to school domains. Meaningful game-oriented learning requires that teachers and students can *articulate* the assumptions of particular educational scenarios and reflect similarities and differences through translations of practices across the involved domains. This is not a simple task. In order to address this challenge, this chapter has outlined a theoretical framework for understanding how the practices and explicit frames of game-oriented learning unfold across school and non-school domains. Thus, the framework and the cases presented here can hopefully be used for further analysis and facilitation of game-oriented learning, which is always present in the contingent continuum between imagined possibilities and the taken-for-granted aspects of existing pedagogical practices.

NOTE

[1] The seven phases are: deciding the paper's profile; planning which articles to write, delegating responsibilities, and setting deadlines; doing research; selecting, managing and editing photos; focusing the article; writing the article; layouting the paper; and sending the paper to print.

REFERENCES

Acker, V. (2007). *The French educator Célestin Freinet (1896–1966): An inquiry into how his ideas shaped education*. Lanham, MD: Lexington Books.

Andrews, R. (2010). *Re-framing literacy: Teaching and learning in English and the language arts*. London: Routledge.

Barron, B. J., Schwartz, D. L., Vye, N. J., Moore, A., Petrosino, A., Zech, L., & Bransford, J. D. (1998). Doing with understanding: Lessons from research on problem and project-based learning. *Journal of the Learning Sciences, 7*(3–4), 271–311.

Barth, F. (2002). An anthropology of knowledge. *Current Anthropology, 43*(1), 1–11.

Barton, D., & Hamiton, M. (2000). Literacy practices. In D. Barton, M. Hamilton, & R. Ivanic (Eds.), *Situated literacies: Reading and writing in context* (pp. 7–15). London: Routledge.

Bourgonjon, J., & Hanghøj, T. (2011). *What does it mean to be a game literate teacher? Interviews with teachers who translate games into educational practice*. Proceedings of the 5th European Conference on Games Based Learning, Athens, Greece.

Bruner, J. (1996). *The culture of education*. Cambridge, MA: Harvard University Press.

Buckingham, D. (2007). *Beyond technology: Children's learning in the age of digital culture*. Cambridge, MA: Polity Press.

Bundsgaard, J. (2009). *A practice scaffolding interactive platform*. Proceedings of the 9th International Conference on Computer Supported Collaborative Learning, Rhodes, Greece.

Bundsgaard, J. (2018). Using technology to scaffold progressive teaching. In Z. Babaci-Wilhite (Ed.), *Promoting human rights in education through STEAM*. New York, NY: Springer.

Bundsgaard, J., & Fougt, S. S. (2017). Faglighed og scenariedidaktik. In T. Hanghøj, J. Bundsgaard, M. Misfeldt, S. S. Fought, & V. Hetmar (Eds.), *Hvad er scenariedidaktik?* [What is scenario-based education?]. Århus: Århus Universitetsforlag.

Bundsgaard, J., Misfeldt, M., & Hetmar, V. (2011). Hvad skal der ske i skolen? Et bud på en prototypisk situationsorienteret curriculumlogik. *Cursiv, 8*, 123–142.

Burn, A., Schott, G., Carr, D., & Buckingham, D. (2006). *Computer games: Text, narrative and play*. Cambridge, MA: Polity Press.

Dewey, J. (1916). *Democracy and education*. New York, NY: Palgrave Macmillan.

Dewey, J. (1922). *Human nature and conduct: An introduction to social psychology*. New York, NY: Henry Holt & Company.

Dewey, J. (1938). *Experience and education*. New York, NY: Palgrave Macmillan.

Fine, G. A. (1983). *Shared fantasy: Role-playing games as social worlds*. Chicago, IL: University of Chicago Press.

Fougt, S. S. (2009). *Didaktisk design af interaktive assistenter*. Copenhagen: Aarhus University.

Freinet, C. (1941). *L'Éducation du travail*. Cannes: Édition Ophrys.

Freinet, C. (1969). *Pour l'ecole du peuple: Guide pratique pour l'organisation materielle, technique et pedagogique de l'ecole populaire*. Paris: Maspero.

Gee, J. P. (2003). *What video games have to teach us about learning and literacy*. New York, NY: Palgrave Macmillan.

Gee, J. P. (2011). Reflections on empirical evidence on games and learning. In S. Tobias & J. D. Fletcher (Eds.), *Computer games and instruction*. Charlotte, NC: Information Age Publishing.

Goffman, E. (1961). Fun in games. In E. Goffman (Ed.), *Encounters* (pp. 15–72). London: The Penguin Press.

Goffman, E. (1974). *Frame analysis: An essay on the organization of experience*. New York, NY: Harper & Row.

Hanghøj, T. (2008). *Playful knowledge: An explorative study of educational gaming* (PhD dissertation). University of Southern Denmark, Odense.

Hanghøj, T. (2011). Emerging and clashing genres: The interplay of knowledge forms in educational gaming. *Designs for Learning, 4*(1), 22–33.

Hanghøj, T. (2013). Game-based teaching: Practices, roles, and pedagogies. In de Freitas, S. Ott, M. M. Popescu, & I. Stanescu (Eds.), *New pedagogical approaches in game enhanced learning: Curriculum integration*. Hershey, PA: IGI Global.

Hanghøj, T., & Brund, C. E. (2010). *Teacher roles and positionings in relation to educational games*. In Proceedings for the 4th European Conference on Game-Based Learning, Copenhagen, Denmark.

Hanghøj, T., Bundsgaard, J., Misfeldt, M., Fought, S. S., & Hetmar, V. (Eds.). (2017). *Hvad er scenariedidaktik?* [What is scenario-based education?]. Århus: Århus Universitetsforlag.

Hanghøj, T., & Hautopp, H. (2016). *Teachers' pedagogical approaches to teaching with minecraft*. ECGBL 2016: 10th European Conference on Games Based Learning, Paisely, Scotland.

Henderson, L. (2008). *Praksisfællesskaber i undervisningen. Elevers deltagelsesformer i undervisning baseret på PracSIP'en: Redaktionen* (MA thesis). Aarhus University, Copenhagen.

Huizinga, J. (1950). *Homo ludens: A study of the play element in culture*. Boston, MA: Beacon Press.

Kent, C. (Ed.). (1990). *Entrepreneurship education: Current developments, future directions*. New York, NY: Quorum Books.

Mills, K. A. (2010). A review of the "digital turn" in the new literacy studies. *Review of Educational Research, 80*(2), 246–271.

Misfeldt, M. (2010). 'Forestillet læringsvej' i IT-baserede pædagogiske udviklingsprojekter. *Dansk Pædagogisk Tidsskrift, 58*(4), 42–52.

Misfeldt, M. (2013). *Instrumental genesis in geogebra based board game design*. In Proceedings for CERME 8, the 8th European Conference of Mathematics Education CERME, Antalia, Turkey.

New London Group. (1996). A pedagogy of multiliteracies: Designing social futures. *Harvard Educational Review, 66*(1), 60–92.

Pelletier, C. (2009). Games and learning: What's the connection? *International Journal of Learning and Media, 1*(1), 83–101.

Petraglia, J. (1998). *Reality by design: The rhetoric and technology of authenticity in education*. Mahwah, NJ: Lawrence Erlbaum Associates.

Purcell-Gates, V., Duke, N., & Martineau, J. A. (2007). Learning to read and write genre-specific text: Roles of authentic experience and explicit teaching. *Reading Research Quarterly, 42*(1), 8–45.

Salen, K., & Zimmerman, E. (2003). *Rules of play: Game design fundamentals*. Cambridge, MA: The MIT Press.

Scribner, S., & Cole, M. (1973). Cognitive consequences of formal and informal education. *Science, 182*(4112), 553–559.

Sefton-Green, J. (2013). *Learning at not-school*. Cambridge, MA: The MIT Press.

Shaffer, D. W. (2004). Pedagogical praxis: The professions as models for post-industrial education. *Teachers College Record, 106*(7), 1401–1421.

Shaffer, D. W. (2006). *How computer games may help children learn*. New York, NY: Palgrave Macmillan.

Sinclair, J., & Coulthard, M. (1975). *Towards an analysis of discourse: The English used by teachers and pupils*. London: Oxford University Press.

Squire, K. (2011). *Video games and learning: Teaching and participatory culture in the digital age*. New York, NY: Teachers College Press.

Stigler, J. W., & Hierbert, J. (1999). *The teaching gap: Best ideas from the world's teachers for improving education in the classroom*. New York, NY: Free Press.

Wegerif, R. (2004). The role of educational software as a support for teaching and learning conversations. *Computers & Education, 43*(1), 179–191.

Wenger, E. (1998). *Communities of practices: Learning, meaning, and identity*. Cambridge: Cambridge University Press.

Wilson, C. D., Taylor, J. A., Kowalski, S. M., & Carlson, J. (2010). The relative effects and equity of inquiry-based and commonplace science teaching on students' knowledge, reasoning, and argumentation. *Journal of Research in Science Teaching, 47*(3), 276–301.

FILIPA DE SOUSA

3. GAME-BASED LEARNING IN THE DIALOGICAL CLASSROOM

Videogames for Collaborative Reasoning about
Morality and Ethics in Citizenship Education

ABSTRACT

This chapter focuses on game-based learning (GBL), and the way a commercial videogame was used to foster collaborative reasoning about morality and ethics in citizenship education. A high school class was video recorded for four weeks, and the data was analyzed to investigate how students collaboratively reasoned in the GBL situation. Post-interview data were also considered. The study found that collaborative reasoning was mediated both by the videogame and the dialogical interactions facilitated by the teacher. Students appropriated both bottom-up and top-down reasoning processes and positioned themselves to anchor practical and conceptual knowledge. This research proposes a learning model that describes the anchoring process as an important tool for promoting content understanding and collaborative reasoning in learning across contexts with GBL.

Keywords: videogames, game-based learning, collaborative reasoning, citizenship education, multiliteracies, dialogism

INTRODUCTION

The design of interest-driven and technological learning environments for active learners is on the agenda for the educational models of the 21st century. Considering how learning happens not only inside classrooms but through different contexts, the multiliteracies paradigm points to a need for developing engaging school activities that take students' out-of-school practices into consideration (The New London Group, 1996). Young people are massive users of new technologies, namely videogames, with 25% of the European online population playing them at least once per week (Interactive Software Federation of Europe, 2012). According to the same source, the sociocultural perception of videogames is also changing, with more than half of European parents thinking that videogames stimulate their children's skills. Despite this, only 7% of all respondents classify videogames as informative or educational. While some researchers defend the idea that games designed specifically for educational purposes are better suited for learning (e.g., Marino & Hayes, 2012), reports from organizations like Becta—British Educational Communications and Technology Agency (2001) and TEEM—Teachers Evaluating Educational Multimedia (McFarlane, Sparrowhawk, & Heald, 2002) have highlighted many strengths related to using commercial off-the-shelf (COTS) videogames in classroom settings, such as developing students' thinking skills, fostering engagement and motivation, and promoting collaboration. Some researchers contend that COTS videogames can be used to provide extended, multimodal learning and create teaching opportunities in alignment with the notion of multiliteracies (Gerber & Abrams, 2014; Jordan, 2011; LaCasa, Martinez, & Mendez, 2008). This is also the case with citizenship education, as some commercial videogames provide very consistent ethical frameworks that, together with their rich narrative storylines, can promote ethical and moral reflection (e.g., Zagal, 2009; Simkins & Steinkuehler, 2008).

More research detailing the learning processes involved in learning through GBL using COTS videogames is required. This chapter presents an empirical study from an everyday classroom where a teacher uses a COTS videogame as a tool for teaching morality and ethics in a citizenship education course. Without intending to merely defend or reject the use of videogames as educational tools, this research focuses on collaborative reasoning processes when students are guided through dialogical teaching practices during GBL. The present study asks the following research question: how do students using a commercial videogame in citizenship education collaboratively reason while learning about ethics and morals?

THEORETICAL FRAMEWORK

Multiliteracies Pedagogy and Dialogical Approaches in Citizenship Education

The complexity and diversity of the teaching and learning processes in the highly technological society of the 21st century require an expanded definition of literacy. The multiliteracies pedagogical approach has risen as a response to this need (New London Group, 1996), providing students with abundant opportunities for using multimodal resources as they become active meaning-makers, constantly remaking signs and transforming meaning in nonlinear environments. This comprises examining diverse multimodal information, critically exploring, and becoming effective communicators (Cope & Kalantzis, 2009; Cooper, Lockyer, & Brown, 2013). Teaching under this pedagogical strand includes four dimensions (New London Group, 1996):

- Situated practice encourages learners to share and expand upon the learning process by drawing on their experiences; namely, valuing previous knowledge, interests, and relationships developed outside school settings.
- Overt instruction encourages learners to take ownership of their learning, facilitating the development of a metalanguage in direct and explicit lessons.

- Critical framing encourages students to develop critical thinking skills, to recognize learning contexts, and to relate what they have learned to broader contexts.
- Transformed practice encourages learners to apply what they have learned, and to redesign and expand knowledge into other contexts.

Learning in a multiliteracies approach embraces three components: the designed, designing, and the redesigned (New London Group, 1996). *Designing* implies developing a metalanguage to address the available multimodal designs representing the world (i.e *the designed*); the *redesigned* is the outcome of designing. The circulation of the described designing process is the essence of collaborative learning, with one person's designing becoming a resource for another person's available design (Cope & Kalantzis, 2009).

The multiliteracies approach resonates with the goals of citizenship education; namely, encouraging students to form their own opinions, make their own moral decisions, and be held critically accountable for those decisions and opinions in different contexts (Schuitema, van Boxtel, Veugelers, & ten Dam, 2011). This disciplinary field also uses plurality dialogical environments, as "students need to understand that there are multiple perspectives on moral and social issues and that their own view is only one of many possible perspectives" (Banks, 2004, as cited in Schuitema et al., 2011, p. 86).

The dialogic model for reasoning contends that meaning-making happens by the inter-animation of multiple perspectives (Mercer & Howe, 2012). This suggests a relation between dialogue and reasoning that moves thinking skills from the territory of the individual to a common social ground; hence, the concept of collaborative reasoning. Dialogues around technology emphasize the process of externalization, where "collective thought is transformed creatively by an individual to become a participation in a context-creating dialogue to intervene to improve the cognitive affordances of the technological mediation of shared thinking" (Wegerif, 2006, para. 31).

Mediation, Morality, and Game-Based Learning

From a sociocultural perspective, the moral function is a form of mediated action where the moral agent gradually achieves, uses, and appropriates mediational means to position himself toward moral situations (Tappan, 2006). Sociocultural theorists refer to the importance of both physical and psychological mediational means (Vygotsky, 1978). In the present study, the mediational tools are not only physical (the videogame) but also mental (the discourse). Moral agency is described in relation to the students' use of mediational means to reason collaboratively about the game in relation to ethical and moral issues. Vygotsky's theoretical framework posits, "All the higher functions originate as actual relationships between individuals" (1978, p. 57). For this study, reasoning is evidenced by the responses that students construct during interactions designed to develop collaborative moral reasoning in a dialogical context.

Using a sociocultural approach to study GBL, the focus is on describing the dialogical position of the students' and teacher's discussions about the videogame. Wegerif (2006) argues that the use of Information and communications technology (ICT) resources can induce both broadening and deepening of the quality of learning dialogues. Videogames are used as tools for mediating discussion and negotiation, also facilitated by the classroom culture and the students' identities (Egenfeldt-Nielsen, 2006).

Analytical Concepts

Analyzing knowledge construction implies considering temporality aspects. Two analytical concepts are useful for analyzing student participation as it unfolds during the learning activity: appropriation and positionality.

Appropriation. From a sociocultural perspective, the path to appropriation involves inherent tensions between the tool and its use within a particular context. The study of videogame use in a formal, educational setting allows the observation of how students and teachers appropriate the tool in this new context. The introduction of what may already be a known tool from an out-of-school context in a classroom setting merges two realities, creating a new context for learning. Wertsch (1998) explains that neither mastery nor appropriation of skills and tools is to be assumed to extrapolate from one context to another. Mastery develops from the use of a tool in a particular setting, but appropriation—which Wertsch defines as "the process (…) of taking something that belongs to others and making it one's own" (p. 53)—requires movement to cross contexts. These movements are intertwined with several aspects of the social context where the activity takes place (Lund & Rasmussen, 2008). Bridging outside-school practices and classroom elements (as in the present study) may set up a rich environment for studying how appropriation happens.

Positionality. The concept of positionality enlightens the process of how participation is enacted across the learning process. Rasmussen (2005) says, "Learning is perceived as participation in different subject practices where the pupils take on positions in relation to the task including the use of different types of resources and representations" (p. 39). Positioning students as authoritative and accountable for their contributions also supports their participation as learners (Greeno, 2006). This study aims to understand how students assume different roles and social identities over time, positioning themselves while appropriating the videogame and other classroom activities. This concept helps understand the evolving positioning in relation to the game content, the school content, the other participants, and the learning activity itself.

EMPIRICAL RESEARCH ON COLLABORATIVE GAME-BASED LEARNING

Three strands of research emerge when reviewing contributions to the field of GBL. The first focuses on how videogames follow important educational principles that are good for learning, claiming that people learn through the act of playing videogames. Videogames allow for immersive, participatory, and emotionally engaging experiences where agency and active learning are central. Learning is viewed as a bottom-up process where conceptual knowledge can be developed through the embodied experience of playing games (Gee, 2003). However, it is hard to find empirical confirmation about specific content learning by simply playing COTS videogames. Useful here is the distinction between learning to play and playing to learn (Arnseth, 2006). In "regular play" the emphasis is on the activity of playing, and learning may be regarded as integral to mastering an activity (i.e., gameplay). This activity does not necessarily lead to content knowledge. In playing to learn (as in educational games), the emphasis is on learning, and some content or skill should be an outcome of gameplaying.

The second strand of research defends the need to design educational videogames specially conceived to promote academic content learning. Some educational videogames engage players with scientific concepts while attempting to maintain the enjoyment of the gaming experience (Shaffer, 2006; Sanchez, 2013). For example, Arici (2008) shows how a student group using an educational game learned more science concepts after two weeks, compared to another group traditionally taught the same curriculum by the same teacher. Results also showed higher engagement and intrinsic motivation, and that the students remembered more academic content after two months. In most educational games, learning is a top-down process where academic theoretical content is prioritized and applied along with the action of the game. Consequently, players often perceive the gameplay as a school-like task, which may be less engaging.

The third strand of research addresses GBL as a complex educational experience that transcends the act of playing videogames in the classroom, whether educational or not. In this context, GBL is an educational setting including not only the game but other activities related to the game. In themselves, tools are not effective or ineffective. Learning happens when the videogame is used as a mediational resource. The environment around the videogame, namely peer interaction and group work, is extremely important for negotiating and constructing knowledge (Egenfeldt-Nielsen, 2006). Teacher interventions must also be considered when analyzing task appropriation and results (Rasmussen & Ludvigsen, 2010; Mercer & Howe, 2012). This assumption aligns with the literature on how new technology in classrooms requires advanced pedagogies (Verenikina, 2010).

Research on collaborative GBL has developed significantly in the last decade, but still lacks investigation related to clarifying its pedagogical aspects (Kronenberg, 2016). The present research follows previous studies, aiming to investigate the "processes of intersubjective meaning-making and how technological affordances mediate or support such processes" (Suthers, 2006, p. 332). Studies on computer-supported collaborative learning have suggested that technology encourages shared experiences and dialogue in ways that facilitate richer learning situations. Among others, Guðmundsdóttir et al. (2014) verified how the use of digital tools in the classroom opened a dialogical sphere where personal and shared meaning could be negotiated. Lacasa, Martinez, and Mendez (2008) studied how other literacy classroom activities associated with gameplay contributed to the development of narrative thought. Erhel and Jamet (2013) demonstrated how providing gameplay learning instructions elicited deeper learning than entertainment-based instruction without negatively impacting motivation. Hanghøj (2013) stressed the importance of instructional aspects in GBL, introducing the term "game-based teaching". He reflected on the dynamic aspects of GBL, emphasizing the intervention and positioning of teachers—namely guiding and scaffolding the students for learning purposes—during GBL (Hanghøj & Brund, 2010).

An overview of research about the GBL from a sociocultural stance concluded that collaboration, debriefing, and discussion are crucial to understanding, and that the role of the teacher is "imperative for the learning experience" (Egenfeldt-Nielsen, 2006, p. 205). Silseth (2012) showed the importance of dialogical aspects of collaborative learning when using GBL. He showed that mobilizing broader aspects, such as identity issues and a multiplicity of voices in a dialogical sense, helped determine the learning trajectory. Silseth and Arnseth (2011) demonstrated how recruiting voices from the out-of-school context was relevant during GBL.

This seems particularly relevant in the context of citizenship education, as dialogue and debate are central forms of participation in that context. Wegerif (2006) modified the "Initiation—Response—Follow-up" (IRF) educational exchange to IDRF, where the D represents the concept of engaging in dialogue before response. Blevins, LeCompte, and Wells (2014) explored the effectiveness of an online civics education gaming program. Presenting both quantitative and qualitative data, they suggested positive gains in students' content knowledge and highlighted the importance of teachers' roles in implementing civics education through gaming formats. The present study aims to examine how this may be achieved with COTS videogames.

METHODS

Classroom Observation

The study followed a Portuguese high school class of 14 students (five boys and nine girls, aged 18–22 years) for one month (7 lessons). The class utilized a COTS videogame named *The Walking Dead* (Telltale Games, 2012) to learn about morality and ethics in a citizenship course. Using this COTS videogame instead of a pro-social educational videogame bridged multiple contexts, as it is the type of game students play during leisure times. Bridging in- and out-of-school contexts aligns with the multiliteracies approach. Getting students to mobilize relevant everyday knowledge while contributing to the social construction of knowledge is of great value, but is difficult for many teachers to obtain (Silseth, 2017). A COTS videogame provides levels of engagement that are difficult to obtain with educational games (Egenfeldt-Nielsen, 2006). Though containing graphic, violent scenes, the violence in *The Walking Dead* is subordinated to the narrative. Additionally, the game offers an open narrative where the story unfolds according to the player's decisions. Many choices within the game concern moral dilemmas, providing the opportunity to teach ethics.

The class activity was inspired by a Norwegian teacher's practice (Staaby, 2015) and was presented by the researcher to the Portuguese teacher. Neither this teacher nor her students had any previous experience with GBL. However, the teacher considered its value to engage her students, namely a class from a vocational course with severe motivational and disciplinary problems. The school board authorized the project based on the same interest. All participants were 18 or older, consented to participate in the project, acknowledged that participation was voluntary, and understood that withdrawal from the project was possible at any time.

The activity consisted of stopping the gameplay at five crucial decision moments presenting moral dilemmas, and discussing the imminent decisions by referring to curricular ethical theories. The Portuguese teacher adapted the activity to her personal teaching style, the profile of her students, and the Portuguese curriculum. Unlike the Norwegian teacher, she presented all the theoretical content before starting the gameplay, creating handouts adapted to the students' profile with brief explanations of three ethical theories determined by the Portuguese curriculum, as follows:

- Utilitarianism: acting considering what is useful to the greatest number of people.
- Psychological egoism: acting considering one's individual interests.
- Deontology: acting considering universal goodwill toward others.

Classes were observed and video recorded. During the first three lessons (176 minutes), the teacher introduced and explained the different ethical theories. During the final four lessons (311 minutes), the students collaboratively played the videogame. The game action was projected on a screen while students took turns at the controls. When the game was stopped, students were asked to reflect on the actions available by using the ethical theories provided by the teacher. For the first three dilemmas, the teacher led classroom debates. For the final two dilemmas, students worked in small groups, instead. These groups analyzed the game dilemma under the perspective of one pre-assigned ethical theory and wrote down conclusions. No ethical theory was considered right or wrong; they were presented as justifications underlying the possible decisions. For all the dilemmas, after discussions, the students voted on what to do using an online application, *Kahoot* (https://kahoot.com/). Options in *Kahoot* were not right or wrong; they were created by the teacher to reflect the different ethical views. After using *Kahoot*, the game resumed according to the decision made by the majority. In the final class, the teacher led a plenary discussion about the GBL activity and how it contributed to the learning goals. Participants were later interviewed by the researcher concerning the same topic. These interviews were audio recorded.

Data Analysis

The data corpus consisted of eight video recorded classes (487 min), 13 audio-recorded interviews (256 min), and extensive field notes. The data analysis focused on the video recordings of the discussion episodes (88 minutes), which were treated as the primary data and analyzed using methods from micro-analytic approaches of moment-to-moment interactions, such as thematic analysis (Braun & Clarke, 2008) and interaction analysis (Jordan & Henderson, 1995). The field notes and semi-structured post-interviews, combined with ethnographic descriptions, served as supplementary data to frame and connect the micro-analysis in a dialectical way. Video data was analyzed against the ethnographic information, and the video analysis informed the global understanding of the context for the present study, particularly considering the school context and the profile of the students.

The analysis considered not only the gameplay experience but the whole dialogical setting in its interdependences. First, the discussion episodes were entirely transcribed and translated into English. Second, thematic analysis was used to identify the themes frequently referred to during discussions (Braun & Clarke, 2006). To study how reasoning evolved during the activity, the researcher isolated the class discussions in short time frames and analyzed them relative to the primary themes from the thematic analysis. Several discussion episodes were then excerpted to reveal how the resources served as mediational tools for reasoning by linking the different themes along the learning trajectory. Those excerpts were analyzed using methods inspired by interaction analysis (e.g., Furberg & Ludvigsen, 2008; Lund & Rasmussen, 2008). The interaction analysis focused on moment-to-moment interactions (talk and activities) to clarify how each example of talk or action was up taken by others in the construction of collaborative reasoning.

The analysis also considered temporal and sequential aspects of the learning trajectory, using the concepts of appropriation and positionality to reveal the mediational processes by which participants built up collaborative reasoning along a trajectory of participation.

RESULTS

Data analysis demonstrates how both the videogame and the dialogical approach mediated the processes of reasoning. In the analysis of the first two excerpts, the researcher describes how both worked together to create a frame for the students' reasoning. In a third excerpt, the researcher describes how reasoning unfolded in a collaborative way.

The Nature of the Videogame as an Educational Tool

The first excerpt illustrates how reasoning was influenced by the nature of the videogame as an educational resource. Unlike other media, videogames offer active participation through interactive fiction, with players assuming the character's role and directly performing actions that impact outcomes in the game. In the study, participatory experiences helped mediate the process of reasoning. In Excerpt 3.1, Lucas, a student, expresses his opinion about what the main character (Lee) should do in the game when facing a difficult decision about himself and another game character (Clementine).

Excerpt 3.1.

1	Lucas:	Teacher, because that is…the world…teacher, imagine that I am alone in the world, right? Imagine, now I'm…I am Lee now! I am alone with Clementine. And they're all now…they are all zombies, right?

In the excerpt, Lucas refers to the game narrative as if the story was happening to him. The use of the first person and the enthusiastic tone of his voice indicate a participatory movement where Lucas is projecting himself emotionally. These episodes are common throughout the gameplay, indicating appropriation of the game narrative. Positionality was also an important aspect. The word "imagine" transports the action out of the game narrative and into an imaginary situation. Lucas commutes from the role of a student interacting with his teacher and presenting an argument to the position of a game character living a difficult apocalyptic situation requiring decision-making. Episodes like this illustrate how participatory mechanisms of videogames assist with appropriation and positionality while contributing to reasoning in GBL.

The Importance of a Dialogical Approach

The second excerpt illustrates how the students' response to the dialogical approach within GBL also contributed to collaborative reasoning. The teacher and the students debate whether to save a child or an adult, both being attacked by zombies in the game.

The students react when the teacher introduces a new alternative to the discussion (not saving anyone). A student links the teacher's prompt and the theory of psychological egoism (line 2). The teacher wants the student to explain how he came to that conclusion (line 3). Several students try to explain it (lines 4–12), with the teacher asking questions (lines 5, 8 and 10). By the end of the excerpt, as the teacher sums up the discussed idea for the whole class (line 13), another student, Iuri, interrupts her with a different opinion. Instead of continuing, the teacher immediately asks him to continue. The dialogical approach here is remarkable because Iuri's position is diametrically opposed to the teacher's initial suggestion.

Excerpt 3.2.

1	Teacher:	Look, what if we don't save anyone?
2	Lucas:	That would be egoism, and it won't fit, teacher!
3	Teacher:	Egoism why? How is that egoism?
4	Joaquina:	He [Lee, the main character] is thinking only about himself.
5	Teacher	If we wouldn't help anybody, why is that an egoistic attitude? Here, let's hear these girls, here ((turns to Joaquina and Carolina)).
6	Joaquina:	They needed help, and we didn't...
7	Carolina:	They were only thinking about themselves [Lee's group in the game].
8	Teacher:	And why wouldn't you do it, why wouldn't you help?
9	Joaquina:	By fear.
10	Teacher:	Why?
11	Joaquina:	(inaudible) in danger...also.
12	Teacher:	Not to get ourselves in danger, very well, Joaquina. You must speak louder. (...)
13	Teacher:	That would be the egoist's attitude. He'd only think of himself.
14	Iuri:	But we must help!
15	Teacher:	Tell us, Iuri!

Throughout this excerpt, students use the opportunities provided by the dialogical context to explore and express their opinions using concepts from ethical theory. The excerpt also illustrates how dialogical contexts can impact both the students' external talk (participation) and internal voice (reflecting and reasoning) while developing collaborative reasoning. When the teacher created multiple perspectives on the situation, the students reacted by taking different perspectives and appropriating the contributions of others to build arguments. The interchangeable use of "they" and "we"/"you" in the dialogue expresses appropriation movements toward the videogame. The students position themselves not only as players but as learners applying theoretical concepts to understand the game content in different ways.

Reasoning Processes—Anchoring Conceptual and Practical Domains

To study how collaborative reasoning evolved during the activity, class discussions were analyzed in relation to four main themes that emerged from the previous thematic analysis, as follows:

- Game narrative: students discussing the videogame plot and the characters attitudes and behaviors (e.g., "...They are all zombies now, right?").
- Real life situations: students addressing examples of situations possible in real life, both real-life events or hypothetical ones (e.g., "...If you were in a house that caught fire...")
- General moral considerations: students elaborating on moral considerations (e.g., "...We are all human beings, old or not, so we must...")
- Curriculum content: students referring to theoretical concepts that are part of the school curriculum (e.g., "...He is being completely utilitarianist [*sic*]!")

The researcher analyzed the sequences of moment-to-moment interaction as they occurred and discovered how the discourse constantly moved between these four themes, constantly linking the game narrative to other situations and ideas.

In Excerpt 3.3, participants are still discussing whether to rescue the little boy or the adult. When the game was stopped, the immediate, general answer was, "The child". The teacher wanted to know why, and the students' justifications relied on reasons like, "He is younger", or "He has lived less", as well as some more abstract concepts like, "The future relies on the children". During the debate, however, one voice spoke up against this general opinion. Lucas argued vehemently that the adult should be saved. He argued that the adult was stronger and, consequently, better able to help the rest of the group fight back against the zombies. Also, Lucas claimed, only three adult men in the group were capable of fighting zombies, and a child wouldn't be helpful. The following excerpt is part of a passionate debate maintained for about 11 minutes. The excerpt occurred two minutes into the discussion and illustrates how different themes were used during the class discussion.

Excerpt 3.3.

1	Lucas:	Then there will come more zombies. And there are only three [men] to … to help. (*Lucas has three fingers up.*) And then, do not forget that the others are elderly. Now, if you support the one that is already a grown-up, right?
2	Isabel:	And I let the child die…
3	Lucas:	He will, will then give further support for you to get to fight the others.
4	Isabel:	And I let the child die… (*overlapping*)
5	Lucas:	No! Imagine. Then think, you are stuck here by that door, and over there they were almost picking up a child, right? I'll pick you up, quickly, here, from the door, for us to get to be two to…to destroy.
6	Isabel:	But in this case, you can only save one person! You yourself said that the man was only about the leg, while the child was…seized by the shoulder…. So, the man can get away from it much more rapidly than the child.
7	Teacher:	So that's a utilitarianism perspective, or not? (*to Lucas*)
8	Lucas:	Mine?
9	Teacher:	Yes.
10	Lucas:	Sure.
11	Teacher:	It is the utility that there is under consideration there.
12	Marco:	It would always be possible to save more lives if it is the man.

Lucas explains why saving the adult is more valuable for the group. Isabel is more concerned about the child (lines 1–4). Then, at line 5, Lucas strengthens his argument with an example from real life. The teacher attempts to link a theory (line 7), a move that Lucas accepts. Finally, a third student, Marco applies the theoretical reasoning back to the game context: utilitarianism holds that any possible action should consider the possible benefit for the greatest number of people (line 13).

Here, the discourse flows between contexts. The excerpt begins with a reference to the game narrative, but in line 5, the discussion leads into another context: Lucas uses the word "imagine", and the discourse departs from the symbolic world of the game to a more reality-based context. He invokes a hypothetical situation from real life to serve as an example. However, Isabel, overlapping, pulls the discourse back to the fantasy world of the game narrative. Then, the teacher brings the discourse to a conceptual level (line 7), encouraging the students to use a metalanguage to address the problem. She departs from the concrete level (game narrative) and moves to a more abstract and conceptual framework (ethical theory). Marco's contribution (line 12) indicates evidence of understanding, as he reformulates the teacher's suggestion in a remark very close to that of the previously learned theory. That he applies this knowledge to the concrete consequences within the game story reveals an ability to relate conceptual knowledge to a practical application.

The students' reasoning followed patterns of alternating themes in cycles: bottom-up movement from concrete examples to conceptual reflections, and top-down movement back to the concrete level again.

The teacher encouraged the students to expand the learning process by picking up the game as an available design and drawing on real-world experiences and sharing personal opinions (lines 1–6). Simultaneously, the teacher established a metalanguage to address the problem (lines 7 and 11). This created a critical framework allowing the students to creatively apply what they had learned to redesign and expand knowledge into broader contexts (lines 5–12).

The analysis also reveals how appropriation and positionality were part of the students' reasoning while moving between contexts.

- Students constantly appropriated the game narrative as a personal experience, especially when linking the game's narrative to their real-life experiences. They also appropriated the contributions of others to build arguments. Throughout the discussion, the debate became even more passionate, with clear signs of engagement. The students interrupted each other, gesticulated, and even got irritated, manifesting exasperation in their body language, facial expressions, and tones of voice. The way new connections between contexts seemed to lend an emotional resonance to the debate also aligns with the concept of appropriation.
- Moving through contexts, especially between conceptual knowledge and its practical application, invited the students to change between different positions. Sometimes students positioned themselves as the characters in the game, and connected emotionally with the needs of the characters they identified with. Many other times, the participants positioned themselves as students, analyzing the game dilemma through a theoretical scope. Finally, the students also positioned themselves as players, deciding what should happen in the game.

DISCUSSION

The design of this GBL activity aligns with a multiliteracies approach. The results illustrate the use of multimodal literacies to combine the videogame with a theoretical framework, students' personal experiences, and critical thinking. The teacher used overt instruction to facilitate the development of the metalanguage used to address the moral dilemmas in the game. She did this not only directly—by providing the theoretical content in advance—but also throughout the dialogue. The teacher created a situated practice where the students could share and expand the learning process by drawing on real-world experiences and their personal opinions. The relationship established between acting in the game and acting in real life allowed the students to extend their knowledge to broader contexts within a critical framework. Throughout the activity, the teacher encouraged the students to creatively apply what they had learned to redesign and expand knowledge into other contexts, developing a transformed practice (NLG, 1996).

The analysis also illustrates how the videogame contributed to the breadth and depth of the classroom dialogues (Wegerif, 2006). GBL resources, both intellectual and physical, were appropriated as mediational tools for reasoning, and those tools contributed to the positioning of students throughout the activity.

- The interactional aspects of appropriation consist of individuals borrowing something from others and investing it with their own intentions (Wertsch, 1998). The analysis reveals how students related themselves to the arguments of others, to the game narrative, and, no less important, to the teacher's instructions and the learning goals. Results show the students appropriating the videogame narrative as a "personal scenario" for reasoning, with the dialogic model supporting this by encouraging the emergence and discussion of different opinions and perspectives.
- The dialogic approach also contributed to positionality; namely, leading students to assume different roles and perspectives over the course of discussions. The results show students changing positionality by assuming different roles to make sense of the different proposed tasks (Rasmussen, 2005): actively playing the game, following the game action, taking active part in how the narrative unfolds by making decisions, participating in plenum and small group debates, performing writing tasks, or using apps to vote for decisions.

In the analysis, the terms bottom-up and top-down reasoning were used as empirical concepts referring to the following movements:

- *Bottom-up reasoning* refers to moments when, departing from practical situations (concrete game context or real-life examples), the students and the teacher engaged in debates leading to more abstract conceptual reflections (moral issues and linkages to curriculum content).
- *Top-down reasoning* refers to moments in the dialogue that began by referring to conceptual theoretical issues (morality and ethics) but ended up applying those abstract or symbolic issues in a practical context.

The analysis illustrates how bottom-up and top-down movements represent a dialectical movement between practical and conceptual knowledge that seems to have an impact on learning by anchoring knowledge across different contexts. I call this in situ construction of a mixed-use of bottom-up and top-down reasoning that characterized the participant's engagement the *anchoring process*. This process is defined here as two-way reasoning, connecting theoretical knowledge to contextualized practices, and contextualized practical actions to more theoretical understanding.

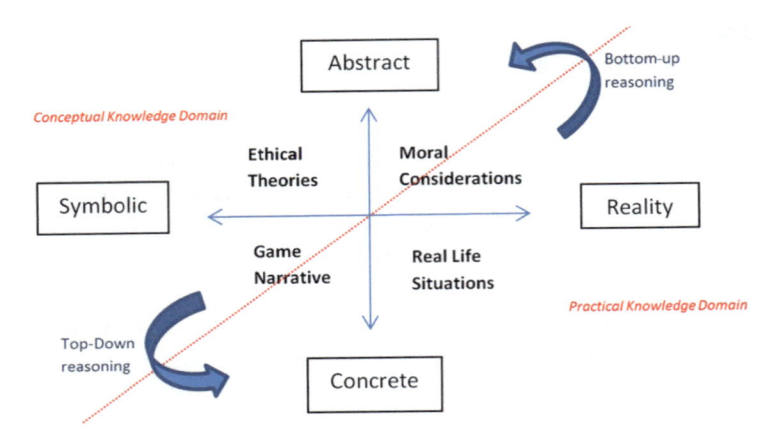

Figure 3.1. Model of the anchoring process

Figure 3.1 shows four themes identified in the students' discussions: game narrative, real-life situations, moral considerations, and ethical theories. The top half of the model represents abstract ways of reasoning, distinguishing between morality and ethics. Here, the terms are used in the context presented in the class (by the teacher and through the handouts): morality as related to behavior and practical actions, and ethics as the philosophical study that theoretically reflects on the morality of human conduct. According to these definitions, the students are reasoning in the moral plane when they refer to moral justifications for their actions (more connected to reality), and about ethics when they reflect on the principles and rules that they used for a decision (more symbolic).

The bottom half of the model indicates the concrete application of these abstract ideas, which can be applied in two different contexts: a more symbolic one (in the game story) and a more real context (in real-life situations, brought up as examples during the dialogue).

The horizontal axis represents how participants moved between referring to symbolic and reality-based elements in their reasoning: on the symbolic side, we have their talk about the fantasy world of the game ("They are all zombies now".) and the use of ethical theories as general concepts and representations of cultural standards of morality ("For me, that is utilitarianism".). On the right side, more reality-connected applications of reasoning are represented; for example, when participants use examples of real-life situations in their discourse ("Imagine you are in a house that started on fire") or when they refer to moral considerations taken from a more contextualized and humanized perspective ("We must protect the child because the child is weaker").

The vertical axis represents movements within the discourse that vary between reasoning using abstract elements like moral and ethical aspects and more pragmatic thinking using real-life situations or the game narrative.

The model illustrates the reasoning anchoring process by representing how the discourse shifts between themes, anchoring the conceptual and practical domains of knowledge. The conceptual domain of knowledge refers to symbolic and abstract elements referenced within the discourse, while the practical domain of knowledge includes discourse that refers to real and concrete situations. The dotted red line in the model represents a virtual division between these two domains. The described movements between domains are identified as bottom-up and top-down reasoning. They appear as arrows in Figure 3.1 and are both dialectical parts of the anchoring process.

This research demonstrates how the studied classroom activity created an intertwined trajectory where both bottom-up and top-down processes were equally important. This aligns with core issues in citizenship education for the 21st century, as established by UNESCO (1998), "Citizenship education needs also to be taught in ways that bring out the ever-constant link between knowledge and practice. The interaction between concepts and action gradually produces the ability to think in terms of values and to refer to them" (n.p.). On the one hand, this disciplinary domain intends to teach students how to reason from abstract concepts and understand the practical implications of different theoretical traditions, resembling a top-down approach. On the other, citizenship education is also about learning through everyday experience using bottom-up reasoning. It encourages using concrete experiences from real life to permit reasoning about, and abstraction of, conceptual elements for moral and ethical development.

Recently, Silseth (2017) restated the value of mobilizing students' relevant everyday knowledge and assigning students roles where they are acknowledged as contributors to the social construction. He refers to this a valuable but difficult practice for most teachers. The significance of the present study relies on clarifying a method of achieving this through using videogames and the anchoring process.

CONCLUSION

This study aligns with recent research on GBL, highlighting the importance of dialogical designs for the implementation of videogames in educational settings. Mediation is an important concept for understanding how a gameplay experience was transformed into a learning situation. Results demonstrate that both the game (physical tool) and the dialogical context (intellectual tool) worked as mediational tools for reasoning. The analytical concepts of appropriation and positionality were used to show how this occurred. Students appropriated the game as a personal narrative and used their colleagues' contributions to build their own perspectives. They also moved between different positions within the tasks, either acting as engaged players or as students applying academic content.

The participatory experience of the videogame encouraged engagement in better-quality dialogues, leading to deeper learning. Students used classroom discussion as a tool to mediate different themes in the discourse and used shifts between those themes to apply significance to their collaborative meanings. In doing so, students used both bottom-up and top-down reasoning processes. The analysis of the participation trajectory revealed how a collaborative, mixed use of these two methods of reasoning served as an anchoring process, linking theoretical and everyday knowledge to facilitate content understanding and, consequently, deeper learning.

IMPLICATIONS AND FINAL REFLECTIONS

The observed participation trajectory and the final metacognitive reflections from the participants (i.e., the final class debate and the interviews) provide evidence of some degree of curricular understanding and sense-making.

During the post interviews, all the students indicated they found the GBL practice very interesting and motivating. They mentioned that it made the classes "different", "more dynamic", and "more fun". However, no practice, no matter how innovative or motivating, suits all learning contexts. Participants also mentioned that GBL would not suit all teachers or all subjects; nor, in the researcher's opinion, is it likely to suit every student.

The practice was considered innovative and transgressive, breaking the routine of everyday theoretical approaches. It is, however, unclear whether videogames would be as motivating if they were routinely used in school.

Students acknowledged that the participatory nature of videogames makes them different than other media (e.g., movies), saying, "In the movie, it is only those circumstances, we can only talk about what we saw. (…) The videogame gives us several options and all of us chose differently". Students related this to increased learning possibilities, saying, "This way I could put things into practice, like, I understood much more".

The students also referred to the importance of the other activities surrounding the game, often commenting on the importance of the debates: "After we debated and saw each other's perspectives, what each one of us thought about it…many of us have different ideas and we could talk about them and show our opinion, and that… helped a lot!"

Most students pointed out the dialogic aspect of the debates. This exposure to multiple views and opinions increased the quality of the dialogues for learning, to paraphrase Wegerif (2006). The students referred to this, saying, "We see the perspective of each of us, and it is much better because we get to see each one's opinion and better understand the content".

The teacher's role during GBL was also included in the meta-reflections of the students. They acknowledged the teacher's importance by saying, "The teacher had an important role because she never let the content die. In all situations and debates, she always included those three aspects [the ethical theories]".

Furthermore, the students stressed that game-based activities could help them learn about other contexts:

> Here I realized things that we, in the games, we can put into practice. I thought, like, playing was only playing, and adapt … and I realized that many options that we took during the game, it's sometimes the options that we have in our daily life. And I think that is very important, hot damn! [*sic*]

Despite their ability to differentiate between contexts, the students tended to agree that reasoning processes in games and real life are similar and that learning was possible from the game experience, especially if mediated by debates and structured tasks.

The immersive experience of the videogame appears relevant to the reasoning processes, although one might expect that the arguments voiced in teacher-led discussions wouldn't match spontaneous discussions around gameplay outside the school context. Both the instructional aspect and providing a framework for reasoning seem important for GBL. The results indicate that by taking a dialogical approach, educators may enhance deeper learning by assisting reasoning through an anchoring process in learning dialogues. The model of the anchoring process in GBL presented here offers a possible representation of the dynamics underlying the dialogical approach to teaching ethics using videogames. Possible extrapolation to other domains of knowledge might be of future interest.

REFERENCES

Arici, A. D. (2008). *Meeting kids at their own game: A comparison of learning and engagement in traditional and three-dimensional muve educational-gaming contexts* (PhD dissertation). Indiana University, Bloomington, IN. Retrieved June 21, 2016, from http://search.proquest.com/docview/287987558?accountid=14699

Arnseth, H. C. (2006). Learning to play or playing to learn: A critical account of the models of communication informing educational research on computer gameplay. *Game Studies, 6*(1), n.p.

BECTA. (2001). *Computer games in education project report.* Retrieved October 24, 2017, from http://consilr.info.uaic.ro/uploads_lt4el/resources/htmlengComputer%20Games%20in%20Education%20Project%20Report.html

Blevins, B., LeCompte, K., & Wells, S. (2014). Citizenship education goes digital. *The Journal of Social Studies Research, 38*(1), 33–44.

Braun, V., & Clarke, V. (2008). Using thematic analysis in psychology. *Qualitative Research in Psychology, 3*(2), 77–101.

Cooper, N. A., Lockyer, L., & Brown, I. M. (2013). Developing multiliteracies in a technology-mediated environment. *Educational Media International, 50*(2), 93–107.

Cope, B. E., & Kalantzis, M. (2009). Multiliteracies: New literacies, new learning. *Pedagogies: An International Journal, 4*(3), 164–195.

Egenfeldt-Nielsen, S. (2006). Overview of research on the educational use of video games. *Nordic Journal of Digital Literacy, 1*(3), 184–213.

Erhel, S., & Jamet, E. (2013). Digital game-based learning: Impact of instructions and feedback on motivation and learning effectiveness. *Computers & Education, 67*, 156–167.

Furberg, A., & Ludvigsen, S. R. (2008). Students' meaning-making of socio-scientific issues in computer mediated settings: Exploring learning through interaction trajectories. *International Journal of Science Education, 30*(13), 1775–1799.

Gee, J. P. (2003). *What video games have to teach us about learning and literacy?* New York, NY: Palgrave Macmillan.

Gerber, H. R., & Abrams, S. S. (Eds.). (2014). *Bridging literacies with videogames.* Rotterdam, The Netherlands: Sense Publishers.

Greeno, J. (2006). Authoritative, accountable positioning and connected, general knowing: Progressive themes in understanding transfer. *Journal of the Learning Sciences, 15*(4), 537–547.

Guðmundsdóttir, G. B., Dalaaker, D., Egeberg, G., Hatlevik, O. E., & Tømte, K. H. (2014). Interactive Technology: Traditional Practice? *Nordic Journal of Digital Literacy, 1*(9), 23–43.

Hanghøj, T. (2013). Game-based teaching: Practices, roles, and pedagogies. In S. deFreitas, M. Ott, M. Popescu, & I. Stanescu (Eds.), *New pedagogical approaches in game enhanced learning: Curriculum integration* (pp. 81–101). Hershey, PA: IGI Global.

Hanghøj, T., & Brund, C. E. (2010). Teacher roles and positionings in relation to educational games. In B. Meyer (Ed.), *ECGBL 2010 Proceedings* (pp. 115–122). Reading: Academic Publishing Limited.

Interactive Software Federation of Europe. (2012). *The video games in Europe consumer study.* Brussels: Ipsos MediaCT. Retrieved March 4, 2015, from http://www.isfe.eu/sites/isfe.eu/files/attachments/euro_summary_-_isfe_consumer_study.pdf

Jordan, B., & Henderson, A. (1995). Interaction analysis: Foundations and practice. *The Journal of the Learning Sciences, 4*(1), 39–103.

Jordan, E. T. (2011). *Place for video games: A theoretical and pedagogical framework for multiliteracies learning in English studies* (PhD dissertation). Michigan Technological University, Houghton, MI. Retrieved October 22, 2017, from http://digitalcommons.mtu.edu/etds/88

Kronenberg, F. A. (2016). Selection criteria for commercial off-the-shelf (cots) video games for language learning. *Journal of Language Learning Technologies, 42*(2), 52–58.

Lacasa, P., Martinez, R., & Mendez, L. (2008). Developing new literacies using commercial video games as educational tools. *Linguistics and Education, 19*, 85–106.

Lund, A., & Rasmussen, I. (2008). The right tool for the wrong task? Match and mismatch between first and second stimulus in double stimulation. *International Journal of Computer-Supported Collaborative Learning, 3*(4), 387–412.

Marino, M. T., & Hayes, M. T. (2012). Promoting inclusive education, civic scientific literacy, and global citizenship with videogames. *Cultural Studies of Science Education, 7*(4), 945–954.

McFarlane, A., Sparrowhawk, A., & Heald, Y. (2002). *Report on the educational use of games.* TEEM (Teachers Evaluating Educational Multimedia). Retrieved May 18, 2016, from http://questgarden.com/84/74/3/091102061307/files/teem_gamesined_full.pdf

Mercer, N., & Howe, C. (2012). Explaining the dialogic processes of teaching and learning: The value and potential of sociocultural theory. *Learning, Culture and Social Interaction, 1*(1), 12–21.

Rasmussen, I. (2005). *Project work and ICT: Studying learning as participation trajectories* (PhD dissertation). University of Oslo, Oslo.

Rasmussen, I., & Ludvigsen, S. R. (2010). Learning with computer tools and environments: A sociocultural perspective. In K. Littleton, C. Wood, & J. K. Staarman (Eds.), *International handbook of psychology in education.* Bingley: Emerald Group Publishing Limited.

Sanchez, E. (2013). A model for the design of digital epistemic games. In N. Reynolds & M. Webb (Eds.), *Proceedings of the X world conference on computers in education* (pp. 257–264). Torun.

Schuitema, J., van Boxtel, C., Veugelers, W., & ten Dam, G. (2010). The quality of student dialogue in citizenship education. *European Journal of Psychology of Education, 26*(1), 85–107.

Shaffer, D. W. (2006). Epistemic frames for epistemic games. *Computers & Education, 46*(3), 223–234.

Silseth, K. (2012). The multivoicedness of game play: Exploring the unfolding of a student's learning trajectory in a gaming context at school. *International Journal of Computer-Supported Collaborative Learning, 7*(1), 63–84.

Silseth, K. (2017). Students' everyday knowledge and experiences as resources in educational dialogues. *Instructional Science, 46*(2), 291–313. Retrieved October 24, 2017, from https://link.springer.com/article/10.1007/s11251-017-9429-x

Silseth, K., & Arnseth, H. C. (2011). Learning and identity construction across sites: A dialogical approach to analysing the construction of learning selves. *Culture & Psychology, 17*(1), 65–80.

Simkins, D. W., & Steinkuehler, C. (2008). Critical ethical reasoning and role-play. *Games and Culture, 3*(3–4), 333–335.

Staaby, T. (2015). *Game-based learning the walking dead: Moral philosophy after the apocalypse.* Oslo: Norwegian Centre for ICT in Education. Retrieved May 3, 2016, from https://iktipraksis.iktsenteret.no/sites/default/files/files/TWD_English.pdf

Suthers, D. D. (2006). Technology affordances for intersubjective meaning making: A research agenda for CSCL. *International Journal of Computer-Supported Collaborative Learning, 1*(3), 315–337.

Tappan, M. (2006). Moral functioning as mediated action. *Journal of Moral Education, 35*(1), 1–18.

Telltale Games (Writer), & Telltale Games (Director). (2012). The walking dead (Episode 1) *Season 1.* San Rafael, CA: Skybound Entertainment.

The New London Group. (1996). A pedagogy of multiliteracies: Designing social futures. *Harvard Educational Review, 66*(1), 60–92.

UNESCO. (1998). *Citizenship education for the 21st century.* Retrieved October 24, 2017, from http://www.unesco.org/education/tlsf/mods/theme_b/interact/mod07task03/appendix.htm

Verenikina, I. (2010). *Vygotsky in twenty-first-century research* (pp. 16–25). World Conference on Educational Multimedia, Hypermedia and Telecommunications, Chesapeake, VA.

Vygotsky, L. S. (1978). *Mind in society: The development of higher psychological processes.* Cambridge, MA: Harvard University Press.

Wegerif, R. (2006). *A dialogical understanding of the relationship between CSCL and teaching thinking skills.* Retrieved May 28, 2016, from http://citeseerx.ist.psu.edu/viewdoc/download?doi=10.1.1.125.4619&rep=rep1&type=pdf

Wertsch, J. (1998). *Mind as action.* New York, NY: Oxford University Press.

Zagal, J. P. (2009). *Ethically notable video games: Moral dilemmas and gameplay* (pp. 1–9). Breaking New Ground: Innovation in Games, Play, Practice and Theory, Proceedings of DiGRA 2009. Retrieved from http://www.digra.org/dl/db/09287.13336.pdf

JOHANNA ÖBERG

4. DESIGNING FOR INCREASED PARTICIPATION BY USING GAME-INFORMED LEARNING AND ROLE-PLAY

Pupils as Co-Researchers in a Study on Democracy

ABSTRACT

A learning activity inspired by game-informed learning was designed with the aim of promoting participation and critical thinking. The observed learning activity was analysed in order to understand how pupils act within the given and created roles, frames, and positions. The learning activity was based on role-play, in which the pupils assumed the role of co-researchers. The implemented role-playing activity included gamification elements (e.g. rewards, narrative, and feedback). We explored the question: How does game-informed learning promote participation? A total of 15 pupils participated in the activity over the course of 16 weeks. When role-playing as co-researchers, the pupils choose their own research question and research methods. The process of this research game was documented in 16 field notes, two interviews with the participating teachers, and several observations. This data was analysed according to Goffman's and Mead's concepts of role. The findings indicate that several factors affect pupils' engagement in the role of co-researchers: being perceived as professionals, interacting and communicating in a new location and setting, giving and receiving feedback, and being recognised through the results obtained. The study contributes to the understanding that a design focused on such factors can facilitate children's participation.

Keywords: game-informed learning, co-researcher, participation, role-play, critical thinking

INTRODUCTION

Citizens today encounter an abundance of information—information they may not be equipped to handle. Because everyone is free to add to the information available on the Internet, the vetting and peer reviewing of that information is in many cases nonexistent. The art of critically reviewing sources and extracting the correct information is a necessity in modern society. Moreover, as a result of the digital era, more information is made available each day. The ability to sort and filter this information is becoming a necessity to avoid information overload, information anxiety, etc. (Bawden & Robinson, 2009). Members of a democratic society require the ability to think critically, understand the complexity of society, and evaluate contradictory and incomplete information in order to arrive at sound conclusions, make intelligent decisions, and thereby participate fully in civic life (Nickersson, 1990). The skills needed for citizenship are, according to Kellett (2010), the capacity for judgment, social agency, and the ability to communicate one's views.

Allowing children to share opinions about matters that concern them is one of the cornerstones of the United Nations Convention on the Rights of the Child (UNICEF, 1989). Articles 12 and 13 of the convention state that a child has 'the right to express its views freely in all matters affecting the child' and that 'the child shall have the right to freedom of expression', respectively. This is further emphasised by, for instance, the Swedish national curriculum (Skolverket, 2011), which states that every pupil should be able to participate in democratic processes and to utilise critical thinking in their everyday life. Långström and Virta (2011) demonstrated that schools have difficulties fulfilling the requirements of both educating pupils to be citizens and simultaneously developing their critical thinking skills. In the present study, a participatory approach was chosen in order to foster pupils' critical thinking skills and a collective sense of accomplishment.

This study focused on role-play as a gamification strategy. Pupils were given the opportunity to take on the role of co-researchers in a research project. Role-play can fulfil a number of functions, such as changing attitudes, exploring subjects, arousing interest, providing motivation, teaching skills, developing communication, testing alternative behaviour, and helping with personal conflicts and problems (Van Ments, 1989). The participating pupils were not familiar with the work of researchers. Their conceptions were based on pictures of Albert Einstein and men in lab coats. Against such a background, the pupils were informed about the role and appearance of modern researchers, and we decided that in order to assume the role of researchers, they would role-play as co-researchers for the duration of the project.

The learning activity designed for this study was inspired by game-informed learning (GIL; Begg, Dewhurst, & Macleod, 2005), which suggests that educational processes should be informed by the experience of gameplay. The main focus of a game-informed learning activity is that the learner is actively playing a role in a narrative scenario containing a challenge or a task; the learner's role is consistent and recognisable within that specific environment (Begg, 2008). GIL has many similarities with the better-known area of epistemic games (EG). The main difference is that EG was first developed as a digital tool/game in which the participant plays the role of a professional performing daily work tasks, solving problems, and so on (Shaffer, 2006). The important principles of game-informed learning, according to Begg, Dewhurst, and Macleod (2005), are to facilitate the pupil's contextual identity, to develop the pupil's own motivation set in an environment with feedback, to give the pupil an opportunity to make choices in a safe setting, and to establish a believable interaction with the surroundings (expanded on below, in the Design section). Gaining personal knowledge regarding a situation or set of conditions is important, because it can help to rouse concern and attention and thereby create the starting point for a willingness to act. This may be one of the prerequisites for developing pupils' competence for taking action and changing their behaviour (Jensen, 2002). Allowing pupils to actively participate in learning activities may strengthen their interest along with their knowledge (Jensen, 2002).

In this study, the researchers sought to design a learning activity that would facilitate pupils' participation, critical thinking, and experience of doing research, here in the role of co-researchers. This goal was promoted by knowing that to successfully engage pupils, the mode of inquiry needs to be grounded and to fit within pupils' own lived experiences and their epistemologies (Pahl, 2011).

Because pupils' changes in behaviour and increased participation would be subtle and hard to pinpoint, a specific analytical method was employed. The pupils' interactions and reactions were analysed by categorising them into different roles, frames, and positions. Goffman (1974) stated that every interaction or activity can be viewed in different frames. These depend on whose perspective the activity is viewed from: an onlooker, or a specific person in the frame at a specific moment. Goffman (1981) also discussed the different positions a person can assume within a role. Building on the work of Mead (1934) and Goffman (1959, 1974, 1981), this chapter uses the concepts of role, frame, and position to conceptualise and categorise observations made during this learning activity that we call the research game. These concepts, in turn, influenced the chapter's focus on certain aspects and features of GIL.

This study used the aforementioned concepts of Goffman (reinforced by the work of Mead, as explained in more detail in the Background and Theory section) as a theoretical framework with which to analyse the pupil's experience of the learning activity described below as 'The Research Party'. The study asked the question, How does a game-informed learning activity promote participation?

The factors that affected the pupils' engagement in their role as co-researchers will be analysed. These factors cover control, rewards, environmental surroundings, and more.

BACKGROUND AND THEORY

In this section, the history and theory will be presented in order to outline some of the key concepts of the study, which include participation, role-play, GIL, and the methods of analysing role, frame, and position.

Participatory Research

In the late 1990s, child research changed drastically (James & Prout, 1997; James, Jenks, & Prout, 1998). Instead of seeing children as objects that are a part of the same childhood, meaning that each childhood was seen as identical, they began to view children as individuals. Research was being conducted not only *on* children but *with* and *for* children. Participatory approaches in social research are currently becoming more common; for example, studies are now including children as participants (Bradbury-Jones & Taylor, 2013), as 'designers' (research by children; Alderson & Morrow, 2011; Lundy, McEvoy, & Byrne, 2011), and as researchers (Hunleth, 2011; Kellett, Forrest, Dent, & Ward, 2004; Hillén, 2013). However, some research that is labelled 'participatory' is instead conducted in a more traditional manner, that is, *on* the children and not *with* them (e.g. Holland, Renold, Ross, & Hillman, 2010).

The degree of child participation in research is often graded according to 'the ladder of participation' (Hart, 1997; see Figure 4.1), which is based on 'the ladder of citizen participation' (Arnstein, 1969). The first three steps (manipulation, decoration, and tokenism) on Hart's ladder do not involve the children in a manner that is consistent with participatory research; the children are present mainly for show. The present study occupies the sixth step of the ladder, with the research being initiated by adults and the questions being addressed by children within a specific framework, in this case democracy.

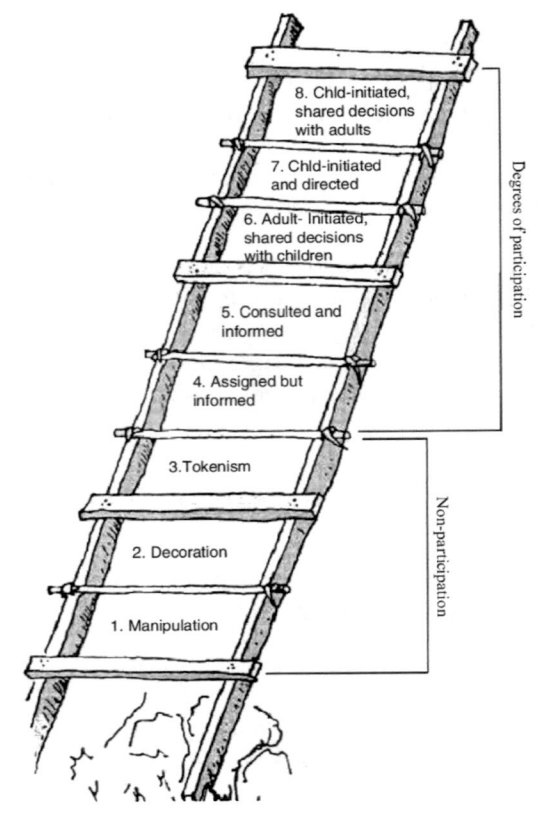

Figure 4.1. The ladder of participation (Hart, 1997)

Co-researching is a participatory research method in which the subjects under investigation are also the investigators. Giving children the opportunity to be co-researchers enables them to practice various skills, such as investigating, employing critical thinking, taking responsibility, and forming and expressing opinions. By strengthening these important skills, children can become responsible citizens; for example, they gain the ability to critically assess their surroundings (Kellet, 2010).

Critical Thinking and Participation

As previously mentioned, members of a democratic society require the ability to think critically, understand the complexity of society, and evaluate contradictory and incomplete information in order to arrive at sound conclusions, make intelligent decisions, and thereby participate fully in civic life. Even though the term 'critical thinking' is broad and a subject for discussion in many academic texts (Larsson, 2011), Långström and Virta (2011) showed that the term refers to both the ability and the inclination of a person to ask critical questions regarding sources of information. Thus, critical thinking includes abilities and behaviours that examine the reliability of information, distinguish between relevant and irrelevant information, identify gaps and attitudes, check up on various arguments' validity, and distinguish between facts, values and opinions. Ennis (1987) showed the complexity of critical thinking, which includes both a mental attitude and a set of skills. Nickersson (1990) identified the need and benefits of developing critical thinking skills for the individual (as well as society) in areas such as work, education, economy, and culture. Critical thinking also contributes to having realistic expectations and the ability to solve global problems.

Game-Informed Learning (GIL)

Begg, Dewhurst, and Macleod (2005) introduced game-informed learning to differ from game-based learning by suggesting that the educational processes should themselves be informed by the experience of gameplay. By contrast, in game-based learning the process includes one or several games. Gee (2003) shared this opinion on games being exciting, engaging, and compelling, encouraging individuals to repeatedly attempt difficult tasks, but Gee maintained that the mechanism providing these activities does not have to be delivered in what would be defined as a game. Begg (2008) explained, furthermore, that game artefacts such as scores, counters, countdowns, and conditional blocks could be useful elements in the learning process but that they are not mandatory. These principles of successful gameplay build on the established learning practices developed by Kolb (1984) and Lewin (1948).

Gamification has been a trending topic among researchers for the past several years. The number of published research papers on gamification has significantly increased on a year to year basis since 2010. Gamification occurs when the designer implements gaming elements in order to increase the usage, users, and their engagement. These elements are most often badges, achievements, leader boards, rewards, narratives, and feedback that motivate the user to keep using the service (app, website, customer program, etc.) (Hamari et al., 2014). This can of course also be implemented into learning activities in order to promote learning, engagement, and participation.

Begg et al. (2005) stated that game-informed learning activities are effective when the following criteria are met:

1. The backstory gives students the opportunity to emotionally engage with and build the character role within the current environment.
2. Essential feedback increases the feeling of agency and students' willingness to learn.
3. Students are given the opportunity to act and make decisions in a perceived real setting without dealing with potential consequences.
4. Students perform according to the role in the setting.
5. Students perceive the setting as a real experience so that they can develop emotional attachment to the character role and thereby enhance the learning experience.

The authors argued that gaming and learning involve similar processes and that it is valuable to integrate the learning principles of games into teaching practice (Begg et al., 2005), making education more playful. The processes that occur in successful gameplay—the development of the player, the appreciation of challenges and goals, the interaction with those challenges to meet those goals, and the lessons picked up in the process—lead to refined approaches and practices (Begg, 2008).

Role-Play

Role-play is an approach that can be used to acquire attitudes, knowledge, and skills in a range of disciplines, such as medical (Hargie, Dickson, Boohan, & Hughes, 1998; Steinert, 1993; Mann et al., 1996; Skelton, Hammond, Fitzmaurice, & Wiskin, 1997; Henderson & Johnson, 2002; Wagner, Lentz, & Heslop, 2002; Wylie, Hallam-Jones, & Daines, 2003), school science (Aubusson, Fogwill, Barr, & Perkovic, 1997; Hildebrand, 1989), and human resources (El-Shamy, 2005).

Van Ments (1989) defined role-play as follows:

> The idea of role-play, in its simplest form, is that of asking someone to imagine that they are either themselves or another person in a particular situation. They are then asked to behave exactly as they feel that person would. As a result of doing this they, or the rest of the class, or both, will learn something about the person and/or situation. In essence, each player acts as part of the social environment of the others and provides a framework in which they can test out their repertoire of behaviors or study the interacting behavior of the group. (Van Ments, 1989, p. 186)

Role-play can take different forms, and the present study employed co-researching as a form of role-play in which the pupils acted out the role of a co-researcher. The performed research was real (see Table 4.1), whereas the researcher profession was assumed. The pupils were given goals along the way and given the freedom to explore their role as co-researchers.

Some of the key aspects of role-playing games (RPGs) were present in this research game. We created a distinct narrative in which the pupils were co-researchers in a study of democracy within their own community. The pupils progressed through the narrative by learning new things and then employing them during their research. They got to make choices based on what they learned, and these choices then shaped the rest of the narrative. Throughout the narrative, the pupils were given feedback on the choices they made, they were tested on the knowledge and skills they gained, and their acquired skills opened up new choices for them (e.g. performing the analysis, conducting the interviews, gathering the data).

Role, Frame, and Position

This section presents an overview of the study's core concepts. Bakhtin's (1981) research on connections between identity and utterance showed that every social grouping has its own language, that is, its own jargon, which is dependent on its members. Mead (1934) discussed the phenomenon of the "generalised other" and the way it determines how social groups behave and interact with other groups.

> It is in the form of the generalized other that the social process influences the behavior of the individuals involved in it and carrying it on, i.e., that the community exercises control over the conduct of its individual members; for it is in this form that the social process or community enters as a determining factor into the individual's thinking. (Mead, 1934)

Pupils that assume a new role should behave in conformity with what they know about this role, according to Mead's teachings about the generalised other (Mead, 1934), just as youths behave differently and adapt (or not) to experienced 'regulations' when they are at their grandparents' home or at soccer practice, performing the role of either grandchild or soccer player. But the concept of the generalised other also indicates that this behaviour should be slightly different from person to person. Not everyone has exactly the same image of how a researcher looks, acts, and talks. When the learning experience feels more like a game, pupils may find it more engaging and participate more actively.

Bakhtin (1986) stated that people, in dialogue with society, develop their roles and their selves through many forms of utterance, whether verbal, written, or acted. According to this framework, as pupils assume a new role, they also start to develop their own selves. Goffman (1959) was of the same basic opinion that selves develop in conjunction with others, but he made the distinction that it is a specific role that is developing, the one that we are 'acting' there and then. We are actors playing roles on life's great stage. When first coming into contact with a new role, the actors play their role based on how they think it should be played, that is, based on preconceptions about the generalised other (Mead, 1934). This is in agreement with other writings by Goffman (1974), which argued that each scene, each moment, can be described within a frame. This framing is something that is performed subconsciously; we are playing a 'role' whenever we act and interact with others. We behave differently when we are at work and when we are at home, when we are with our children and when we are with our parents. From the vantage point of a third-party onlooker, this frame can be viewed and analysed from different perspectives, and the analysis may have different results depending on the perspective.

Goffman (1981) discussed the breakdown of parts between two-party talks. The parts are not only speaker and hearer but can be divided into several other positions, such as animator, author, and principal for the speaker, and (un)ratified recipient and (un)addressed recipient for the hearer. This further breakdown can be assumed for any role that the person assumes and that gives the person their position (Marinova, 2004).

According to Bakhtin (1981), every social group has its own language. A person can belong to several different social groups at the same time and as such will have a different jargon for each group. The pupils placed in the role of co-researchers, which is a new social group, may also have adapted their language accordingly.

The five criteria for effective learning from GIL can be related to the role, frame, and position described above. The 1st (the backstory gives students the opportunity to emotionally engage with and build the character role within the current environment), 2nd (essential feedback increases the feeling of agency and students' willingness to learn), and 4th (students perform according to the role in the setting) criteria are related to the role, because the backstory and good feedback helps pupils engage in their role. The 4th and 5th (students perceive the setting as a real experience so that they can develop emotional attachment to the character role and thereby enhance the learning experience) criteria are related to the frame. Changing the setting (e.g. surroundings) for the pupils allows their perception of the situation to be changed within the same role. The 3rd (students are given the opportunity to act and make decisions in a perceived real setting without dealing with potential consequences) criterion is related to the position, which enables the pupils to act fully as co-researchers and make the decisions they believe a co-researcher would. The generalised other can be related to the 4th criterion, meaning that the pupils will perform according to how they interpret the role.

DESIGN

The design of the research game was inspired by game-informed learning (Begg et al., 2005). In the design of an effective game-informed learning activity, a number of criteria should be met (see the Game-Informed Learning section) to facilitate the students' connection to context, character role, feedback, and identity as well as their emotional involvement.

The five GIL design criteria (GIL #1–5) presented above were considered throughout the design process.

The research game was initiated in a university environment, the workshops were held in the university's classrooms, and the pupils were given security badges. These aspects of the design strengthened the role of a co-researcher, with all its benefits, including unsupervised access to technical devices, maintained classrooms, and fruit. This, combined with the introduction meeting and the consent form signed by the parents, contributed to creating a believable backstory.

The pupils had access to two researchers and a participating teacher during each session; this enabled the pupils to get feedback, support, and supervision throughout the research game (GIL #2). The learning activity was designed to fulfil the criteria throughout the research game (which was subdivided into three parts: preparation, performance, and postprocessing). The outcome of the learning activity is described in the next section.

Preparation: The idea was to start the collaboration with three workshops to develop a collective view of this activity, what research and researchers can be, and the craft of doing research, all of which gave pupils the opportunity to build a character role (GIL #1). More specifically, the first workshop addressed issues such as what the name of the group should be, the difference between everyday and scholarly knowledge, and the distinction between qualitative and quantitative research. The second workshop contained planned subjects like choosing and using different perspectives (perspective indulgence) on situations and research ethics. The last workshop highlighted cooperation with the recipient, choices made, selections, bias, fooling, and the importance of source criticism for everyone. During these workshops, the pupils also delved into different ways of gathering knowledge by conducting mini-studies. These mini-studies were performed using interviews, observations, and/or surveys to study the university students and their campus (GIL #3).

Performance: The next part was designed for the group to jointly decide on a research question and come up with strategies for how to gather information and knowledge that would help them answer the question. The planning was designed to enable the pupils to find their own way by deciding on the methods and procedures themselves (GIL #4). The researchers were available for support if the pupils wanted it.

Postprocessing: The last part was designed to allow the pupils to work in smaller groups together with the researchers and teachers. This activity would help them discuss their various views, possible conclusions, and how to present these conclusions to an audience (GIL #5).

RESEARCH GAME

First, two months prior to the project's commencement, an information meeting was held in order to disseminate the outlines of the project, perform the set-up, describe the pupils' rights of participation, and collect consent forms from the parents. The pupils came from the three different eighth-grade classes in the school and were selected to participate by the school's teachers. The participating school is located in one of the larger city districts of Stockholm, in an area that is well known for its high density of ICT colleges, corporations, and think tanks. The school is ethnically diverse, with 650 pupils, including the kindergarten; the age range in the school is 1–16 years, and the eighth-grade pupils are 14–15 years old.

A large amount of data was collected during the research game, from video recordings to the participants' notes and the written report. This chapter focuses primarily on the researchers' observations and field notes, not on the actual results of the pupils' investigations, in the sense that results only consists of the content of the pupils' conclusions regarding their research questions.

After completing the project, follow-up interviews were conducted with the two teachers associated with the project. One of them was an initiator of the project, and the other was a participant in the weekly project meetings. The teachers were asked to answer questions about differences between the participating pupils and groups of pupils taught in a traditional way and about the factors that may have affected these pupils' engagement.

Preparation: Workshops

After arriving at the department on the university campus, the 15 pupils were divided into four prepared subgroups with representatives from each of the three different eighth-grade classes in them. The subgroups were the same during the three first workshops, which focused on introduction to research. Discussions were held about what observations and interviews mean in connection to science and how they differ from 'candid camera' (observations) and sports interviews (interviews). Pens, notepads, and security badges were handed out to each pupil. The name 'The Research Party' was chosen by the pupils because of the Swedish parliamentary elections taking place at the same time. The researchers led the workshops and discussions but gladly followed the pupils' 'sidetracks'. The frame for the research question, democracy, was introduced and was to be discussed at a later time.

The first couple of workshops emphasised three different ways one can collect data: surveys, interviews, and observations. Using the different methods, mini-studies were performed on university students during the workshops. This gave the pupils the opportunity to practice 'doing science'. The outcome of the different mini-studies was shared with everyone, providing an opportunity to illustrate ethical issues and the different methods' pros and cons.

Performance: Data Collection

It was decided that the pupils' research question would address the topic of democracy. They were asked to approach this topic first on their own, then in beehives (small groups), and finally all together as a large group. After the large-group discussion, the pupils still had not decided on a research question. Because of the time limitation, the researchers helped the pupils formulate several research questions and presented them to the pupils at their next meeting. The pupils chose the following as their research question: *What meaning does democracy have for people in their everyday life?* Because the pupils wanted to pursue different methods, this topic was then subdivided and studied by the pupils in three substudies, as follows (collected data is shown in Table 4.1):

Substudy 1. Interviews with pupils, parents (etc.), and senior citizens.
This substudy was divided into three themes:

- What understandings and experiences do children, adults, and senior citizens have of democracy and participation in their everyday life, including experiences in their school?
- What experiences do children, adults, and senior citizens have of taking environmental responsibility in everyday life, including experiences in their youth?
- How do children, adults, and senior citizens use technology for participation today as well as when they were children?

Substudy 2. Observations.
- What responsibility do fellow pupils take for their (school) environment?

Substudy 3. Surveys.
The survey consisted of six questions:

- (1) What is your age?
- (2) What is your gender?
- (3) Is politics important to you?
- (4) How often do you think there should be elections?
- (5) How often should there be referendums?
- (6) At what age should citizens have the right to vote?

Over a period of four weeks, the studies were conducted by the pupils in the local mall, a nearby retirement home, and their school. The pupils, through their own interest, added a substudy about trash left behind by humans. This was called 'Traces from People' and contained photographs taken by the co-researchers of trash, graffiti, and damage throughout the school.

The three studies were performed together by the group in different configurations, and the fourth was completed by the initiator.

Table 4.1. The studies performed, their goals, and the data collected

Name	Study 1	Study 2	Study 3	Study 4
	Interviews	Observations	Surveys	Traces from people
Goal	Study the ways in which people can exert influence, now and before	Study the reaction to violations of the no-littering rule	Study people's opinions on election, voting age, referendums, and the importance of politics	Study traces from people throughout the school environment
Data collected	16 interviews, 24 people interviewed [2 interviews with senior citizens; 2 group interviews with pupils grade 4 (6 pupils in total); 2 group interviews with pupils grade 9 (6 pupils in total); 10 interviews with parents/adults.]	2 sessions, app. 30 minutes each. +4 teachers interviewed	263 in total. 160 pupils from 9 to 17 years old 103 adults	Approximately 80 photos

This large amount of data was collected by the pupils as a group effort. The researchers helped by suggesting the minimum amount of data required for each substudy.

Postprocessing: The Co-Researchers' Analysis and Presentation of Conclusions

The beginning of the analysis was led by the researchers. By using templates with questions like 'What similarities and differences do you see?' we could focus the pupils' attention on how to analyse the interviews. After this, the pupils had to use their own judgment in order to choose a question from the surveys, a question where the results were of interest to them and analyse it in a similar way as they had analysed the interviews. All the conclusions the pupils could draw from sitting in pairs and analysing 'their question' were written on a whiteboard, which was divided into the gender and age categories from the survey. The pupils wrote their results in the appropriate category. Then, we observed the results in their entirety to determine if we could draw any conclusions about the report, viewing it critically. Whereas nine pupils worked on conclusions, six volunteered to work on the upcoming presentation at the National Museum of Science and Technology. The latter group relied on the other group's ability to analyse the results and communicate their findings. The final presentation for 'The Research Party' would not take place for another two months, but because the invitation to present at the museum arrived after the research game had started, this division into groups had to be made in order to finish on time. Between this first presentation and the final one, at the university, the work was focused on writing a report on the project. In order to hold the project together and keep all the participants on the same page, we and the school decided to hold three extra meetings, relying on the whole group's agency for action to be able to communicate their findings.

The additional meetings were held at the school, and the pupils left ordinary lectures in order to work on the report together. The work up to the final presentation also included writing a communiqué that was sent to the press and various other media sources. The final presentation was held at the Department of Computer and System Sciences at Stockholm University. The audience consisted of 60 of their classmates, the entirety of their teaching staff, the headmaster, the area manager, representatives from Stockholm city administration, and staff and researchers from the department.

REFLECTIONS ON AND ANALYSIS OF FIELD OBSERVATIONS

In this section, we present our observations from the meetings with the pupils and our analysis of how their behaviour may have been influenced by the learning activity. We also include the teachers' observations from the interviews, presented as quotations below. By using the concepts introduced in the background section, we, as the participating researchers, categorise our observations into different roles, frames, and positions. All quotations are translated from the teacher interviews, which were conducted in Swedish.

Role

It was important from the start to signal that this was not a regular school activity. We did so by consciously not including the accompanying teachers in the planning and not giving the teachers any information before the pupils as well as dealing with school connected issues at other times. With the goal of positioning the co-researchers (pupils) and the researchers as the participants and the teachers as more of suppliers or companions.

Throughout the learning activity, the pupils were addressed not as 'pupils' but as 'youths' or 'co-researchers'. The purpose of this project for the pupils in their pupil-role was not clear at first; we did not have answers regarding what the end product would look like, because we wanted the pupils to decide. It also took a while for them to get information about how they were to be graded by the teachers. From the perspective of a co-researcher role, the task was clear: *What interests you (as a young person) when it comes to the subject of democracy?*

Moreover, we took time to engage in discussion and take decisions together in the group in order to enhance the pupils' agency for the role. The pupils started to take more responsibility after they were put in this new situation and environment.

They used their knowledge about how they thought a researcher should act and behave (generalised other) in order to play their role; this was also noticed by the teacher:

> They got a sort of pupil maturity; some became pupils in a different way. Especially on the days they were walking away [to campus]. They gathered without an adult, found out where we were supposed to be, something they don't do when it is something in school.

Another thing that was noticed by the pupils was the difference in how things were done. Our workshops consisted more of discussions and questions than of lectures. A pupil commented after the second workshop that they did not have to copy the whiteboard; instead, they had time to reflect and think.

In the beginning of the collaboration with the pupils, they behaved in a reserved manner, holding back a bit. They also seemed relatively passive when it came to their engagement in the subject and question formulation. The pupils had difficulty coming up with ideas about what they could research. However, with time, ownership of the project shifted more towards the pupils, perhaps after the purpose became clear to them and they realized it wasn't a question of right or wrong. Our management of the project, which took the form of papers with instructions to writing which tasks that were left to do on the whiteboard, transformed into something new. Now, we were supporting the pupils' work on their presentations and report as well as challenging and questioning their thoughts and ideas.

As the pupils more fully inhabited their role as co-researchers, they started to exhibit new skills. They thought critically about their own work and were motivated to do a good job, as the quote below illustrates:

> Critical thinking and motivation, as I said, and confidence that the pupils themselves get a sense of accomplishing a rather difficult task.

They were excited to be able to influence how they used their time, controlling both the goal and the journey towards the end.

> They controlled both the journey and then also the goal. It is not so common that they are allowed to do that.

During the research game, continuous feedback was given by the participating researchers and teachers, as well as by representatives from the community. Feedback is an important step, because it motivates pupils to learn and to strengthen their sense of ownership (Begg et al., 2005). Feedback was given in several ways:

- The audience asked questions during their presentations.
- The audience applauded their results when presented.
- The participating researchers gave feedback during the report-writing phase, but the pupils were responsible for writing the report.

By giving the pupils essential and constructive feedback, we could see signs of their active agency and interest. When the audience and moderator asked questions that had not been prepared, the pupils formulated their own answers based on what they had discovered during their observations and reflections.

During their last presentation, the pupils were eager to answer the questions first and to communicate their own views. They wanted to show what they knew, and they used language suitable for the scientific setting when answering. They were fully engaged in their co-researcher role.

Frames

We noticed that the university campus influenced them. They were still within the same role (that of co-researchers), but their experiences from the research game had changed their perspective. They had discovered that legitimate research could be based on the interests of youth and that they were the only people who possessed the desired knowledge. This new perspective on knowledge (and learning) might have given the pupils a new frame for understanding what learning can be and who performs the learning. Their behaviour was more serious while they were working in our well-kept rooms, with all their technology, than when we met them in their school classrooms.

The teachers also noticed that the change in learning environment affected the pupils' behaviour. The pupils' perceived stress and pressure encouraged them to take the situation more seriously and act accordingly; they wanted to do a good job.

> Somehow the way we worked changed the group and changed the pupils. [...] It became different when they were able to go away and do something for real, like the research project. [...] [Schoolwork] is also for real, but it is still in the old environment, where they are familiar. Now they got to go to the university campus, phrase research questions regarding democracy and discuss in a different environment. They simply got more time. They became very worried about the result, they did not know if they were going to cope. They had a quite high pressure on them which contributed that they took the situation more seriously, I think.

We also noticed that the pupils started to view the issues from different perspectives. One of the co-researchers wanted to investigate how a senior citizen would answer if they were interviewed and asked the same questions as the younger people (*Substudy 1*). This pupil initiated and followed through with the interviews at a retirement home in the vicinity.

They were surprised about some of the things they discovered during their research. They commented that some of the age groups defined for the surveys didn't answer as they had expected. For example, for the question concerning voting age, respondents in the older-age categories thought that the age for voting should be lowered.

In order to finish both the report and the final presentation, a total of five additional meetings were held. These meetings were needed because the extra presentation at the museum had used up meeting opportunities that were not accounted for at first. The meetings were based on the pupils' volunteering. The researchers were available in a room, and the pupils were allowed to leave their scheduled classes in order to come and write the report and presentation. Although one could speculate that the pupils showed up only in order to skip their scheduled classes, we did observe a lot of activity and responsibility in order for them to finish before the deadline. They conversed about what was finished, what still needed to be done, and who needed help.

During the research process and towards its conclusion (the compilation of the written report and final presentation), we observed an increase in the co-researchers' ownership of the findings. At the beginning of the process, they needed help to come up with ideas for a research question, but towards the end, all the pupils wanted to take responsibility for the conclusions. For the first presentation at the museum, only six pupils wanted to be presenters; they had the opportunity to speak to the moderator over Skype before the presentation, asking their own questions about the proceedings, and got to practice the setup. For the final presentation (for which participation was still voluntary), all the pupils wanted to participate in some way; each pupil presented the part that they felt most responsible for during the writing of the report. This took place without a major rehearsal. Many of them felt nervous, but their ownership over the process made them feel confident enough to go through with their part in the presentation, contributing and communicating their findings and conclusions.

Positions

When we first met, the pupils started to assume the role of co-researchers but remained essentially in the role of pupils. They were at first more interested in knowing how they would be judged for their work, how to get certain grades, and how participation in the project would affect their other subjects. Towards the end, when they were writing the report and preparing the presentation, their position had changed. They now wanted to tell people about what they knew, and they were interested in the results of their research. Moreover, they had developed additional questions that they wanted to explore. They had positioned themselves both as lecturers with something to say and as co-researchers with more questions that needed to be investigated.

They positioned themselves as co-researchers who listened to feedback in order to improve their work. Providing continuous feedback to the pupils enabled them to overcome their doubts. According to the interviewed teachers, they did not act as they usually did while in the role of pupils, when they used less nuanced language and were often scared of asking questions or thinking for themselves.

> During these circumstances ['The Research Party'] the doubts existed as well.
> They do not dare to express themselves, they do not dare to think, do not know
> if they are doing it right or wrong. But here they were actually able to work
> through it. They got ... it became more intense. And they got the confirmation

too: 'You're on the right track, you're on the right track'. And this doubt that they have, and had then, in some way they were able to work with it. And this helped them in some ways, instead of just being a burden.

Acting as professionals also changed the pupils' language, especially in official contexts. During presentations, their accent diminished, and they spoke more clearly. This indicated that the pupils changed their position during official presentations.

> Some of the pupils did no longer have an accent when speaking Swedish, they talked a bit more clearly, some of them that do have an accent, and they spoke a better Swedish. They stood up in front of other people, if there had only been classmates there they might have still had an accent, but now there were a few others there and teachers. They took another role; they took a position. They positioned themselves somehow as a lecturer and that you noticed.

Furthermore:

> They stood up for something that they had done, not only proud and haughty but they believed that this was something important. That they had come up with something.

When presenting their results, they felt an emotional tie to them; they were *their* results. They stood up for them and defended them; they believed they had discovered something new. It was important for the pupils that the message they conveyed was the correct one; they helped each other out during the presentations in order to convey the correct message.

The pupils started to show tendencies and qualities that are uncommon for pupils in their age group. These qualities signified a stronger sense of ownership over the research, an important step towards assuming the identity of a co-researcher. These tendencies are summarised below:

- The pupils volunteered for the panel debate.
- The pupils came to the writing sessions in order to finish their report instead of going to scheduled classes.
- The pupils stayed to answer questions after the presentations without being asked.
- The pupils performed the interviews, surveys, and observations in a professional and serious manner. This was the case even though they had to approach both older pupils and strangers at the local shopping mall, which can be hard for teenagers to do.

The pupils grew accustomed to their role as co-researchers and were able to position themselves as lecturers. They wanted to convey their knowledge to others (volunteering for panel debates, taking the time to finish the report, staying after presentations to answer more questions). They could also assume a different position, as an interviewer, still being in the co-researcher's role, when asking questions both to older pupils and to adults they met at the mall.

Teachers' Perspectives on the Research Game

Several factors influenced the pupils' ability to take on the role of co-researchers. For example, 'real' researchers were involved, a large portion of the work took place at the university, and the school's teachers and administrators were supportive.

As the quotations from the teacher interviews in the Observations and Analysis section make clear, the time, location, and expectations, both their own and others', were important for the success of this project. Beyond the practical issues, the opportunity for the pupils to get feedback and to develop their reasoning regarding their doubts and thoughts was also shown to have an impact on the pupils' success as co-researchers.

Both teachers mentioned that the freedom the pupils experienced was important. Whether it was the freedom of choosing the journey, the goal, or which questions to answer or ask was not as important as the pupils' general sense of freedom of choice.

One of the teachers mentioned that the approach contributed to a broader perspective on knowledge that will help the pupils develop their motivation and critical thinking skills. That, in combination with improved confidence, gave them the ability and willingness to attempt more difficult tasks:

> It [the project] has contributed to reinforce their way of thinking when it comes to education and knowledge. It has probably helped them a bit to understand what knowledge can be used for. And then to understand what relationship one can have to knowledge, one can have a relationship without things being definitely right or wrong. One can learn more; raise more questions where knowledge is not black or white. That is the relationship they have experienced. I think that is the most important. I think, I believe that it will in turn, help them to develop their critical thinking and their motivation.

DISCUSSION

With the design setup influenced by GIL (and intending that the educational process be viewed as gaming), we hoped to leverage the exciting, engaging, and compelling nature of games.

The game-inspired approach we chose to utilise was role-play. Role-play is a good method for teaching new skills and trying out projects that may otherwise be unavailable to participants because of their age or career, so we chose to let our pupils role-play as co-researchers. In this setting, they were able to formulate their own questions and decide which methods to use when performing their research.

There are of course other factors that could have affected the pupils. Suddenly, there were more adults around who were interested in their work, reporters who were visiting or interviewing them, and participating researchers who were taking the pupils seriously. However exploratory, this learning activity may offer some insight into how GIL-based activities can inspire learning and how learning activities can be designed. These insights are described in the paragraphs below.

Using children as co-researchers involves several challenges and issues that need to be addressed. There is naturally a power difference between the researchers and the co-researchers because of the difference in knowledge. As a result of letting the pupils decide on the research question and research methods, part of the power shifted towards the pupils. Because the children were minors, they needed to be protected; we addressed this by having a teacher accompany them during the meetings. We also made sure that whenever they split into smaller groups, there was always an adult with them. The pupils' lack of research competence required a training program, so workshops were used to give the pupils some knowledge and experience in basic research methodology.

It came up during both of the teacher interviews that this project was supported by both the headmaster and teachers. From a school point of view, they were generous about allowing more time when we needed it. From a researcher's point of view, the school structure, with its schedules, delays caused by classes ending late, and field trips affecting that week's meeting, resulted in less time going into the project than we had counted on.

By applying role, frame, and position as the categories under which the learning activity was analysed, the pupils' participation could be observed and their actions could be placed in the correct category. The findings from this analysis indicate that several factors associated with the different categories affected the pupils' engagement in their role as co-researchers. The following are examples of these factors:

Role: Being perceived as professionals.
Frame: Interacting and communicating in a new location and setting.
Position: Giving and receiving feedback; being recognised through the results obtained.

These factors can of course also be connected to successful gameplay. For example, in role-playing games, the narrative is an important factor for immersion and for perceiving the game as real. This was addressed in several ways, such as by changing the location and setting to more researcher-related ones, by treating the pupils as professionals, and by giving feedback to make the role believable. These important factors need to be considered when designing learning activities that focus on facilitating pupil participation, thereby viewing the gaps in the present learning environment (school setting).

If the target is a knowledgeable pupil who is interested in their schoolwork, we need to design subject areas and teaching methods accordingly. We need to facilitate pupils' pursuit of their own questions in an area and their ability to come up with their own means of reaching the knowledge goals. By arranging the opportunity to present and get feedback from the community, pupils' motivation to engage in the learning activity can be strengthened.

CONCLUSIONS

Active citizens are the foundation of a democratic society. Kellet (2010) argued that in order to be active citizens, we need a few sets of skills, namely the capacity for judgement, social agency, and the ability to communicate our views. These skills need to be developed and practiced in school; the problem is that today's school system does not provide opportunities for this practice (Långström & Virta, 2011). To be able to practice these skills and approaches, pupils need access to other roles, frames, and positions.

At first, the pupils in our study were locked into their traditional pupil role, which led to several consequences. Because of this, the pupils had a hard time adjusting to their new role, and it took them some time for them to start asking questions and behaving as co-researchers. Over the course of the research game, the traditional role was unlocked and was replaced by the co-researcher role.

The change in setting and location enhanced the fact that they were no longer just pupils but also co-researchers. We made sure to talk to and meet the pupils as professionals. This also enhanced their feeling of being more than just pupils. Furthermore, the pupils' new freedom to make their own decisions and work in an unsupervised environment encouraged them to be more responsible and behave maturely. They could embrace the role of being more than a pupil; they acted as co-researchers. They also participated actively, showing that they found the research game exciting, engaging, and compelling.

Through gamification in the form of role-play, the following advantages could be observed:

- Increased participation
- Increased interest
- The experience of an authentic environment and authentic research practices

As co-researchers, the pupils gained experience in communicating their findings, expressing their thoughts, analysing their own results, and making their own decisions. These are experiences they later in life may have use of, which may be different from knowledge gained that they have only read about and not practiced.

Learning-activity design that focuses on providing access to roles, frames, and positions is needed. Both Mead and Goffman argued that the self is developed in the midst of interaction with others; pupils need to possess a view of themselves other than that of the traditional pupil in order to be active as students and citizens. Design influenced by GIL can contribute to the process of facilitating pupils' participation in both school and society.

Gamification and role-play have strong potential to increase participation, but more research is needed.

ACKNOWLEDGMENTS

I would like to thank the City of Stockholm, FlashPoll, and the University of Stockholm for providing the financial means to perform this research. My greatest appreciation goes to Kista Grundskola and the participating pupils for their effort and participation. I would also like to acknowledge Associate Professor Patrik Hernwall, the other researcher involved in this project.

REFERENCES

Alderson, P., & Morrow, V. (2011). *The ethics of research with children and young people: A practical handbook*. London: Sage Publications.

Arnstein, S. R. (1969). A ladder of citizen participation. *Journal of the American Institute of planners, 35*(4), 216–224.

Aubusson, P., Fogwill, S., Barr, R., & Perkovic, L. (1997). What happens when students do simulation-role-play in science? *Research in Science Education, 27*(4), 565–579.

Bakhtin, M. M., & Holquist, M. (1981). *The dialogic imagination: Four essays*. Austin, TX: University of Texas Press.

Bakhtin, M. M., Holquist, M., & Emerson, C. (1986). *Speech genres and other late essays*. Austin, TX: University of Texas Press.

Bawden, D., & Robinson, L. (2009). The dark side of information: Overload, anxiety and other paradoxes and pathologies. *Journal of Information Science, 35*(2), 180–191.

Begg, M. (2008). Leveraging game-informed healthcare education. *Medical Teacher, 30*(2), 155–158.

Begg, M., Dewhurst, D., & Macleod, H. (2005). Game-informed learning: Applying computer game processes to higher education. *Innovate: Journal of Online Education, 1*(6), 6.

Bradbury-Jones, C., & Taylor, J. (2015). Engaging with children as co-researchers: Challenges, counter-challenges and solutions. *International Journal of Social Research Methodology, 18*(2), 161–173.

El-Shamy, S. (2005). *Role play made easy: 25 structured rehearsals for managing problem situations and dealing with difficult people*. San Fransisco, CA: Pfeiffer.

Ennis, R. H. (1987). A taxonomy of critical thinking dispositions and abilities. In J. B. Baron & R. J. Sternberg (Eds.), *Teaching thinking skills: Theory and practice* (pp. 9–26). New York, NY: Freeman and Company.

Gee, J. P. (2003). What video games have to teach us about learning and literacy. *Computers in Entertainment, 1*(1), 20–21.

Goffman, E. (1959). *The presentation of self in everyday life*. Garden City, NY: Double Day.

Goffman, E. (1974). *Frame analysis: An essay on the organization of experience*. New York, NY: Harvard University Press.

Goffman, E. (1981). *Forms of talk*. Philadelphia, PA: University of Pennsylvania Press.

Hamari, J., Koivisto, J., & Sarsa, H. (2014). *Does gamification work? A literature review of empirical studies on gamification* (pp. 3025–3034). In System Sciences (HICSS), 47th Hawaii International Conference on IEEE, Waikoloa.

Hargie, O., Dickson, D., Boohan, M., & Hughes, K. (1998). A survey of communication skills training in UK schools of medicine: Present practices and prospective proposals. *Medical Education, 32*(1), 25–34.

Hart, R. A. (1997). *Children's participation: The theory and practice of involving young citizens in community development and environmental care*. London: Earthscan.

Henderson, P., & Johnson, M. (2002). Assisting medical students to conduct empathic conversations with patients from a sexual medicine clinic. *Sexually Transmitted Infections, 78*(4), 246–249.

Hildebrand, G. (1989). Creating a gender-inclusive science education. *Australian Science Teachers Journal, 35*(3), 7–16.

Hillén, S. (2013). Forskning med och av barn. In B. Johansson & M. Karlsson (Eds.), *Att involvera barn i forskning och utveckling*. Lund: Studentlitteratur.

Holland, S., Renold, E., Ross, N. J., & Hillman, A. (2010). Power, agency and participatory agendas: A critical exploration of young people's engagement in participative qualitative research. *Childhood, 17*(3), 360–375.

Hunleth, J. (2011). Beyond on or with: Questioning power dynamics and knowledge production in child-oriented research methodology. *Childhood, 18*(1), 81–93.

James, A., Jenks, C., & Prout, A. (1998). *Theorizing childhood.* Cambridge, MA: Polity Press.

James, A., & Prout, A. (1997). *Constructing and reconstructing childhood: Contemporary issues in the sociological study of childhood.* London: Routledge.

Jensen, B. B. (2002). Knowledge, action and pro-environmental behaviour. *Environmental Education Research, 8*(3), 325–334.

Kellett, M. (2010). *Rethinking children and research: Attitudes in contemporary society.* New York, NY: Continuum International Publication Group.

Kellett, M., Forrest, R., Dent, N., & Ward, S. (2004). "Just teach us the skills please, we'll do the rest": Empowering ten-year-olds as active researchers. *Children & Society, 18*(5), 329–343.

Långström, S., & Virta, A. (2011). *Samhällskapsdidaktik: för utbildning i demokrati och samhällsvetenskapligt tänkande.* Lund: Studentlitteratur.

Larsson, K. (2011). *Kritiskt tänkande i samhällskunskap. En studie som ur ett fenomenografiskt perspektiv belyser manifesterat kritiskt tänkande bland elever i grundskolans år 9. Studier i de samhällsvetenskapliga ämnenas didaktik nr 11.* Karlstad: Karlstad University Studies.

Lundy, L., McEvoy, L., & Byrne, B. (2011). Working with young children as co-researchers: An approach informed by the United Nations convention on the rights of the child. *Early Education & Development, 22*(5), 714–736.

Mann, B. D., Sachdeva, A. K., Nieman, L. Z., Nielan, B. A., Rovito, M. A., & Damsker, J. I. (1996). Teaching medical students by role playing: A model for integrating psychosocial issues with disease management. *Journal of Cancer Education, 11*(2), 65–72.

Marinova, D. (2004). [Papers from the Special Session in Honor of Erving Goffman (Professor at the University of Pennsylvania 1968–1982)] Two approaches to negotiating positions in interaction: Goffman's (1981) footing and Davies and Harre's (1999) positioning theory. *University of Pennsylvania Working Papers in Linguistics, 10*(1), 17.

Mead, G. H. (1934). *Mind, self, and society: From the standpoint of a social behaviorist* (Works of George Herbert Mead, Vol. 1). Chicago, IL: University of Chicago Press.

Shaffer, D. W. (2006). *How computer games help children learn.* New York, NY: Palgrave Macmillan.

Skelton, J., Hammond, P., Fitzmaurice, D., & Wiskin, C. (1997). The acceptability of whole-context role play. *Education for General Practice, 8*, 206–212.

Skolverket. (2011). *Läroplan för grundskolan, förskoleklassen och fritidshemmet.* Stockholm: Skolverket.

Steinert, Y. (1993). Twelve tips for using role-plays in clinical teaching. *Medical Teacher, 15*(4), 283–291.

UNICEF. (1989). *Convention on the rights of the child* (United Nations Treaty Series). New York, NY: UNICEF.

Van Ments, M. (1989). *The effective use of role-play: A handbook for teachers and trainers* (Revised ed.). New York, NY: Kogan Page.

Wagner, P. J., Lentz, L., & Heslop, S. D. (2002). Teaching communication skills: A skills-based approach. *Academic Medicine, 77*(11), 1164.

Wylie, K., Hallam-Jones, R., & Daines, B. (2003). Review of an undergraduate medical school training programme in human sexuality. *Medical Teacher, 25*(3), 291–295.

KRISTINE ØYGARDSLIA

5. STORIES ABOUT HISTORY

Exploring Central Elements When Students Design Game Narratives

ABSTRACT

This chapter explores what characterizes the narratives of games designed by students in a classroom setting and how this ties to educational outcomes. The chapter builds on video data from one sixth-grade and one seventh-grade class that designed computer games about topics from their social studies curriculum, as well as the games they created. Constructionism and a design-theoretic perspective are the main theoretical concepts informing this chapter, with the main assumption that the game design processes and the games themselves reveal what the students value and emphasize. The video data is analyzed with a focus on the organization of the social interactions. It is argued that the narrative is a key factor for learning and engagement when designing games and that the following characteristics can be observed in how the students work on game narratives: (1) content learning while shaping the game narrative; (2) exploring alternative versions of history, often testing the limits of what is legitimate to include in a school setting; (3) emphasizing the story when presenting their group's games and evaluating those of the other groups; (4) working on narrative skills; and (5) challenging stereotypes.

Keywords: narrative, classroom game design, game-oriented learning

INTRODUCTION

Will this game have a story, or is it just going to be one of those silly games? (Vera, 12-year-old game designer)

We can do that afterwards—but first we need to fix the story. (Scott, 12-year-old game designer)

That is what I said! *I told them both* that we should have worked more on the story! (Marius, 12-year-old game designer)

From tales around the campfire in prehistoric times to the computer screens and the classrooms of young people today, storytelling has been tied to learning. When it comes to games, the narrative offers one of the main advantages utilized by the medium to foster both engagement and learning. As early as 1954, Mood and Specht stated, "A virtue of gaming that is sometimes overlooked by those seeking grander goals [...] is its unparalleled advantages in training and educational programs. A game can easily be made fascinating enough to put over the dullest facts" (pp. 12–13).

This chapter aims to explore the role of the narrative when elementary school students, aged 11 and 12 in this case, design their own games related to history topics from their social studies curriculum. There are two main reasons for this focus. First, research on learning from game design has often concentrated on learning programming or other subjects related to science, technology, engineering and mathematics (STEM) (Hayes & Games, 2008), and some scholars have called for research on learning from designing games in relation to other subjects (Good & Robertson, 2006; Ke, 2014; Oldaker, 2010). Despite the few studies on learning from designing narratively driven games, their results have been promising. Good and Robertson (2006) argue that game design in narratively driven learning environments can foster learning, reflection, and skill development, calling it "an ideal environment to practice and refine narrative skills" (p. 2). By creating computer games in the classroom, the students have to create a well-developed plot and interesting characters and write a dialogue that will fit well with the game story. The authors also note that as computer games constitute an important part of young people's everyday lives, there are both motivational appeals to creating games and its social aspect, as it is possible for the young game designers to receive feedback from their peers (Good & Robertson, 2006, p. 2). Research on story-driven games in English classes has shown that students can design sophisticated stories with interactive story-authoring tools (Carbonaro et al., 2008). Using the engine from Neverwinter Nights, Robertson and Good (2005) indicate that game creation in the classroom has positive educational outcomes, such as improving self-esteem, narrative skills, and motivation.

The fact that creating game narratives contributes to the students' motivation to perform the task ties to the second main reason for focusing on learning from game narratives. Throughout the game design process in this study, the students clearly emphasized the importance of developing a good game story. This was not only observed when working on the game design but also when playtesting and evaluating one another's games. As this was clearly an essential factor to the students, the significance of understanding the role of narratives in classroom game design is highlighted in this chapter.

This chapter aims to provide a deeper understanding of how the design of game narratives might tie to learning by posing the following research question: What characterizes the students' way of working with narratives in the game design process, and how is this made visible in their social interactions and finished computer games?

To explore this issue further, three short episodes are analyzed from the students' design of games about history topics from their social studies curriculum, as well as one game about the Middle Ages that was created by two sixth-grade students. Through the analysis of the students' interactions, the excerpts are chosen to show how the students worked with game narratives in the different stages of the game design process. The episodes are not isolated events but present recurring events in the data material. The games are analyzed to exemplify how significant aspects of learning from creating game narratives are not only perceived in the students' social interactions but also in the games themselves.

BUILDING BLOCKS OF STORYTELLING:
NARRATIVE, FANTASY, AND CURIOSITY

According to Malone (1981) and later emphasized by Dickey (2006), the *narrative* is one of the three important factors for creating an intrinsic motivation for learning, along with *fantasy* and *curiosity*. In this section, these elements are briefly explored to further understand the impact of the game narrative in relation to learning.

The role of the narrative in games has been a subject of debate, raising questions, such as whether the narrative and interactivity oppose each other, as well as its possible methodological implications for game researchers (see, e.g., Jenkins, 2004). Nonetheless, many scholars would argue that stories constitute an important element of games; it has even been contended that many games *are* stories (Egenfeldt-Nielsen, Smith, & Tosca, 2008). While the terms "story" and "narrative" are often used interchangeably, the narrative can be defined as "a succession of events. Its basic components are: the chronological order of the events themselves (story), their verbal or visual representation (text), and the act of telling or writing (narration)" (Egenfeldt-Nielsen et al., 2008, Kindle location 4603).

The narrative has been closely linked to computer games, summarized as offering opportunities for "reflection, evaluation, illustration, exemplification, and inquiry" (Conle, 2003; Eisner, 1991, as cited in Dickey, 2006, p. 248). However, there are various ways of integrating the narrative into the gaming experience, which both game research and educational psychology often explain through the difference between *intrinsic* and *extrinsic motivation*. While players who are driven by intrinsic motivation have an inner urge to keep progressing in the game, players who are extrinsically motivated are stimulated by external factors that are unrelated to the game play, such as points, badges, or rewards. According to Dondlinger (2007), the narrative is an important factor for creating intrinsic motivation, as a narrative context might contribute to situate the activity, establish rules, and implement the learning content that is related to the narrative. Kangas (2010) supports this argument; based on reviews on narration, the author argues that narratives comprise a way to make sense of the world while learning (p. 2) and that narration can be perceived as part of creative learning.

Fantasy can be tied directly to learning, as done by Rieber (1996), who writes that if the fantasy of the game is interesting, it will make the learner seek a resolution when presented with a problem, as long as the "solution seems possible and within reach" (p. 50). In Fine's research on role-playing games, he emphasizes that although fantasy can be viewed as "content divorced from everyday experience" (1982, p. 3), this does not mean that it is completely separate from the mundane world of players or game designers; on the contrary, fantasy is "constrained by the social expectations of players and of their world" (p. 3). Gee (2007, pp. 40–41) notes that if a game is played critically, it is possible to observe how the designed world reflects identities and social relationships in the modern world. Although fantasy is designed content, it cannot be separated from the identities, relationships, and everyday lives of players and designers. This matter might be important to remember when researching on the learning properties of computer games in a formal educational environment, with an already established school culture and a set of references and expectations.

Another important point that ties the game narrative to learning is *curiosity* (Malone, 1981). Curiosity is often driven by the narrative, compelling the player to ask, "What is going to happen next?", which might be propelled by interesting plot hooks that urge the player to make a choice or take action (Dickey, 2006). Curiosity can also relate to an important concept presented by Simons (2007), who notes that game narratives can be platforms for thought experiments and explorations of how history might unfold under different circumstances (para. 17).

UNDERSTANDING NARRATIVES IN STUDENTS' GAME DESIGN

Salen and Zimmerman point out that "games reflect the values of the society and culture in which they are played because they are part of the fabric of that society itself" (2004, p. 516). According to Flanagan and Nissenbaum (2014), games embody the values and the beliefs of their designers and might function as "cultural snapshots: they capture beliefs from a particular time and place and offer ways to understand what a given group of people believes and values" (Kindle location 178). The narrative, together with other game elements, such as character representation and the actions available to the player, should be considered. The relevant aspects of the game narrative that should be explored relates to what the game story is, who the player character is and what their motivations and goals are, and what happens along the way (Kindle location 779). Throughout the game design period in the study presented, these were choices that the students had to make to proceed with their task.

Two theoretical approaches that emphasize the importance of the students' choices in the design process are *constructionism* and the *design-theoretic perspective*. The main idea behind constructionism is that knowledge is actively constructed and done best while the learner creates something that he or she finds meaningful (Papert & Harel, 1991). This idea has informed much of the research on game design and learning (Kafai, 2006; Kafai, Ching, & Marshall, 1997) and has implications for how learning should be perceived. Kafai and Burke (2015) suggest that learning from designing games can be grouped into three dimensions when viewed from a constructionist perspective. These consist of the personal dimension or "the academic and attitudinal outcomes that making games can provide to learners" (p. 314); the social dimension, focusing on answering the question, "What does game making rather than just playing offer young learners in terms of not only collaborative making but also gaining a wider appreciation of designing for an audience?" (p. 315); and the cultural dimension, which asks how children making their own computer games can change the perspectives of what is seen as good play (p. 315).

When perceiving learning from a design-theoretic perspective (e.g., Selander, 2008a; Selander & Kress, 2010), what the students choose to include in or exclude from the design process is emphasized (Selander & Kress, 2010). In the process of designing, students acquire information that they transform together, forming it into new representations (Selander & Kress, 2010), which can be computer games, for example. These representations "show their choices, what they perceive as central of peripheral [...] indicates what students value as natural or divergent, important or unimportant, central or peripheral, necessary or unnecessary and so on" (Selander, 2008b, pp. 274–275). In other words, designed content can be viewed as "a window onto its maker" (Jewitt, 2013, p. 252). Analyzing not only the *process* of designing game narratives but also the games themselves can therefore reveal what young game designers themselves regard as important and emphasize in the process. This aspect is vital because one of the main benefits derived from creating computer games in the classroom, as perceived from a constructionist perspective, is that learning can then be tied to a project that the *students themselves* find meaningful.

METHODS

The data was collected in a small elementary school in the eastern part of Norway. The sixth-grade class (11-year-old students) consisted of seven boys and three girls, while six girls and six boys comprised the seventh-grade class (12-year-old students). The students designed their own computer games in the classroom, related to the following topics from the history component of their social studies curriculum: the Renaissance, European explorers, the Viking Age, and the Middle Ages. This aspect is related to the competency aims stating that students should be able to "tell others about the main characteristics of social development in Norway from the Viking period and to the end of the Danish-dominated period, and explain in detail a key topic from this period" (Utdanningsdirektoratet, 2013b, p. 8); "present trips of discovery and exploration made by Europeans" (p. 8); and "elaborate on central characteristics of the following epochs: the Middle Ages, the Renaissance and the Enlightenment in Europe" (p. 8). Additionally, *digital skills* are considered basic, which in social studies include creating multimedia products, exploring websites, and searching for information (Utdanningsdirektoratet, 2013b, p. 6).

Inspired by a design-based research approach (e.g., Reimann, 2011), the author of this chapter developed a website that included short challenges related to game development (Figure 5.1), in addition to written and short video tutorials. The written and the video tutorials were related to several aspects of designing the games, such as creating the game story and characters, creating the game world, writing dialogue and events, and playtesting the game. The tutorials and the challenges were related both to the technical aspects of using the software *RPG Maker VX Ace* (Enterbrain, 2011) and game design tips and tricks. Regarding the game narratives, the instructions prompted the students to consider when and where the game story would unfold and to think thoroughly about the conflict of the story by asking themselves, "What is the aim of the protagonist, and what obstacles does the protagonist have to face to achieve this aim?".

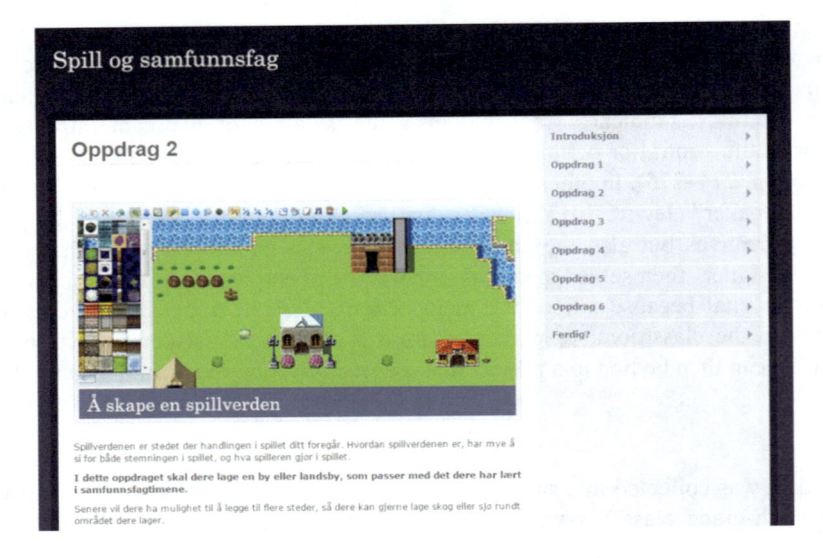

Figure 5.1. Screenshot of the developed webpage

The data was collected in three phases over seven days in total. First, in the initial observation phase, only observation notes were taken. Second, during a two-day game design period for each class, the students used the developed learning resources while creating games. The third phase allotted a one-day game design period for each class, about two months after the original game design period, when the students already knew the basic principles of designing games.

The data was collected using three video cameras, amounting to a total of 75 hours. Two cameras were stationary and recorded a three-person group at all times during the game design process. One of these two cameras was placed in front of the student group in focus, recording their interactions, while the other was placed behind the student group, recording the screen. The third, hand-held camera recorded classroom interactions and events that occurred in the other groups. Additionally, observation notes were used to support the categorization and the analysis of the data material. The students' finished computer games were also collected and used to support the analysis.

The collected data was organized in a content log (e.g., Derry et al., 2010), which included narrative summaries of the events, supplemented by rough transcriptions of the dialogues, as well as the formation of categories. Here, *sensitizing concepts* were utilized. This method draws attention to the central aspects occurring in social interactions (Bowen, 2006), instead of providing clear definitions of codes and categories (Blumer, 1954). The sensitizing concepts used were based on both the theoretical foundation of the research project and the patterns observed in the data.

The selected parts of the video data were transcribed by using a modified version of the Jeffersonian Transcription Notation (*Appendix*) and translated into Norwegian, emphasizing the meaning of the students' utterances rather than the syntax and the exact words that they used. The episodes selected for in-depth analysis in this study were chosen as they drew attention to various, central, and recurring aspects of how the students worked with game narratives in the process. The video data was analyzed with a focus on the social organization of the activity (e.g., Francis & Hester, 2004), emphasizing the interactions among the students, such as pointing, gazing, and positioning (e.g., Goodwin, 2007), as well as *how* the students used artifacts in the game design process.

FINDINGS: LEARNING FROM DESIGNING GAME NARRATIVES

This section presents three episodes occurring at different stages of the game design process. The first two examples are from the three-person group making a game about the Viking Age, focusing on *content learning* while creating the game narrative, as well as *exploring alternative versions of history.* It also touches on a common characteristic observed when designing game narratives—how the students often create game narratives that could be perceived as *pushing the borders of what is legitimate to include in a school context* and could be contested by both teachers and classmates. The third episode is taken from a playtesting session, where the concept of *creating a clear game story* is brought up. Finally, a short analysis of one of the computer games is presented, with a focus on refining *narrative skills* and how the computer game design can *challenge the stereotypical design.*

Content Learning While Designing Game Narratives

One of the most central characteristics of learning from creating game narratives is how the students utilize and build on their knowledge about the historical topic in focus. They actively construct knowledge through discussions and the use of knowledge artifacts to make the games as historically accurate as possible, expanding their knowledge about curricular topics along the way. The following episode shows how three students, at the initial stage of the period, are prompted by the game medium to expand their knowledge about a curricular topic, which would inform the further construction of the game narrative.

Casper, Peter, and Samuel are developing the story of their game about The Battle of Stiklestad. They have made a new game map and are prompted by the game design tool to name it. Casper is sitting in the middle, controlling the keyboard, while Peter and Samuel are on each side, watching the screen.

Excerpt 5.1. Participants: Casper, Peter, and their teacher Catherine

1	Casper	E:eh what should we call it? ((*looks at Peter*))
2	Peter	°A country°
3	Casper	((*looks down at the book*)) Where did he flee to then?
4	Peter	(No it says in the book) (5.0) ((*turns and looks at some people in the classroom and comments on the activity*))
5	Casper	Yes (3.0) ((*points at a paragraph in the textbook and reads aloud*)) «in 1026[1] the Danish King sail (.) sailed against Norway he wanted to conquer back the kingdom that Olav had taken (twelve) years earlier (2.0) when Olav understood that (the Danish King's army was) much larger than his own» (.) it doesn't say where he fled↑
6	Peter	((*lifts his head and looks at another side of the classroom*)) Catherine↑
7	Casper	((*lifts his head and looks at another side of the classroom*)) Catherine↑
8	Peter	It does not say where King Olav fled (6.0) we can google it though ((*looks at the screen and starts googling it*))
9	Catherine	((*walks up to the students and stands behind them*)) What is it?
10	Casper	Well it says here ((*points at the page in the book*)) the town he will flee to ((*turns towards the screen*)) >no what are you doing?<
11	Peter	We'll google it
12	Casper	No ((*turns back to the book and points*)) it says he should flee (.) you know (.) «in 1028 the Danish King sailed against Norway he wanted to conquer back the kingdom that Olav had taken twelve years earlier (.) when Olav understood that the Danish King's army was much larger than his own he decided to flee» >but it doesn't say where he fled< ((*turns his head and looks up at Catherine*))

Catherine continues to read the textbook, while both Casper and Peter use Google to search for the answer. After a break, Catherine comes back with another textbook, reads it, and then tells them that King Olav fled to Russia.

In this episode, Casper starts by asking what the game map should be called, after being prompted by the game software to name it (line 1). He then turns to the textbook on the desk beside him, wondering where King Olav fled to as this should be what they should name the game map. He then starts reading aloud from the textbook (line 5). Peter looks up and calls their teacher, Catherine, with Casper following (lines 6 and 7). Peter suggests that they start googling about the question of where King Olav fled to (line 8); Casper disagrees, instead reading aloud the textbook passage to Catherine, ending with "he decided to flee". This is followed by his comment to Catherine, "it doesn't say where he fled" (line 12). Catherine continues reading the textbook to find the answer, while Peter and Casper start searching for the answer on Google. After a break, Catherine comes back to tell them that King Olav fled to Russia, which the students then use as the name of the game world.

The students' starting point for constructing the game narrative is their inquiry about a historical fact—where King Olav fled in 1028 after finding out that the Danish king's fleet was much larger than his own. They need this information to construct the game as they want to make this country part of the game world, which would also have implications for the rest of the game narrative. The game design process itself leads the students to seek more information about a curricular topic, the Viking Age in Norway, as they need this knowledge to construct the game. From a design-theoretic perspective (Selander, 2008a), this starts the students' process of transforming their knowledge into what would later be formed as a representation, the computer game.

In this episode, the students expand their knowledge about King Olav as they need to know which country their game map should be based on. This is an example of how students learn academic content from making games, what Kafai and Burke (2015) call the personal dimension. Academic content learning using knowledge artifacts is a common pattern in the data material. Before the same student group makes a game about the Crusades, they use a world map on the wall as a starting point for a discussion about where the Crusaders traveled; the conversation about geography is mixed with creating a story about the dangers that the Crusaders would encounter along the way. Another student group uses both textbooks and Google to find out the name of Leonardo da Vinci's teacher when making a story about the Renaissance. The student groups frequently use textbooks to make their stories about the great explorers historically accurate.

At the end of the first game design session, a teacher comments that the students excel at basing the games on what they have learned about the topic and using textbooks and materials that they had earlier produced themselves to guide the game design. However, she also mentions that as the game design period progresses, they delve more into "the game world". This is witnessed in the next episode.

Exploring Alternative Versions of History

While the students use competency aims from the curriculum as a starting point for creating game narratives, their narratives often evolve into *alternative versions of history*. The episode captured in Excerpt 5.2 follows shortly after the first, where Casper, Peter, and Samuel have recently learned that King Olav fled to Russia to escape the Danish king's army. They have just made a game map called Russia.

While the activity starts with a focus on the content—discussing the history of King Olav—the nature of the activity changes as Peter uses this information to suggest that

Excerpt 5.2. Participants: Peter, Casper, and Samuel

1	Peter:	Then we have to work with Russia
2	Casper:	Eh ye:es
3	Peter:	But (.) what is it they will actually be (h)doing there↑
4	Samuel	(We need water or [something there then) ((*points at the screen*))
5	Peter	[We make a <u>pub</u>↑ we have to make a <u>pub</u>
6	Casper	Yes
7	Peter	In Russia they drink a lot of vodka [((*looks at Casper*))
8	Casper	[Yes
9	Casper	(xxx) ((*looks at Peter*)) And then he can walk around and (.) create a lot of people in a <u>pub</u>↑ (.) and then he asks would you like to be my soldier (.) and then we can conquer back <u>Norway</u>↑
10	Peter	And he is so <u>drunk</u> that he says <u>yes</u>↑
11	Casper	<u>Yes</u>↑
12	Peter	<u>Yes</u>↑

they construct a pub, as people drink a lot of vodka in Russia (lines 1–8). Casper agrees with Peter, building on his idea by suggesting that King Olav Haraldsson walks around the pub, asking people for help to reconquer Norway by each becoming his soldier (line 9). While the game's storyline starts to differ from historical facts, Peter enthusiastically builds on this idea, stating, "And he is so drunk that he says yes↑" (line 10). This statement results in a strong display of alignment (e.g., Du Bois, 2007), with Casper looking at Peter and saying "Yes↑", which is echoed by Peter (lines 11–12). What the students choose to make relevant when designing the game should be noted, "In Russia, they drink a lot of vodka" (line 7). This points to a cultural dimension of making games, as the designers themselves in this case choose to build on a stereotypical view of Russians when creating the characters.

The central aspect of this short excerpt is how the students, while starting out with a basis on the curriculum, create a narrative that explores alternative versions of history. In this example, the Battle of Stiklestad is fought by King Olav and an army of Russian soldiers that the king himself recruits from a pub. This aspect of creating game narratives is observed several times in the games made by the students. For example, in the previously mentioned game about the Renaissance, Mona Lisa is the daughter of da Vinci's teacher, and da Vinci is asked to paint her. Although the game ends after da Vinci finishes the painting, the students continue building on the storyline in the process, such as how da Vinci falls in love with Mona Lisa. In Peter, Casper, and Samuel's story about the Crusades, the game's protagonist Henrik ends up battling both crocodiles and Polish bandits on his way to Jerusalem.

Fantasy and curiosity are among the most important factors for building intrinsic motivation for learning (Dickey, 2006; Malone, 1981), and games are well suited for exploring alternative versions of history (Simons, 2007). The presented episode shows another aspect of this point that is often observed in the data material. The students often create game narratives that their classmates or teachers consider inappropriate in the school context, which are therefore often challenged. Nonetheless, the students often passionately follow these storylines.

In the presented excerpt, the students decide to add a pub to the game; several times, students in this class introduce pubs into their game narratives. However, in their attempts, their classmates' reactions vary. While Casper and Peter agree on the idea, other students would quickly stop their group members from doing this, either making comments such as they "don't have time to be fooling around" or changing pubs built in the game into ordinary houses. On a similar note, zombies comprise a recurring theme for some of the sixth-grade students. While the teacher quickly tells them to get their act together as "there were no zombies during the Middle Ages", the theme *does* play a role in the games of the students, such as the student group that introduces a "zombie apocalypse" to the game about the Middle Ages. This results in the students having to spend some time fixing up the game as the teacher would not allow zombies to be part of the game. While one student comments, "This is what happens when you have zombies visiting", another student asks the group during the second game design period two months later, "Was it you who had zombies the last time?"

It should be noted that the affordances of the game might have influenced the students' choices as these *allow* them to add pubs and zombies to the game. While the students' choices are not always approved by either their classmates or their teacher, offering them the option to pursue a narrative that they themselves find interesting clearly seems to be a motivating factor for them, as observed in the enthusiastic dialogue between Peter and Casper in Excerpt 5.2. According to Dickey (2006), the narrative is a core factor for creating an inner urge to progress in the game. From the data material informing this chapter, creating narratives that the students themselves find meaningful seems to be a core aspect of an engaging learning experience. Ito and colleagues (2013) also suggest that connecting academic content learning to what young people find interesting in their spare time might have positive implications for *learning*. However, it could be argued that the discrepancy between what is historically accurate and what the students actually make poses a challenge that should be considered. The teacher's role should therefore be briefly noted, as she performs an important function in keeping the students on track when they stray *too* far from the curricular topic on which they are supposed to work.

Presenting and Playtesting Games

When playtesting the games, the students often emphasize the *game design* aspects, with the story being a recurring element to be commented on. The episode in this section shows how the students, while presenting their games to their classmates, participate in a process where they could increase their understanding about designing game narratives for an audience.

Excerpt 5.3. Participants: Irene, Marius, and their teacher Maria

1	Maria	But did you sort of understand what was your quest from the [beginning
2	Irene	[NO:O
3	Maria	What you should do↑
4	Irene	I did not quite understand what I should do
5	Marius	Because the king tried to kill you because (.) e:h (.) Luna was not a [Christian
6	Irene	[((*nods*))
7	Marius	So then she had to kill the king to not get killed
8	Irene	Yes (3.0) but I did not understand that
9	Maria	That should have been a bit clearer then
10	Irene	Until the end
11	Marius	That is what I said (.) <u>I told them both</u> that we should have worked more on the story
12	Irene	I did not understand until he said it sort of (.) other than that it was <u>very good</u>
13	Marius	<u>Thank you</u>↑
14	Maria	Maybe that is the hard part (.) that those who have made the game sort of have the story in their head (.) and sort of have to understand (.) how they get those who play to see it without (.) to see it by themselves sort of
15	Irene	It is sort of hard for us who don't know what it is (.) what should we do kind of↑

Irene is testing the game created by Marius, Scott, and Vera. Marius is sitting on the side, writing down Irene's comments, while their teacher Maria is sitting next to them.

In this excerpt, the teacher, Maria, starts by asking Irene if she understood from the beginning of the game what her goal was; Irene replies that she did not (lines 1–4). Marius, one of the creators of the game, explains the game story: The king tried to kill the game's character as she was not a Christian, and she therefore had to kill the king to avoid being killed herself (lines 5–7). When Irene states that she did not understand it until the end of the game, Marius emphatically replies, "*I told them both* that we should have worked more on the story" (line 11), referring to the other students in his group. Irene also responds that apart from that, the game "was very good" (line 12). Thus, the students clearly show what they consider important in the game, related to the players understanding what to do.

Kafai and Burke (2015) state that an aspect of learning from designing computer games is the *social dimension* related to the question "What does game making rather than just playing offer young learners in terms of not only collaborative making but also gaining a wider appreciation of designing for an audience?" (p. 315). As presenting and commenting on the games of other groups are important aspects of this project, the exercise offers the students an opportunity not only to reflect on what they themselves value in a game, such as its story, but also the processes involved in implementing these elements in a computer game in a way that the audience would understand.

At the end of the first game design session, the teacher notes, "Now you have worked very effectively for two whole days [...]; imagine how much time it will take to make a whole game!" Isbister (2016) mentions the need to raise public understanding of computer games. As observed here, a narratively driven game design might be an approach that students would find meaningful.

Representations in the Students' Games

While the previous sections have focused on the students' interactions, learning from creating game narratives could also be perceived in the games themselves, which might provide insights into what the game designers value and emphasize (Flanagan & Nissenbaum, 2014). This section explores a game about the Middle Ages, called *Sunniva's Journey to the King*, created by two female sixth-grade students. The game portrays the female protagonist, Sunniva, who is asked by her friend Karl to go on a journey to recover his belongings that the king has stolen. While this game does not show content learning to a substantial extent, as many of the other games do, it depicts other dimensions of constructionist learning that should be noted, specifically, working on *narrative skills* and challenging stereotypes.

Refining narrative skills. Flanagan and Nissenbaum (2014) suggest examining different aspects of narratives as these can help the audience understand the designers. This process includes studying the story's theme, the motivation and the goals of the player character, and the obstacles and the events occurring along the way. With or without the students' knowledge, the narrative structure of the game *Sunniva's Journey to the King* has many parallels to an approach of structuring a story that is well known from games and other forms of popular culture, building on Campbell's (1968) *monomyth* or the *hero's journey,* or Vogler's (1992) *The Writer's Journey.* First, Sunniva is seen on an island with her friend Karl, who asks her to retrieve the possessions that the King has stolen from his family (*the call to adventure*; see Figure 5.2). She is able to refuse but is then called a coward. If she accepts, she can leave the island on a boat (*crossing the first threshold*) before meeting a *non-player character* (NPC) who warns her about the dangers of continuing and gives her an option to go back. If she continues her journey, she will arrive on another island where she will meet another NPC. This character will give her information on how to find the king but will also warn her and give her the option to go back, thus both *meeting allies* and *being tested* (Figure 5.3) before going to the final island. Here, she has to pass the guards in order to enter the king's castle, called the *approach to the innermost cave* (Vogler, 1992). If she touches one of the guards, the game

Figure 5.2. The call to adventure. Translation: "Can you help my family get their belongings back from the king? (1) Yes, I can do that. (2) No, it is too dangerous"

Figure 5.3. Meeting allies and being tested. Translation: "To reach the king's castle, you need to cross the water, and then there is a moat that you need to cross"

reaches the *game over* state, but if she manages to proceed past them, she may enter the castle. Sunniva then has to face the king, who refuses to return the belongings that he stole. The player then has to search for a knife in the castle, so Sunniva can kill the king. She can then *return to her ordinary world*, with the items that the king stole from her friend.

This game does not implement content learning to the same extent as many of the other games in this project. However, creating story-driven computer games in the classroom has also been linked to increased narrative skills (Carbonaro et al., 2008;

Robertson & Good, 2005). The Norwegian subject curriculum states that students should be able to "write narrative, descriptive, reflective and persuasive texts using patterns from sample texts and other sources" and "use digital sources and tools to create composite texts" (Utdanningsdirektoratet, 2013a). In this instance, the students create a game with a sophisticated narrative that draws on a structure used in many works of popular culture, such as games, movies, and books. Such an approach is often observed when students are free to design their own media products, which might contribute to bridging formal learning with young people's own interests (Ito et al., 2013; Jenkins, Ito, & boyd, 2016).

Challenging stereotypes. As observed in the theoretical framework, games can provide insights into what the students emphasize and value (Flanagan & Nissenbaum, 2014; Selander, 2008a). The narrative created by the students features a young girl as the player character (Figure 5.4), a heroine acknowledged by the antagonist king as the only person who has managed to sneak past the guards (Figure 5.5). However, strong female protagonists do not represent the norm in computer games.

According to an earlier study (Williams, Martins, Consalvo, & Ivory, 2009), with data collected from 150 games released over a year, only slightly more than 10% of the primary characters were female. One of the findings from the report was that the number of female game characters (comprising 15%, including supporting characters) was closer to the number of female game developers than female players (Williams et al., 2009, p. 830). The overwhelming number of male characters can be linked to a stereotypical view of players as "young, white males" (p. 831). As suggested by Kafai and Burke (2015), a cultural dimension of designing games is that young designers can challenge what is perceived as good play.

Scandinavian countries are ranked among the top nations worldwide in terms of gender equality (World Economic Forum, 2017). It could therefore be assumed that the games created by the students in this region would reflect this value (e.g., Flanagan & Nissenbaum, 2014). However, it should be noted that most of the games developed by the students portray male player characters. Out of the 16 games made, only two depict female player characters. While the greater numbers of boys than girls in the classes (thirteen boys and nine girls in total) might contribute to this imbalance, with only one all-female group as opposed to several groups consisting only of boys, it seems more likely due to the topic of the assignment given to the students. When the topic involves some European explorers (Magellan, Marco Polo, Vasco da Gama, or Christopher Columbus), these would be the main characters of the students' games, and Viking kings and Renaissance painters would often be the protagonists of the other games. However, as observed in this section's example, the female game designers use topics often associated with male main characters, the Middle Ages, and the *hero's journey* as the focus for a game narrative with a female protagonist. A topic for further research could be to discover how the player characters are portrayed when making games about other topics from social studies, such as civics.

Figures 5.4. The protagonist Sunniva confronting the evil king. Translation: "I will get back the things you have taken from my friend's family"

Figures 5.5. The protagonist Sunniva confronting the evil king. Translation: "Many have tried to get their things back from me, but none has managed to get past the guards"

CONCLUDING SUMMARY

Through the analysis of the students' interactions and the computer games they develop about history topics from the social studies curriculum, this chapter has explored what characterizes the students' strategies of working with narratives in the game design process, as well as how it is made visible in their social interactions and finished games. The following main arguments have been discussed:

First, game narratives might prompt the construction of content knowledge because *in the process* of creating game narratives, the students need to acquire information to make the narratives historically accurate. Second, the students often further engage in the creation of alternative versions of history and may also write game narratives that push the limits of acceptable norms to be followed in a school context. Third, the game narrative is a key focus for the students, not only when *designing* their games, but also when *presenting* these and *evaluating* those of their classmates. This point can lead to an increased understanding of the factors involved in designing a game for an audience. Fourth, creating game narratives might be a way of improving narrative skills. Fifth, this process might contribute to challenging stereotypes and changing what is perceived as good gameplay.

A relevant area of future research could involve further exploring the impact on students' learning outcomes when the narrative they are working on strays too far from historically accurate facts. In this regard, it should again be noted that the teacher's role plays an important part in keeping the students on track with the assigned topic when designing game narratives. The teachers also ask the students important questions in the game design and playtesting process, making the class reflect on the function of the game narrative. Other researchers have noted the importance of the teacher in the process of game-oriented learning (e.g., Silseth, 2012), and while this chapter has not focused on the teacher's role, it is a suggested topic for further research.

Learning from designing computer games has mostly been concerned with learning programming or other STEM-related subjects (Hayes & Games, 2008). However, as this present analysis shows, working with *narratives* is a crucial factor for learning that should be considered. Not only is this aspect emphasized as meaningful by the students, it is also connected to the social and the cultural dimensions of learning (Kafai & Burke, 2015). Robertson and Howells (2008, p. 576) argue that designing games offers opportunities for cross-curricular learning, which is supported by this present study's findings. Learning outcomes of designing game narratives are related to learning both the content of social studies and narrative skills, in addition to the digital skills involved in designing games.

Narrative, fantasy, and curiosity are among the core elements for promoting engagement in and learning from playing games (Dickey, 2006; Malone, 1981). In conclusion, as discussed in this chapter, these also seem to be key aspects for engaging in learning when *designing* games that the students find meaningful.

NOTE

[1] When reading the same text in line 10, he reads this as 1028, which is the historically accurate year.

REFERENCES

Blumer, H. (1954). What is wrong with social theory. *American Sociological Review, 19*(1), 3–10.
Bowen, G. A. (2006). Grounded theory and sensitizing concepts. *International Journal of Qualitative Methods, 5*(3), 12–23.

Campbell, J. (1968). *The hero with a thousand faces* (Vol. 17, 2nd ed.). Princeton, NJ: Princeton University Press.

Carbonaro, M., Cutumisu, M., Duff, H., Gillis, S., Onuczko, C., Siegel, J., Schaeffer, J., Schumacher, A., Szafron, D., & Waugh, K. (2008). Interactive story authoring: A viable form of creative expression for the classroom. *Computers & Education, 51*(2), 687–707. Retrieved from http://doi.org/10.1016/j.compedu.2007.07.007

Conle, C. C. (2003). An anatomy of narrative curricula. *Educational Researcher, 32*(3), 3–15.

Derry, S. J., Pea, R. D., Barron, B., Engle, R. A., Erickson, F., Goldman, R., Hall, R., Koschmann, T., Lemke, J. L., Sherin, M. G., & Sherin, B. L. (2010). Conducting video research in the learning sciences: Guidance on selection, analysis, technology, and ethics. *Journal of the Learning Sciences, 19*(1), 3–53. Retrieved from http://doi.org/10.1080/10508400903452884

Dickey, M. D. (2006). Game design narrative for learning: Appropriating adventure game design narrative devices and techniques for the design of interactive learning environments. *Educational Technology Research and Development, 54*(3), 245–263. Retrieved from http://doi.org/10.1007/s11423-006-8806-y

Dondlinger, M. J. (2007). Educational video game design: A review of the literature. *Journal of Applied Educational Technology, 4*(1), 21–31. Retrieved from http://doi.org/10.1108/10748120410540463

Du Bois, J. W. (2007). The stance triangle. In R. Englebretson (Ed.), *Stancetaking in discourse: Subjectivity, evaluation, interaction* (pp. 139–182). Amsterdam: John Benjamins Publishing Company.

Egenfeldt-Nielsen, S., Smith, J. H., & Tosca, S. P. (2008). *Understanding video games: The essential introduction.* New York, NY: Routledge.

Eisner, E. W. (1991). *The enlightened eye: Qualitative inquiry and the enhancement of educational practice.* New York, NY: Macmillan Publication Company.

Enterbrain. (2011). *RPG maker* (Computer software). Retrieved from http://www.rpgmakerweb.com/

Fine, G. A. (1982). *Shared fantasy: Role-playing games as social worlds.* Chicago, IL: University of Chicago Press.

Flanagan, M., & Nissenbaum, H. (2014). *Values at play in digital games: A theoretical and practical guide to integrating human values into the conception and design of digital games.* Cambridge, MA: MIT Press.

Francis, D., & Hester, S. (2004). *An invitation to ethnomethodology: Language, society and interaction.* London: Sage Publications.

Gee, J. P. (2007). *Good video games + good learning: Collected essays on video games, learning, and literacy.* New York, NY: Peter Lang.

Good, J., & Robertson, J. (2006). *Learning and motivational affordances in narrative-based game authoring* (pp. 37–51). In Proceedings of the 4th International Conference for Narrative and Interactive Learning Environments (NILE), Edinburgh.

Goodwin, C. (2007). Participation, stance and affect in the organization of activities. *Discourse & Society, 18*(1), 53–73.

Hayes, E. R., & Games, I. A. (2008). Making computer games and design thinking: A review of current software and strategies. *Games and Culture, 3*(3–4), 309–332. Retrieved from http://doi.org/10.1177/1555412008317312

Isbister, K. (2016). *How games move us: Emotion by design.* Cambridge, MA: MIT Press.

Ito, M., Gutiérrez, K., Livingstone, S., Penuel, B., Rhodes, J., Salen, K., & Watkins, S. C. (2013). *Connected learning: An agenda for research and design.* Irvine, CA: Digital Media and Learning Research Hub.

Jefferson, G. (2004). Glossary of transcript symbols with an introduction. In G. H. Lerner (Ed.), *Conversation analysis: Studies from the first generation* (pp. 13–31). Amsterdam: John Benjamins Publishing Company.

Jenkins, H. (2004). Game design as narrative architecture. In N. Wardrip-Fruin & P. Harrigan (Eds.), *Game design as narrative architecture* (pp. 118–130). Cambridge, MA: MIT Press.

Jenkins, H., Ito, M., & Boyd, D. (2016). *Participatory culture in a networked era: A conversation on youth, learning, commerce, and politics.* Malden, MA: Polity Press.

Jewitt, C. (2013). Multimodal methods for researching digital technologies. In S. Price, C. Jewitt, & B. Brown (Eds.), *Sage handbook of digital technology research* (pp. 250–265). London: Sage Publications. Retrieved from http://doi.org/10.4135/9781446282229.n18

Kafai, Y. B. (2006). Playing and making games for learning: Instructionist and constructionist perspectives for game studies. *Games and Culture, 1*(1), 36–40. Retrieved from http://doi.org/10.1177/1555412005281767

Kafai, Y. B., & Burke, Q. (2015). Constructionist gaming: Understanding the benefits of making games for learning. *Educational Psychologist, 50*(4), 313–334. Retrieved from http://doi.org/10.1080/00461520.2015.1124022

Kafai, Y. B., Ching, C. C., & Marshall, S. (1997). Children as designers of educational multimedia software. *Computers & Education, 29*(2–3), 117–126. Retrieved from http://doi.org/10.1016/S0360-1315(97)00036-5

Kangas, M. (2010). Creative and playful learning: Learning through game co-creation and games in a playful learning environment. *Thinking Skills and Creativity, 5*(1), 1–15. http://doi.org/10.1016/j.tsc.2009.11.001

Ke, F. (2014). An implementation of design-based learning through creating educational computer games: A case study on mathematics learning during design and computing. *Computers & Education, 73*, 26–39. Retrieved from http://doi.org/10.1016/j.compedu.2013.12.010

Malone, T. W. (1981). Toward a theory of intrinsically motivating instruction. *Cognitive Science: A Multidisciplinary Journal, 5*(4), 333–369. Retrieved from http://doi.org/10.1207/s15516709cog0504

Mood, A., & Specht, R. D. (1954). *Gaming as a technique of analysis.* Santa Monica, CA: The Rand Corporation.

Oldaker, A. (2010). Creating video games in a middle school language arts classroom: A narrative account. *Voices from the Middle, 17*(3), 19–26.

Papert, S., & Harel, I. (1991). Situating constructionism. In S. Papert & I. Harel (Eds.), *Constructionism* (pp. 1–13). Norwood, NJ: Ablex.

Reimann, P. (2011). Design-based research. In L. Markauskaite, P. Freebody, & J. Irwin (Eds.), *Methodological choice and design* (Vol. 9, pp. 37–50). Dordrecht: Springer. Retrieved from http://doi.org/10.1007/978-90-481-8933-5_3

Rieber, L. P. (1996). Seriously considering play: Designing interactive learning environments based on the blending of microworlds, simulations, and games. *Educational Technology Research and Development, 44*(2), 43–58. Retrieved from http://doi.org/10.1007/BF02300540

Robertson, J., & Good, J. (2005). Story creation in virtual game worlds. *Communications of the ACM, 48*(1), 61–65.

Robertson, J., & Howells, C. (2008). Computer game design: Opportunities for successful learning. *Computers & Education, 50*(2), 559–578. Retrieved from http://doi.org/10.1016/j.compedu.2007.09.020

Salen, K., & Zimmerman, E. (2004). *Rules of play: Game design fundamentals.* Cambridge, MA: MIT Press.

Selander, S. (2008a). Designs for learning: A theoretical perspective. *Designs for Learning, 1*(1), 10–22. Retrieved from http://doi.org/10.1080/14626260802312673

Selander, S. (2008b). Designs of learning and the formation and transformation of knowledge in an era of globalization. *Studies and Education, 27*(4), 267–281. Retrieved from http://doi.org/10.1007/s11217-007-9068-9

Selander, S., & Kress, G. (2010). *Design för lärande: ett multimodalt perspektiv* [Designs for Learning: A multimodal perspective]. Stockholm: Norstedts.

Silseth, K. (2012). The multivoicedness of game play: Exploring the unfolding of a student's learning trajectory in a gaming context at school. *International Journal of Computer-Supported Collaborative Learning, 7*(1), 63–84.

Simons, J. (2007). Narrative, games, and theory. *Game Studies: The International Journal of Computer Game Research, 7*(1). Retrieved from http://www.gamestudies.org/0701/articles/simons

Utdanningsdirektoratet. (2013a). *Norwegian subject curriculum.* Retrieved from https://www.udir.no/globalassets/filer/lareplan/engelsk/norwegian-subject-curriculum.pdf

Utdanningsdirektoratet. (2013b). *Social studies subject curriculum*. Retrieved September 4, 2017, from
http://data.udir.no/kl06/SAF1-03.pdf?lang=http://data.udir.no/kl06/eng

Vogler, C. (1992). *The writer's journey: Mythic structure for storytellers and screenwriters*. Studio City,
CA: Michael Wiese Productions.

Williams, D., Martins, N., Consalvo, M., & Ivory, J. D. (2009). The virtual census: Representations of
gender, race and age in video games. *New Media & Society, 11*(5), 815–834. Retrieved from
http://doi.org/10.1177/1461444809105354

World Economic Forum. (2017). *The global gender gap report 2017*. Geneva: World Economic Forum.

APPENDIX: TRANSCRIPT NOTATIONS

Adapted from Jefferson (2004)

(.) Full stop inside brackets:	Micropause of no significant length
(0.2) Number inside brackets:	Timed pause
[ ] Square brackets:	Overlapping speech
((*interaction*)):	Description of non-verbal activity
(xxx):	Talk that was too unclear to transcribe
(word):	Doubtful transcription
? Question mark:	Inquiring intonation
↑ Upward arrow:	Rise in intonation
↓ Downward arrow:	Drop in intonation
:: Colons:	Elongated speech
(h) Bracketed h:	Laugh within the talk
<u>Underlined</u>:	Emphasized talk
= Equal sign:	Continuation of talk
°word°:	Quiet speech
"": Quotation marks:	Reported speech

PART 2

DESIGNS FOR LEARNING

JARI DUE JESSEN AND CARSTEN JESSEN

6. A THEORY OF PLAY DYNAMICS

ABSTRACT

In this chapter, we will present a theory of play dynamics. The effect of play dynamics is to push users into a state of play, which is a special way of being in the world, with a certain framing and disposition towards the world and the actions performed. We believe that humans play solely for fun, and that they seek tools that use play dynamics to push them into a state of play, creating feelings of joy. In this chapter, we will present examples of play dynamics in well-known play tools, from physical movement to computer games. We believe that the concept of Play Dynamics facilitates deeper understanding of why certain play tools work better than others and why.

Keywords: play, play dynamics, games

INTRODUCTION

'Play' is a somewhat amorphous concept, often defined implicitly in academic research. We concur with leading play researcher Brian Sutton-Smith, who summarizes more than 40 years of play studies in the following terms:

> We all play occasionally, and we all know what playing feels like. But when it comes to making theoretical statements about what play is, we fall into silliness. There is little agreement among us…. (Sutton-Smith, 1997)

We do not pretend to entirely end this 'silliness' with this chapter, but we will attempt to clarify how the concept of 'play' can be better understood regarding products designed for play, such as play equipment, board games and computer games. We will present a theory of 'play dynamics', grounded in humanistic play theory and philosophy.

Games, especially computer games, have lately become the subject of scholarly research. We understand and define games in relation to play, and to avoid misunderstandings, we will first investigate the relationship between games and play.

The French theoretician Roger Callois' concepts 'ludus' and 'paideia' (Callois, 1961) are often defined as highly structured (games) and unstructured (play), respectively (Walther, 2003); in that sense, they are two points on a spectrum. Conversely, we define these two concepts on a vertical line—rather than a horizontal one—on which games are a subset of play. Moreover, we regard games as a tool that human beings use to create play. From this perspective, games are only one many

© KONINKLIJKE BRILL NV, LEIDEN, 2019 | DOI:10.1163/9789004388826_007

tools that human beings (of all ages) use to enter a state play, which we see as a specific state of being in the world. In the following, we will explain this "state of being" as the first element of our theory of play dynamics.

PLAY AS A STATE OF BEING

We base the understanding of play presented briefly above on the play theory of philosophers Johan Huizinga (1938) and Hans-Georg Gadamer (1977), and on the ideas of play theoretician Sutton-Smith (1997) that are exponent for a perspective on play that built on German philosopher and poet, Friedrich Schiller's writings about play. Schiller argued that '…Man only plays when in the full meaning of the word he is a man, and he is only completely a man when he plays…' (Schiller, 1793). This understanding of play is substantially different from the one that currently dominates psychology and pedagogy, in which play is first and foremost a means to an end in child development (Singer et al., 2009).

In his book 'Homo Ludens: Man as player', Johan Huizinga describes play as a *separate life sphere* that cannot be legitimized with outer purposes. Play is a self-sustaining phenomenon, which is an end until itself. Compared to other human activities it does not lead to anything; it neither creates nor produces anything, except play.

Play is a free, voluntary activity indulged for its own sake, and although creative, play is unproductive and non-utilitarian. Play has boundaries of space and time, and takes place temporarily outside 'regular life', with its own course and meaning (Huizinga, 1938).

According to Huizinga, play is a difficult concept to define in an academic context because it represents other values than those inherent in science. Scientists usually try to rationalise human activities by determining their purpose, but play does not submit itself to the rational notions:

> …the fun of playing resists all analysis, all logical interpretation […] Here we have to do with an absolutely primary category of life, familiar to everybody at a glance […] We play and know that we play, so we must be more than merely rational beings, for play is irrational. (Huizinga, 1938)

Accepting this line of thinking about play as not rational in a common sense, which Huizinga share with some of the most influential thinkers in modern philosophy (e.g. Nietzsche, Heidegger, Caillois, Gadamer, Derrida), turns much accepted wisdom of human behaviour upside down and pose a difficult question: How are we to explain human activities without reference to rational reasoning?

The claim that play is an end until itself should not be understood to suggest that play is a meaningless act. Although many play activities can appear meaningless (especially for people who are not participating), it is an important point that *play is the purpose of play*. In Gadamer's (1977) words, '[Play] may be a purposeless activity but this activity in itself is intentional'.

Huizinga (1938) describes play as something that takes place 'temporarily', outside ordinary life, in what he calls a 'magic circle'. This magic circle is similar to what Gregory Bateson (1956/2006) has termed 'framing', a linguistic and psychological concept that both delimits a set of meaningful actions like a picture frame—'attend to what is within and do not attend to what is outside' (Bateson, 2006, p. 323)—and at the same time gives instructions on how to interpret the actions within the frame. Bateson formulates it this way after describing how he observed two monkeys play fighting: 'The playful nip denotes the bite, but it does not denote what would be denoted by the bite' (Bateson, 2006, p. 317). This means that when we play, we are in a special sphere and in a special state of mind and we can only understand and react to the actions we take within this sphere. When participating in play fighting, children do not fight for real. It is a violation of the tacit rules of play if they do.

Michael Apter further elaborates when he writes that fundamentally, play is 'a state of mind, a way of seeing and being, a special mental "set" towards the world and one's own action in it' (Apter, 1991, p. 13). In other words, play is a *state of being in the world*, where the regular rules do not apply, because in this state we can do, imagine, and say things without the consequences they would normally result in, and we can imagine things that are impossible in ordinary life. The actions we undertake are framed as 'play', and participants have a playful attitude towards the world and the actions performed within this frame. All that is a well-known fact about play, but the question is, why do human beings behave like this? What purpose accompanies the purposeless?

Huizinga writes that we enter the state of play 'for the fun of it', and in the same manner, Michael Apter writes that we choose to play 'for its own sake and the immediate pleasure which [we] hope it will bring' (Apter, 1991, p. 15). For example, one of the games small children play involves making themselves dizzy by whirling around. Observing children in this activity makes it clear that it is an exciting experiment and very funny even though the child falls repeatedly. For the child, there is no reason for playing the game other than the special feeling it creates in their body and mind. The same is the case for other activities like using a swing, playing ball, playing golf, dancing, or playing computer games, and for the games parents play with infants, like tickling on the changing table. Sutton-Smith describes the latter as a 'paradigm' for play, and also points to what we regard as an important aspect of human play as something plays actively creates:

> ... we postulate as the original paradigm for play, mother and infant conjoined in an expressive communicational frame within which they contrastively participate in the modulation of excitement. We call this a paradigm for all lucid action, because we suggest that other play itself is a metaphoric statement of this literal state of affairs. (Sutton-Smith, 1979)

This description of play as active modulation of moods from the players' point of view is quite a precise definition of what happens when we play, regardless of age. Similarly, Jessen and Lund have defined play as follows:

> Play is actions, which we undertake and participate in with the purpose to create a reality-sphere within which we are free and independently can create and regulate moods (physical and mental states of tension) which provides us with specific, wanted experiences (of delight), socially and individually. (Jessen & Lund, 2008)

This definition points to an understanding of play not only as a special state of being in the world, but as a state of being that the players actively and voluntarily create. However, creating this state requires assistance from certain kinds of tools.

PLAY REQUIRES TOOLS

Jessen and Lund's definition of play implies that an active effort is a premise for play; in their paper, they note that over the course of our lives, we develop the ability to modulate moods, and they emphasise that we use tools to do so.

Play does not come by itself. It demands effort, work, knowledge, and—not least—learning. Play is a state that players create with purpose, and is thus a goal-oriented, intentional human activity. We use countless methods to achieve this state, and knowledge of those methods is indispensable to those who wish to play. As Apter notes,

> One of the most interesting things about play is the tremendous variety of devices, stratagems and techniques which people can use to obtain the pleasures of play. (Apter, 1991, p. 18)

Likewise, people are often willing to make significant financial investments to obtain playful experiences.

Some of the methods of play include games, which are either learned from parents or peers or purchased, as with board games and computer games. Other methods include use of play equipment such as swings or roller coasters. We consider both play equipment and games to be instruments, or 'tools', that specialize in creating play; using these tools assists people in creating and regulating those physical and mental states of tension and moods that we previously defined as play. For example, by following the rules of a street game, there is a good chance that the players will experience play. In this manner, a street game is a tool consisting of specific rules for behaviour, which the players must perform. In the Italian introduction to Huizinga's book "Homo Ludens", Umberto Eco writes that

> "To play the game" means "follow the rules". There is an abstract subject, a game, and then there is concrete behaviour, a performance of play. To play is "to take part in a game". (Eco, 1973)

In their book 'Rules of Play' (2004), Salen and Zimmerman identify a similar connection between games and play. They define the goal of successful game design as 'the creation of meaningful play', later stating that 'Rules [of games] are merely the means for creating play' (Salen & Zimmerman, 2004, pp. 33 and 302). In a subsequent anthology, they argue that 'Games create play: of that there is no doubt' (Salen & Zimmerman, 2006, p. 83). In other words, the purpose of games is to fulfil their function as tools to generate the state of being in the world that we call 'play'.

THE STATE OF PLAY

Games help users to create play, but a deeper conceptual understanding is desirable. We describe play as a special state of being that human beings actively seek to get enter, the *state of play*. To understand this concept, it is important to distinguish between what is normally termed 'playing', and the process of entering the state of play. Activities labelled as play are often more accurately an ongoing search for the state of play, and the experiences this state entails, which are not always straightforward. This is evident in children's play (Hughes, 1999; Jessen, 2003). For instance, when two children meet for the first time, they often try out different play ideas, play equipment or toys, seeking common ground; it may take some time before they find something that works for both of them. This process points to the fact that individual children have their own preferences. Whether a certain toy or a 'play tool' is working—i.e., can bring the player into the state of play—is a question of personal taste. For example, while some people enjoy playing computer games such as Counter Strike—perhaps because it reminds them of their childhood games of 'cops and robbers'—others find these games boring or even repellent due to the violence. Another example that most people have experienced, both as children and adults, is how the same joke sometimes creates laughter and other times falls flat, depending on who the listeners are and on its delivery. In other words, there must be a connection between the tools players use to enter a state of play, and their personal tastes and preferences. For this reason, play tools can differ substantially between cultures and individuals. In general, it is vital that play tools create the right sensations in the user's body or mind. Otherwise they fail, and the player will not achieve the state of play.

Entering the state of play is not an easy task. All play demands (often hard) work in order to be successful. Apart from the state of play being the successful result of a goal-oriented experimentation and search, we also understand it as a special state, where people experience the world in a different way. The framing of actions tells us to have a certain disposition towards those actions (Apter, 1991; Bateson, 2006; Huzinga, 1938). Furthermore, human beings seek special forms of stimulation that push them into the state of play.

PLAY DYNAMICS

Games of any kind are especially good at creating the state of play; they may be understood to embed 'tacit knowledge' of methods for creating specific play experiences. In street games, that knowledge may be a form of cultural heritage handed down from one generation to the next. In modern times, where street play culture and other traditional cultural activities are eroding (Jessen, 2003), there is a need for new tools for play that can be adjusted to modern conditions (Jessen, 2003; Lund & Jessen, 2005; Jessen & Karoff, 2008).

If play is created when players use play tools—whether computer games, playgrounds, toys, or others—it is important to understand which games and play products function by generating play for users, and why some function and others do not. We believe we can gain this understanding by studying what we call 'Play Dynamics'. These are dynamics are embedded in every play tool and only appears when a tool is used, for instance, when users play a game by following the prescribed rules. There are numerous kinds of dynamics, from whirling in circles to the competition in ball games or chess. Here, we will analyse examples of a few play dynamics, and how different play tools make use of them. It is not our intention to create an exhaustive list of such dynamics, which we believe would be impossible because they are continually developed along with play culture.

We believe it can be beneficial for designers to understand what Play Dynamics are, and we believe the concept can create a new research area and a new methodology for discussing and developing toys, games and play equipment.

We have already described one play dynamic above—dizziness—which is a specific reaction in the body that is brought forward and controlled in a game we will call 'body whirling'. The dynamic in this game consists solely of producing a feeling of dizziness, but it appears to be a common method of entering the state of play. Children are not the only ones to use this dynamic: it is evident throughout adult life in settings such as amusement parks.

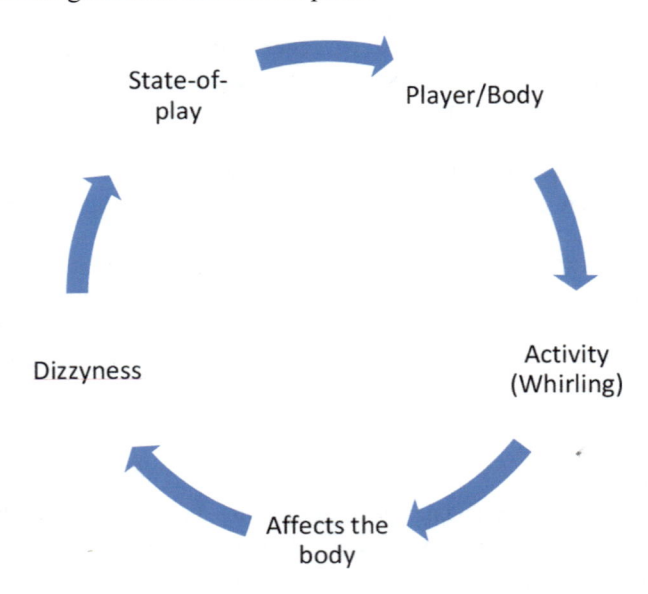

Figure 6.1. An example of how the play dynamic of whirling creates play for the user

Another example is the game of tag, where the play dynamic involves chasing and being chased. Just as body whirling produces dizziness, tag produces a specific kind of feeling in the body based on controlled fear. Those who remember the game will also likely recall the feeling the body produces upon being nearly caught and touched. In that situation, it feels as though the body is taking over and reacting by instinct, producing a state of joy if successful. At its best, the play dynamic of tag is an ongoing movement between nearly being caught and escaping.

To illustrate how play dynamics can function, we will describe a board game called 'Quackle!' We have chosen this game as an example for play tools because it uses only a limited number of play dynamics. Part of the challenge of understanding how play tools work is that they often combine many different play dynamics to create their effects. This is especially true of play tools created for experienced players, as they continually demand new challenges and inputs. However, "Quackle!" is relatively simple.

THE BOARD GAME 'QUACKLE!'

'Quackle!', played by a mixed-age group, is an illustration of play dynamics. Here, we will briefly describe the game; a more thorough description is available in the manual (Alga). Quackle! is a board game for the ages 5 and up. The game employs 12 animal figures, 8 barns and 97 playing cards with pictures of the animals. Players pull a random animal figure from a cloth bag and, after showing it to the other players, hides it away in a barn. One player deals all the cards to the others and places them in a pile face down in front of each person. The game's objective is to get rid of all the cards.

Quackle! runs in rounds, in which the players each turn a card over and place it for all to see. If two cards with the same kind of animal appear, those two players enter a 'battle' in which each player attempts to be the first to make the sound associated with the animal in the other player's barn, e.g., 'Oink' for a pig. The player that loses the battle must pick up the other players cards. The game continues this way until one of the players gets rid of all their cards.

The game appears simple, but requires the players to remember and quickly say the correct sounds when two identical cards are turned, which is more difficult it might appear, even for adults. Thus, the game requires the players to interact in a special way—in Eco's words, to 'follow the rules'. By doing so, players are brought into the state of play—so long as the game is made up of the right rules or play dynamics. Here, we will analyse some of these dynamics.

First, the game uses a play dynamic of mixing many items and making it difficult for players to keep them organised. In Quackle!, players receive multiple inputs— their own animals, those of the other players, and the animals on the cards—and they must remember what is where. Another dynamic is competition, the most common dynamic in games. Players must compete against one other, and this is important for the game to work, because it brings the dynamics of the multiple inputs mentioned above into effect. As with other competitive games, tension builds in the players which is especially apparent among children, but also present in adults. Keeping track of the different animals is not so challenging on its own, but competition forces the players to do so as quickly as possible in their quest to be the first to say the animal sound aloud.

The game also uses a social play dynamic: it utilises the effect of people saying something wrong in the company of others. The fun of the game occurs when players say something wrong. In combination with the other two dynamics, Quackle! forces them to produce incorrect and often strange sounds in a social context, creating laughter and pushes all players into a state of play. Because each player must be very fast in competition with others, they will often not only say the name of a wrong animal, but they will have difficulties pronouncing the name at all. Their tongues do not obey them, and instead of specific sounds, strange noises unintentionally escape their mouths. In other words, the game affects the player physically, much in the same way that whirling does. This way of influencing users is prototypical for play dynamics in games and other play tools.

While other dynamics are identifiable in this game, we believe that this analysis is adequate to introduce the thought process that undergirds the theory of play dynamics. We will now provide another example of play dynamics by briefly analysing the highly successful computer game 'Counter-Strike'.

COUNTER-STRIKE

Counter-Strike was developed as a modification of Valve's Half-Life; it has been and remains a highly successful game. Since its first release in 2000, several follow-up games have been created, of which the latest—released in 2012—retain more than 6% of the total playing time in 2015, making them the second most-played PC games (Statita, 2015). Here, we will focus on how the game pushes players into the state of play through use of play dynamics.

Counter-Strike is a first-person shooter game, where the players see the game world in first-person view on the computer screen and see their teammates and opponents as figures. Participants can play on teams as either terrorists or counter-terrorists. Each team tries to either kill all the players on another other team, or to complete their mission objectives. The most common scenario is that the terrorists must carry a bomb, plant it in a designated location and protect it from counter-terrorists, who try to disarm it before it explodes (A more detailed description is available on Wikipedia).

Counter-Strike resembles the traditional childhood games of 'cops and robbers' or 'cowboys and Indians', which are variations of tag. In Counter-Strike, every time a team wins, the game places the players back in the starting area and revives them if they died during the round. All players that did not die retain their equipment (mostly weapons), while the others lose theirs. The players begin with only a knife and a pistol; whenever they kill someone or win the game, they are issued money to purchase better equipment, such as machine guns or grenades. The game requires significant strategic planning and collaboration and strategic between the players on each team.

We have observed children and young people from the ages of 7 to 16 playing Counter-Strike at home and in computer clubs; here, we present a prototypical play scenario from one of these observations, where a player—'Jack'—is playing online from home:

1. "Jack" must choose a game to join, and then a team. He chooses counter-terrorists.
2. The game loads and Jack prepares to play.
3. The game displays a loading screen. Jack is then placed in the 'buy zone', and for a few seconds the game is paused so that he can buy weapons and other equipment.
4. The game begins.
5. All players run out of the buy zone to different locations on the map. Jack first runs to one of several bomb spots, which he will try to protect from terrorists by shooting at them and trying to 'kill' them. The bomb spots are where the terrorists must place their bombs. If they fail, they lose the game.
6. Jack hides behind an object (a wooden box), waiting for approaching terrorists. His teammates and enemies are moving around the map; most sneak around, hiding behind walls and objects, looking for friends and enemies. Teams communicate (via headphones online from home), and their voices bear witness to the tension building up. Jack is clearly affected. He is physically restless, moving his head, arm and shoulders abruptly. Occasional messages such as 'Enemy spotted' come from Jack's teammates, and he can hear gunshots when they enter gunfights.
7. Jack's first gunfight begins when he sees an enemy and starts to shoot at him. Simultaneously, he is trying to evade the enemy's bullets. His fear is also visible—he literally ducks his head. He is hit several times and loses some of his 'health' (shown on the screen). He cries out loudly, retreats to a more secure location and calls his teammates for help.
8. After a brief break spent hiding in the secure location, Jack walks out again and sees that everything is clear for the moment, as the terrorists took another route. He begins to search for an enemy again walking around the map. Then he receives the message 'Bomb placed', which tells him that the terrorists have been successful in placing their bomb. Immediately he runs to one of the bombsites to see if the bomb and the terrorists are there.
9. A new gunfight begins. Jack quickly kills a terrorist with a 'head shoot' (and receive bonus in game cash for this), but shortly afterwards, he is killed by another terrorist. As 'dead' he is automatically placed in 'observer mode', where he can follow a teammate around and watch him play, but cannot interfere.
10. Soon after, terrorists kill the last counter-terrorist and win the round.
11. A new round begins. Every player receives extra cash to buy weapons.
12. Jack, his teammates and the terrorist team play 15 rounds in total before the game is over, and the game's statistics are presented to determine which team won most often, how many enemies each player killed, and so on.

ANALYSIS OF THE COUNTER-STRIKE SCENARIO

The game has several similarities to street games and sports games. First the player must choose a side; this makes the player feel like part of a team. In the second stage of the scenario presented above, we begin to see tension building, as Jack prepares for play. Often, players from the same team will hold their first quick strategic discussion during the game's short loading time.

By the third stage, players are inside the game world. The freeze time makes it clearer what is waiting for them, and the players can see the world before venturing into it. At this point, each player is also able to upgrade their gear and weapons. Receiving new, better, often specialised gear increases players' expectations. At this stage, the network being built between the teammates is also evident. In the fourth stage, the players see the game map and the objects within it. Now they are able to walk around, and act in the virtual world.

For Jack, the game's objective—to win by preventing the terrorists from placing a bomb—makes him move to the bomb spot. The fear of being caught makes him hide behind an object. He is afraid of being found and shot, and this fear increases as he hears messages of teammates finding people, of gunshots, and so on. Even though the 'fear' is framed by play and the activities occur on a screen, it is obvious that Jack's body is affected. The first gunfight makes this even more evident. Jack's role in the game 'takes over', so to speak, as he sees an enemy and automatically begins shooting. As the enemy shoots back, he automatically tries to hide and duck (even physically). When he is hit several times and flees, the hide-and-seek dynamics clearly emerge. The tension of meeting the enemy, almost 'dying' and then escaping, immerses Jack (and the other players) within the game; they enter the state-of-play. It is not funny in the sense that the players laugh, but is nonetheless a very playful experience. Jack is now fully alert and focused on the game. As he walks slowly and cautiously out of his second hiding place, he discovers that the enemy has taken another route and he is safe once again to roam around the map. This is also visible physically: his shoulders relax, and he appears calmer. Shortly afterwards, he receives the message that the bomb has been placed, meaning that the counter-terrorist team has 45 seconds to find and defuse it, and that Jack—as a counter-terrorist—must be fast, adding a time constraint that increases his tension. He runs to find the bomb.

As this analysis shows, the dynamics of competition between the two teams dominate the game. In many ways, the game can be described as an advanced form of tag. Although the settings and forms of tagging and running are simulated rather than physical, the computer game nonetheless utilises the dynamics of the street game and its effects on each player's body and mind. By mimicking a well-known game, Counter-Strike draws on players' previous experiences to initiate the play dynamic, which is then further developed by the addition of a game world, weapons and other equipment, and the ability to communicate with teammates and develop strategies. Counter Strike continuously renews the experience of 'tag', but does not become boring for the players. As in physical street games, the game evokes 'fear' in players' bodies when they are chased, which is most likely a deep-rooted feeling in human beings. This 'fear' is framed in precisely the same way Bateson suggests when writing about apes who are play fighting. Play dynamics affect the body and mind within a secure frame, evoking the moods and state of being in the world we call play.

By using a virtual game world, Counter-Strike further utilises the dynamic of emergence, where players experience their surroundings as though they are real, becoming part of the world. Edward Castronova described how this works in his book on synthetic worlds (Castronova, 2005), noting that that participants in a game can try to pretend that their actions and experiences are not real, but then they would simply go mad. Instead, players surrender to the experience in the game world, and begin to talk about the avatar as "I".

This is an important understanding of videogames that they have been successful at inspiring players to merge into the game world, and thus are 'in' the game— shooting the enemy, feeling 'fear' and 'running around'. However, at the same time, the players experience the game as something separate from ordinary life, where the actions do not mean what they normally mean.

Counter-Strike uses simple, familiar dynamics to push players into the state of play. These dynamics may be simple formulas, but they allow room for improvisation in every new game, and for ongoing innovation of weapons and equipment. This is probably why the game is still popular 15 years after its first incarnation, even though the fundamental play has not changed substantially. Counter-Strike is in that sense a rare exception in the world of computer games. From our perspective, the reason for this is the game's ability to mimic one of the most basic game formulas available., mimicking not only tag or hide-and-seek, but also 'peek-a-boo', one of the first games learned as children, and according to Sutton-Smith, a 'paradigm for play'. Moreover, to mimic is to use the same play dynamics, not necessarily the same shape or configuration.

CONCLUSION

Perhaps the reader has become interested in *why* various play dynamics works. We believe this can be explained by psychology, biology, human science or similar sciences, but we are not sure this will lead anywhere in connection to game design, because we do not believe there is a universal theory of joy. It is not even the case that all play is joyful, and thus, play dynamics do not only invoke joy, but also other pleasurable feelings, such as the 'fear' in Counter-Strike. Furthermore, a brief observation of what human beings find funny, pleasurable, joyful, engaging, and so on will show that these feelings differ along cultural and individual lines.

We believe that understanding the play dynamics games and play equipment will illuminate new ways of using play dynamics and of further developing the existing ones. In this chapter, we have identified some of the play dynamics used in different games to push players into the state of play. We cannot yet provide prescriptions for the creation of products with good play dynamics; rather, we can only postulate that any product aimed at creating play for users must use play dynamics. Therefore, it is necessary to improve understanding of which play dynamics work best under different circumstances, and how these can be created within games and toys. Future research will reveal more of these dynamics and reveal a deeper understanding of what is at play when we play.

REFERENCES

Apter, M. J. (1991). A structural-phenomenology of play. In M. J. Apter & J. H. Kerr (Eds.), *Adult play: A reversal theory approach*. Amsterdam: Swets & Zeitlinger.

Bateson, G. (2006). *Steps to an ecology of mind: Collected essays in anthropology, psychiatry, evolution and epistemology*. Chicago, IL: University of Chicago Press.

Bourdieu, P. (1997). *Af praktiske grunde*. København: Hans Reitzels forlag.

Caillois, R. (1961). *Man, play, and games* (M. Barash, Trans.). Champaign, IL: University of Illinois Press.

Castronova, E. (2005). *Synthetic worlds*. Chicago, IL: University of Chicago Press.

Eco, U. (1973). Homo ludens oggi. In J. Huizinga (Ed.), *Homo ludens* (foreword). Turin: Guilio Einaudi.

Gadamer, H. G. (1977). *Die Aktualität des Schönen Kunst Als Spiel, Symbol Und Fest*. Stuttgart: Reclam Verlag.

Hughes, L. A. (1999). Children's games and gaming. In B. Sutton-Smith, J. Mechling, T. W. Johnson, & F. R. McMahon (Eds.), *Children's folklore: A source book*. Logan: Utah State University Press.

Huizinga, J. (1938). *Homo ludens: A study of the play-element in culture*. Boston, MA: Beacon Press.

Jessen, C. (2003). *The changing face of children's play culture*. Denmark: LEGO Learning Institute. Retrieved August 15, 2015, from http://www.carsten-jessen.dk/Play_Culture.pdf

Jessen, C. (2008). Læringsspil og leg. In L. B. Andreasen (Eds.), *It og didaktisk design*. København: Danmarks Pædagogiske Universitetsskole.

Jessen, C., & Karoff, H. (2008). *Playware and new play culture*. In Proceedings for BIN Conference, Æstetik og kultur, Island.

Jessen, C., & Lund, H. H. (2008). *En definition af leg*. Retrieved January 15, 2018, from http://carsten-jessen.dk/?page_id=206

Jessen, J. D., & Jessen, C. (2014). Games as actors-interaction, play, design, and actor network theory. *International Journal on Advances in Intelligent Systems, 7*(3–4), 412–422.

Karoff, H. S. (2011). Play media: Children´s tool for play. *Childhood Today.*

Lund, H. H., & Jessen, C. (2005). *Playware–intelligent technology for children's play*. Denmark: Centre for Playware, Technical University of Denmark.

Salen, K., & Zimmerman, E. (2004). *Rules of play: Game design fundamentals*. Cambridge, MA: MIT Press.

Salen, K., & Zimmerman, E. (2006). *The game design reader: A rules of play anthology*. Cambridge, MA: MIT Press.

Schiller, F. (1793). *Über die Ästhetische Erziehung des Menschen. Klassiker Auslegen.*

Singer, D., Golinkoff, R. M., & Hirsh-Pasek, K. (Eds.). (2009). *Play=learning: How play motivates and enhances children's cognitive and social-emotional growth*. New York, NY: Oxford University Press.

Statita. (2015). *Most played game on steam*. Retrieved from https://www.statista.com/statistics/656278/steam-most-played-games-peak-concurrent-player

Sutton-Smith, B. (1979). *Play and learning* (Vol. 3). New York, NY: Halsted Press.

Sutton-Smith, B. (2009). *The ambiguity of play*. Cambridge, MA: Harvard University Press.

Walther, B. K. (2003, May). Playing and gaming: Reflections and classifications. *Game Studies, 3*(1).

HANS CHRISTIAN ARNSETH, THORKILD HANGHØJ
AND KENNETH SILSETH

7. GAMES AS TOOLS FOR DIALOGIC TEACHING AND LEARNING

*Outlining a Pedagogical Model for Researching and
Designing Game-Based Learning Environments*

ABSTRACT

In this chapter we introduce an analytic and normative model of how games can be used as part of dialogic teaching and learning practices in the classroom. In our research during the last few years, we have been analysing how students makes sense of computer games in educational contexts. We have also been concerned with design-based research and with implementing games into more complex learning designs. Based on our experiences we wanted to focus more explicitly on teaching and the importance of the teacher in realizing the potentials of game-based learning. We found that more context sensitive models for implementing games into teaching and learning practices were lacking. Our model is grounded in a sociocultural and dialogic approach to meaning making and we discuss important concepts from this theory such as voice, utterance and artifact. We argue that we cannot expect that games themselves have particular effects on pedagogy and learning. On the contrary, the potentials of games needs to be realised in practice. We also contextualize and ground our argument in international research and in our own studies on the use of games in classrooms, and we argue that games can provide teachers with interesting means for creating more active and reflective learning experiences for students in the classroom. Our learning design model emphasize the interrelationship between instructional categories and it represents a model for planning and carrying out teaching with games in classrooms. Having said that, it can also be a useful model for analysing how games work as part of complex learning ecologies.

Keywords: dialogism, learning design, digital games, education

INTRODUCTION

During the last couple of decades, research on digital games in education has demonstrated how games can be used as effective tools for learning in and across different domains (Gredler, 1996; Gros, 2007; Nash & Shaffer, 2011). In a recent review, Clark, Tanner-Smith, and Killingsworth (2016) argued that digital games enhance students' learning relative to non-game conditions, but these effects vary across game mechanics characteristics and the visual and narrative characteristics of game designs. This is not surprising given the variations among games and game characteristics. However, Clark et al. also have argued that it is important to take into account both the affordances of a digital game and the pedagogical designs beyond it. In this chapter, we introduce a pedagogical model for researching and designing how games can become tools for teaching and learning. Across the educational sciences, teachers are often described as one of the main factors determining students' learning (Hattie, 2009). Particularly important are teachers' abilities to plan learning activities, engage students in productive interaction, and provide coherence in their learning over time (Engle, 2006; Sawyer, 2006). What concerns us here is how this translates into design-based research and teaching with digital games in the classroom. We are particularly concerned with dialogic principles of pedagogy as ways of designing for, carrying out, and analyzing practices with digital games. We use "digital games" as a generic term comprising all types of digital games across platforms. This does not mean that we are ignorant of the fact that different game designs offer different learning opportunities. On the contrary, when using the model to inform learning design and analysis, researchers and teachers need to pay careful attention to the level of fit between the game design and other features of the learning situation.

We know surprisingly little about how we can design learning environments in which games become tools for expansive learning conversations. Apart from earlier work conducted by the authors of this chapter (Hanghøj, 2008; Silseth, 2012; Silseth & Arnseth, 2011), relatively few empirical studies exist that consider dialogic aspects of teaching and learning with games. In summary, there is a lack of knowledge of how teachers and students can utilize games and features of games as relevant tools for talk and learning.

We do not see games as fixed learning machines or as constituents of magic circles (Huizinga, 1950), but rather as flexible artifacts that may take on many different meanings when taught and played across different classrooms. In this way, we are interested in the relationship between the game as an artifact and the dialogic pedagogy used within particular game-based learning environments. Viewing digital games as flexible tools emphasizes the dialogical assumption that learning takes place by allowing knowledge to be continually "constructed, deconstructed and reconstructed" (Wegerif, 2006a, p. 60).

In this chapter, we draw together some of the recent findings from our research; we explicate some of the core dialogic concepts and relate them to digital games; and we try to formulate a set of principles or guidelines for a dialogic pedagogy with digital games, what we term "the GTDT model" (Games as Tools for Dialogic Teaching). Introducing games can also cause disruptions in established pedagogies. The meanings and functions of games cut across formal and informal contexts, but we argue that this can also be a source of discussion and reflection. Disruption constitutes an opportunity to engage in dialogue. Tensions can be about how players experience and make sense of the game and how their experiences connect to curricular topics. They can exist between game narratives and real-world scenarios, for instance, or between how the Cold War is depicted in a game and how it is described in textbooks. Finally, they can exist between game mechanics and real world events, for example, between how city planning is simulated in a game and how it happens in real life. Such tensions can offer new forms of comparison and dialogue, which can be productive in terms of expanding learners' preconceived assumptions, values, and ideas (Thomas & Brown, 2007).

The GTDT model is grounded in a dialogic pedagogy. Dialogic theories originated in the seminal works of Bakhtin and Vygotsky (Wertsch, 1991). These ideas help us to tease out what we believe constitutes important principles for design-based research and a dialogic pedagogy for game- and play-oriented learning. These theories underscore how meaning, thinking, and being are situated in concrete, practical circumstances. Meaning is constituted by context and constitutive of context, and human learning and development is dependent on and mediated by semiotic and material tools. Furthermore, human sense-making is the result of negotiations among different voices and positions, and meaning is the result of negotiations among different participants. Furthermore, meaning and sense are never final. What things mean or how they function can always be reinterpreted and made problematic. From this perspective, games can be used to open up dialogic spaces that offer multiple voices and positions. Following Thomas and Brown (2007), we argue that games can help create complex dialogic spaces in the classroom where different voices can enter into dialogue.

> Within the spaces of virtual worlds, we can begin to see a new way of learning emerge, focused on the ideas of agency and disposition, facilitated by modes of transfer that are no longer about fidelity between worlds, but are about the power of imagination to explore the differences and similarities between them and to use experience to translate those differences and similarities from the virtual to the physical world. (Thomas & Brown, 2007, p. 169)

From this perspective, digital games are tools with flexible meanings, purposes, and functions, which can make them into tailorable and useful tools for teaching and learning. This does not mean that we believe it is easy to implement digital games into educational practices. A range of practical and pedagogical issues makes it challenging to use digital games for learning. Some of these issues are related to the relevance of particular games to learning goals, the amount of time it takes to play games, access to relevant hardware and software in schools, and teachers' digital competence (Van Eck, 2009). We also want to underline that we cannot take for granted that all students are necessarily interested in games, and different pupils might also have different preferences in terms of the games they like to play outside school. Finally, using games in a school context also changes the meaning and purpose of games and game playing, which could impact students' motivation and interest. We believe that to face these challenges, a sound pedagogical framework increases the likelihood of productive uses of digital games in classrooms.

The GTDT model consists of principles and recommendations for designing, analyzing, and using different types of games to facilitate dialogic learning. One of the aims is to facilitate productive interaction in and around games. To support teacher's pedagogical strategies, it is also important to analyze how particular game mechanics, narrative structures, and representational forms are able or unable to support learning through dialogue. For instance, there are important differences between single-player games and multi-player games, with the latter often facilitating more in-game dialogue among players. Still, we argue that in principle all games can become part of dialogic practices, which may foster dialogic spaces that allow participants to identify with new perspectives within a multi-voiced classroom. This is dependent both on specific game features and on how the game is "talked into being" as part of classroom practices.

For instance, an empirical study of a single-player learning game intended to train adults' second language skills showed how the game was used spontaneously to facilitate various types of dialogic learning among students. It helped create a playful frame for learning and generated specific "language events" during lessons, which the teacher could use as resources in the later instructional work (Hautopp & Hanghøj, 2014). The study shows how games can act as contingent and somewhat unpredictable discussion tools. According to Atkins (2006), games are "temporal events that exist only in their dialogic relationship with a player, and a videogame without a player is just so much dead code" (p. 135). The meaning of games is therefore not static and given *a priori* (Arnseth, 2006). Like any other text, game texts have meaning potentials that can be realized in many different ways (Linell, 2009). This also means that it is problematic to assume that particular game designs automatically determine or support specific types of dialogue. Instead, we argue that a model of game-based dialogic pedagogy should identify and describe productive patterns of dialogue in and around games, focus on the dynamics between a game design and its use in the classroom, and specify how teachers can create productive learning trajectories for students. To understand how this might happen, it is necessary to discuss and introduce important dialogic concepts in some detail.

Throughout the chapter, we address how digital games can become talked into being in the classroom. We also discuss how digital games can co-constitute dialogic spaces that offer ways of experiencing and reflecting, enabling players to take the perspective of the other. We argue that the learning opportunities offered by digital games are very much dependent on how they are enacted and articulated. Digital games offer the opportunity for more instrumental teaching and learning where the emphasis is placed on mastering game rules, leveling up, gaining experience points, and winning. However, they also offer opportunities for bringing other voices and positions into the classroom. We argue that the latter is more fruitful in terms of creating powerful dialogic spaces for learning.

The structure of our chapter is as follows: First, we introduce important concepts from dialogic theory. After that, we critically review the relevant literature with a particular focus on the role of the teacher in classroom practices with games. Then, we introduce and describe in detail our dialogic model for designing and analyzing teaching and learning with digital games. Finally, we draw together the main threads of our argument and display how games can help create dialogic spaces and disrupt traditional pedagogies.

UTTERANCE AND VOICE: A DIALOGICAL APPROACH

"Dialogism" is an epistemological approach to the understanding of language, cognition, and meaning-making as something cultural and historical. From this perspective, meaning is always situated in social and cultural life, and every act is seen as a response or an answer to something in this context (Linell, 1998). Dialogism contrasts with what is often coined "monologism", which is a collective term for approaches informed by the idea that meaning resides in language as a formal system of signs (Marková, 1990). A dialogical approach departs from this idea and sees meanings being created in interactions among real people in particular settings (Valsiner & van der Veer, 2000). In a dialogical approach, interaction and context work as guiding principles when studying language, cognition, and meaning-making (Linell, 1998, 2009). The notion of "dialogicality" is perhaps the most basic concept for Bakhtin (1981, 1986; Wertsch, 1991). Put simply, it refers to how an utterance both represents a certain position or the voice of a speaker and an orientation towards a recipient or an addressee. Thus, every utterance has a dual nature. This is also the case for sense-making and how we use language to make sense of one another and the world. In this sense, dialogicality is also an epistemic concept.

In a dialogic approach, important concepts are utterance and voice. These ideas enable us to provide a more nuanced understanding of how signs and tools mediate human activity systems. The notion of "utterance" has been coined precisely to underscore the fact that language is not an abstract system. On the contrary, our idea of language as a system is abstracted from the concrete usage of language *in situ*, and not the opposite, the derivation of meaning from an abstract system of signs. According to Linell (1998), the conceptualization of language as primarily an abstract system represents a bias towards the written word. In contrast, the notion of utterance retains and points out this view of language, namely that meaning is always situated in concrete historical, social, and communicative circumstances. For Bakhtin (1981), the utterance is the unit of analysis when studying human sense-making. It is also the site where the systematicity of language and concrete, situated usage come together.

According to Bakhtin (1981), "voice" refers to the speaking personality or consciousness; it is the person situated in a particular time and space that speaks and thinks. An utterance is produced by a voice; a voice is where the utterance is coming from and how it is responsive towards other voices. A voice is not simply something that persons have; instead, it orients to the other—to a recipient or a context. Bakhtin has also stressed the notion of "multivoicedness". In this sense, meaning is always heterogeneous. This does not mean that all voices are equally important or visible in dialogue. A dialogic approach also entails a critical approach, that is, it emphasizes the importance of scrutinizing why some voices and not others are invoked in particular circumstances.

A take on learning within a dialogic approach has been formulated by Wegerif (2006b, 2007). He has emphasized the importance of creating "dialogic spaces" in educational settings, where students and teachers engage in collaborative activities in which students learn to see a task or topic from others' perspectives. According to Wegerif (2006), teaching should aim at facilitating learning situations in which multiple voices are allowed to inter-animate each other. Wegerif (2006) said that "meaning itself only arises when different perspectives are brought together in a way that allows them to 'inter-animate' or 'inter-illuminate' each other" (p. 146). Meaning is not found in one voice or one perspective, but rather in the way that these multiple voices illuminate each other. This is what we term a dialogical space in the classroom.

We also draw on a socio-cultural perspective. According to this approach, meaning-making is mediated by signs and tools and situated within historically developing human practices (Wertsch, 1991). This enables us to examine in more detail how particular voices are more visible or relevant to certain contexts, as well as how students can become and need to appropriate more hegemonic voices. Doing so will enable them over time to participate in important societal practices. Having said that, it is also an important purpose of education to gain a critical perspective on science, politics, arts, and ethics. We argue that a dialogic approach is particularly relevant to fostering a critical approach toward the organization of social and cultural life.

As mentioned above, the dialogic becomes a concept or a theory of how we make meaning in general, how we understand one another, and how we make sense of our surroundings. If we were to try to reformulate some of these ideas in relation to practical pedagogy, it would seem reasonable to claim that, even though we see language use as always being dialogical, classroom interactions can be more or less dialogic in practice. Thus, certain voices can gain hegemony. Historically, the institutional voice of the school or the curriculum uttered by a teacher in a classroom gains this hegemony. It is important for us to regain this distinction between dialogism as a general theory of communication and learning and dialogic pedagogy as a more practical application of dialogic principles, in that differing ideas should be given voice in a classroom. Our practical dialogic pedagogy does not mean that we believe all voices are equally relevant, interesting, and true, but it means that a teacher should build on student ideas in an explicit manner (Silseth, 2017). It also involves being agreeable to inquiry in a more open context. Moreover, it entails bringing a more explicitly multivoiced text into play in the dialogic space of the classroom—multivoiced in that characters in a game more explicitly represent different and dynamic voices than, for instance, the voices of a textbook.

According to Wegerif (2015), a dialogic pedagogy in the Internet age is dialogic in two senses: dialogue is both a goal for education and the means through which education is realized. He has also stressed the need to articulate and engage with multiple voices, arguing that dialogic argumentation is an important goal and procedure, and students need to be taught how to talk in effective and convincing ways. What is taught also needs to be made relevant to students in one way or another; the form and content need to connect to their social worlds and experiences. A dialogic pedagogy should enable students to reflect on their thinking and identity: on how they make sense of the world and on who they are as participants in a range of different practices in society and culture. A dialogic education should also enable them to reflect on the nature of important institutions in society and how they work. Finally, Wegerif (2015) has argued that new digital technologies should be used to connect to diverse cultural contexts beyond the classroom and to mediate student's inquiries into real world problems.

In the following sections, we review research on digital game-oriented learning in order to summarize important findings that might inform a dialogic game-based pedagogy. We focus on relevant research on how games are used as part of learning designs that emphasize collaboration and dialogue, as well as on research that examines the role and importance of the teacher for students' learning and participation. This review, together with our theoretical approach, will constitute an important ground for discussing a more normative framework for the productive use of games in the classroom.

DIGITAL GAME-ORIENTED LEARNING, COLLABORATION, AND DIALOGUE

It is important to underscore that collaborative learning does not equal dialogue and dialogic learning. Research has demonstrated quite clearly that the implementation of collaboration does not improve learning in and of itself. A rationale for collaboration is that it is supposed to stimulate learners to explicate their knowledge (van der Meij, Albers, & Leemkuil, 2011). Theoretically, collaboration should foster the articulation of knowledge, but playing a game in a dyad does not guarantee that a player will discuss issues that are relevant to their task. Indicative is the analysis of the discussion protocols by Van der Meij et al. (2011), which showed that much discussion involved superficial game features, such as movements in the game. In addition, the authors proposed that scripted collaboration, in which partners are assigned a specific role or task, can improve learning (see also Hummel et al., 2011; Weinberger, Ertl, Fischer, & Mandl, 2005). We agree that scripted collaboration in relation to the educational use of computer games can be a promising combination. It would also be interesting to investigate whether the integration of scripted collaboration into a narrative provides added value.

Gee (2004) has argued that, when participating in a game, you need to orient toward, adopt, and learn the frames that the designer of the game has constructed for you. However, to participate competently, you also need to learn how to use the resources in the game creatively to move forward in the game. In addition, the player can do things in the game that were unanticipated by the designer (as, for instance, seen in the practice of glitching[1] or uploading Let's Play videos on YouTube). Thus, an element of agency in many games makes them different from other cultural tools, such as books (Silseth, 2012). Players use their own experiences and knowledge when creating meaning and understanding game play, and games provide a set of values or belief systems that make it possible for players to enact different identities (DeVane & Squire, 2008; Hayes, 2007; Shah, Foster, & Barany, 2017).

However, as research has shown, there can also be some challenges in implementing games as learning resources. Fields and Enyedy (2013) have shown how gamers being positioned and acknowledged as experts in classrooms requires much interactional work by participants. As Squire (2005) has shown, a teacher's informed use of computer games in their classroom can create a situation in which some students feel uneasy when having to perform identities in school that are developed around game play in settings outside school. According to Hanghøj (2011), students might experience genre clashes in regard to what they expect of a computer game. When presented with the educational computer game *Global Conflicts: Latin America*, different classes of secondary students expected to explore a complex interactive game world, but several students were turned off by the lack of in-game actions and the considerable chunks of text to be read, which in many ways resembled the familiar design of a textbook. This demonstrates how computer games, which have a clear pedagogical purpose, belong to a different genre than the commercial games that students play outside school. A learning environment in which students are provided the opportunity to engage with an educational game might create a conflict of interest between the teacher's assumption (that the educational game will motivate and engage students) and the students' expectations (that the educational game will offer the same experiences provided by commercial games played outside school). Thus, realizing games as learning resources requires well-considered learning designs in which the teacher clearly articulates the aim of playing and reflects on multiple aspects that might influence the success or failure of game-based learning.

THE TEACHER AS FACILITATOR

Research has shown the crucial importance of the teacher in planning, framing, enacting, and assessing game-oriented learning environments (Freitas & Maharg, 2011; Freitas & Oliver, 2006; Hontvedt, Sandberg, & Silseth, 2013; Wouters & van Oostendorp, 2013). For example, the teacher might have an important role in bringing together different players' divergent experiences with the game, guiding them through the process of connecting game play to the curriculum, and making the process relevant for students as learners (Squire & Barab, 2004). Sandford and colleagues (2006) have explored the use of commercial games in education. Their study document how a teacher's knowledge of the curriculum and competence in applying it in practice is more significant for students' learning with a game than teachers' competence in playing the game in question. The findings also show that the success of game-based learning in educational settings is highly dependent on a teacher's awareness and interpretation of students' capacities, as well as on whether the teacher manages to strategically use games as resources for obtaining well-articulated learning objectives. Computer games are not good learning resources by themselves; rather, they are thematizable artifacts that must be realized as learning resources in practice (Linderoth, 2004).

Silseth (2012) has shown how the teacher has a crucial role in constituting the computer game as a learning resource. Competence in playing computer games outside school might be relevantly invoked when students engage in game play as part of curriculum-guided teaching. However, the findings show that such competence might not be enough to foster subtle understanding of the topic addressed in the game. The constitution of a computer game as a learning resource is a highly collaborative activity in which multiple resources for meaning-making are in play and shed light on what might be characterized as student–teacher interactions that contribute to students' subtle understanding. The findings also show how a teacher could use resources in the game (personal and concrete stories from different sides of the conflict) when facilitating discussions on different aspects of the curricular topic. By making the students use personal stories from the game as resources for providing accounts and evaluations of what happened during game play, the teacher creates dialogic spaces in which the different voices of the conflict inter-animate each other. In addition, the findings show that, to realize the potential of game-based learning in educational practices and enable students to develop comprehensive understanding of the topic addressed in the game, it is important for the teacher to find ways of creating a learning environment that connect in-school and out-of-school experiences with a topic.

Similarly, Silseth and Arnseth (2011) have shown how participants use stories, categories, and inscriptions to construct different learning selves that have significance for students' participation when they play *Global Conflicts: Palestine*. Conflicts among the relevance of the different learning selves occur. Some learning selves are seen as relevant by the teacher and others by students; however, these learning selves stand in a dialogical relationship to each other. This type of negotiation has implications for students' participation, but students also have agency in this process. In addition, the study suggested that students would not uncritically embrace games as tools for learning in school, that the relevance of using a game for learning about a curricular topic is negotiated through student–teacher interactions, and that game-based learning should be seen with regard to how students are constructed as learners.

Focusing on teachers' pedagogical approaches to games, Hanghøj and Hautopp (2016) have shown how teachers adopted quite different positions when teaching a *Minecraft* curriculum at three different primary schools. The findings suggest that teachers' positioning toward game-based teaching can be categorized in terms of an "executive approach", which reflects a high degree of teacher control of the game setting, as well as the teachers' limited curricular knowledge of the game;

an "improvisational approach", which suggests a student-centered and open-ended exploration of the game world with a limited focus on curricular aims; and, finally, a "transformational approach", in which the teacher takes ownership of *Minecraft* as a design tool to develop new curricular content to meet local needs and aims. The findings indicate that teachers' pedagogical approaches to games are highly important in terms of framing what counts as legitimate curricular aims and practices in the classroom. Moreover, the findings emphasize that teachers need to acquire basic game literacy in relation to specific games in order to adapt games to their existing teaching repertoires and avoid either "being played by" or "playing against" the game in question. Based on the findings described above, we will now characterize and describe a pedagogical model for researching and designing how games can become tools for teaching and learning.

GAMES AS TOOLS FOR DIALOGIC TEACHING (THE GTDT MODEL)

In our model, we address several issues; some are classical didactical categories and others are more specifically related to games. The classical questions in didactics circle around what should be learned, how it should be taught, and why it should be taught and learned. The recommendations of our framework articulate the need for making some of the principles of a dialogic pedagogy relevant to game-oriented learning. We want to try to identify and support specific forms of dialogue in and around games and connect games to specific learning goals and objectives. The GTDT model considers aspects as shown in Figure 7.1.

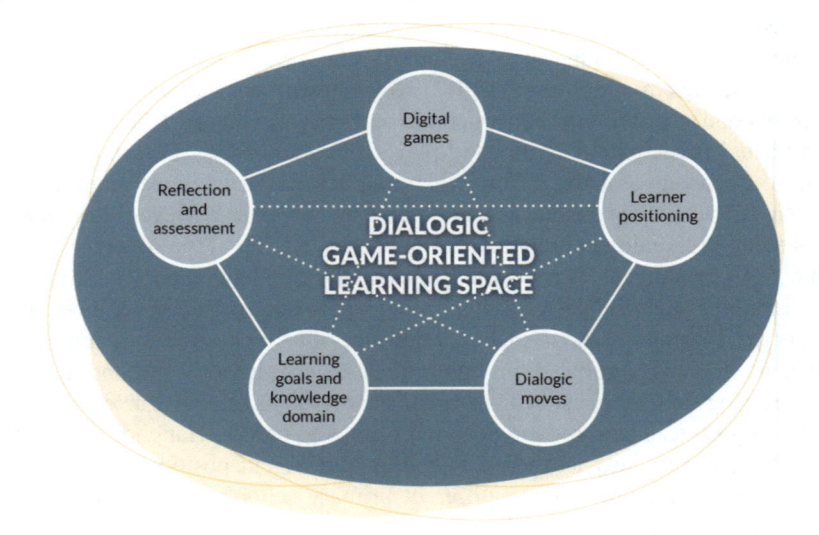

Figure 7.1. The GTDT model

The model consists of five different dimensions that should be taken into account to create a dialogic space for learning. This is where the actual practice of game-oriented learning and teaching through dialogue is realized in action. We briefly go through all these dimensions in detail before we draw them together and provide examples. The model is not sequential in any strict sense. Teachers need not start with the learning goals; they could have an idea about a game that might be interesting, or the pupils themselves and their interests could even constitute the starting point for planning an activity.

1. The *learning goals and knowledge domain* are about what the teacher wants to achieve with the activity and what in what direction he or she wants the activity to develop. It can be about learning a skill, learning about a particular domain, or learning about a particular concept. These things can also be intertwined in one activity. It is of course useful to anchor the learning goal in the curriculum. In regard to this dimension it is also crucial to consider how knowledge is structured, about what constitute important concepts and how they are related to one another as part of a system. It is crucial to be able to assess whether a game or a feature of a game can mediate a certain concept correctly or accurately and, if not, how the particular contrast can be made into a specific topic for reflection.

2. *Reflection and assessment* relates to how students and teachers talk about experiences in the game and relate their experiences to particular learning goals. Reflection is also about assessing what happened and connecting experiences in a game to situations and practices beyond the game. Reflection can be metaphorically oriented, focusing on differences, or metonymic, focusing on similarities across contexts. Reflection and assessment can be both formative and summative; they can be done during or after an activity.

3. *Digital games* come in many shapes and genres. Sometimes the sheer availability of games can be overwhelming. It is useful to learn from other teachers' experiences in terms of what games might be relevant for realizing different learning goals. We find it useful to distinguish among the representations in the game, the game narratives' given voice, and the actual game mechanics. Representations can be about how, for instance, certain events, milieus, or phenomena are represented in the game. Narratives are about how the game tells certain stories about events. Mechanics are about how the game plays out and responds to actions, and how participants can make sense of that.

4. *Learner positioning* is about the learner and the experiences he or she brings to the particular game-oriented activity. It is crucial for the teacher to have some idea about what experiences students have with particular games, what kind of identities they usually take on in different subjects and activities in the classroom, and their motivation and engagement relating to game-based learning. What students do in game-oriented learning activities is always mediated by their previous experiences, and the teacher needs to build on and challenge those precepts.

5. *Dialogic moves* are about the particular mediating tools the teacher can make use of when talking to students. These forms of talk can support, challenge, or problematize students' accounts, thereby fostering conceptual and personal development through dialogue. These moves can be the following types of utterances: explaining, clarifying, justifying, elaborating, deliberating, exploring, and revoicing. The dialogic effect of these utterances cannot of course be predicted in advance. Their functioning in dialogue depends on how students and teachers negotiate the meaning of such resources in joint learning activities.

Now, these dimensions are drawn into and become part of what we called a dialogic space. The dialogic space is constituted by participants using and orienting toward these dimensions and relating them to one another as part of an educational practice. In and through participation in this dialogic space, the meaning and sense of these dimensions become available to participants, and the space is constructed as a meaningful and perhaps productive learning activity for students. This meaningful framework enables students relate their game play to certain purposes and to connect what they experience in the game with the overall goals of the lesson. Creating and maintaining the space provides the integrating principle for the classroom activities. It is what ties all the other activities together. Thus, the learning goals should not be introduced as fixed. Instead, students should be encouraged to explore and develop their understanding of the topic in question. The teacher can shift among introducing topics, questions, and learning tools; asking questions; clarifying issues and requesting clarification; encouraging students to predict what will happen; summarizing activities; encouraging comparisons; and pointing to relevant knowledge.

PLANNING FOR GAME-ORIENTED LEARNING IN THE CLASSROOM

After having introduced the different dimensions in our model, we illustrate how they can be used when planning and realizing game-oriented learning activities in the classroom. In teaching and in design-based research, we usually start with the learning goals, but as mentioned, the model does not prescribe this particular sequence. What is it that the teacher wants the students to learn, and how can games be employed to reach these goals? Let us say that the teacher wants students to learn about geometry in mathematics. Many specifically designed computerized learning tools are tailored to this topic, but the teacher can also use *Minecraft* to support this aim. When *Minecraft* become integrated within the framework of a dialogic game pedagogy, the learning goals and the game become dialogically related and one makes no sense without the other within the context of the classroom. Using *Minecraft* can enable the teacher to realize other goals, as well, namely connecting to pupils' interests and situating the knowledge domain within a broader context.

Now, in relation to game elements, we mentioned three aspects. Which one of these is highlighted also depends on the learning aims. For instance, if the learning aim is to learn about Renaissance architecture, *Assassins Creed III* might be a useful and relevant learning tool. Particularly the representational and narrative aspects of the game become important resources for developing students' understanding. Students can learn about Renaissance architecture or ways of life during this particular period and connect these representations to knowledge about architecture or history.

In regard to reflection, there is a need for the teacher to enable students to reflect on their actions and experiences and to monitor whether what they know and learn are aligned to authorized ways of learning and knowing. In this sense, reflection also involves self-assessment. Promoting reflection in and on game play is crucial to help students create relevant meanings from their game play. By addressing and articulating particular game situations, teachers can help students build new knowledge and challenge their existing beliefs and values. This also allows assessment of how students relate to the relevant knowledge that develops through game play. In this activity, assessment is built into the actual game play and the reflection on game play in group or whole-class discussion. Of course, this does not mean that the teacher cannot or should not use more summative forms of assessment.

In terms of learner positioning, the teacher needs to consider students' previous experiences. If pupils in the classroom are very good at playing *Minecraft*, it might be useful to give them roles and assignments as experts, which can help other students who do not have the same experience. Of course, the entire class of students does not have to play the same game. The teacher can also design work in group with different games and then compare and contrast in whole-class sessions. Learner positioning can also be about how particular learners get to play certain roles and positions in the game. The teacher can use different kinds of approaches here, for instance, designing activities where a student plays a role in a game that contrasts with other identities, thereby creating opportunities for comparison and reflection and, perhaps, sustained engagement.

How the teacher supports and talks with students represents another crucial issue. In our model, inquiry and dialogue are crucial goals; therefore, we encourage teaching methods that involve reciprocity and multiple perspectives and positions. Thus, the use of the storyline or representations of architecture in *Assassin's Creed* needs to become an object of reflection and dialogue. The teacher can encourage students to inquire into particular aspects of the game as a text; he or she can also inspire students by asking specific questions to guide their inquiry—preferably not closed questions but rather open questions that encourage active exploration. These experiences then become the starting point for more elaborate dialogues within groups or the class. Here, students are encouraged to give voice to their experiences in the game and inquiries into the game as a textual artifact. Their voice requires recognition by the teacher, but it can of course be problematized. Finally, the teacher can encourage students to reflect on how different voices relate to one another and form different genres, activities, or practices. This latter approach encourages students to develop meta-media literacy.

As suggested in the relational model, there may be many different pedagogical strategies when teaching with a game. In some cases, the emphasis may be deductive, for example, when students are first introduced to specific curricular concepts or topics (e.g., the Israeli–Palestinian conflict) before exploring the phenomenon on their own by playing the game *Global Conflicts: Palestine* (Silseth, 2012). In other cases, the emphasis could be more inductive, for example, by letting middle-school students first actively explore a commercial game, such as the action role-playing game *Torchlight II*, and articulate what challenges they encountered in the game and how they could improve their in-game tactics before making it clear how specific mathematical knowledge (e.g., of fractions or percentages) might provide students with in-game advantages when utilizing their game resources (Hanghøj, 2015).

Summarizing the GTDT model and the above discussion, we suggest the following educational design principles for educators, which are aimed at fostering dialogic spaces in and around students' game experiences. Thus, dialogical game pedagogy emphasizes teachers' ability to do the following:

- Facilitate dialogue through open and authentic questions, which relates to both specific game experiences and learning aims. Through dialogue, students' game experience should become meaningful in relation to specific curricular topics. Likewise, teacher-led dialogue should develop students' curricular knowledge so that they better understand or make more informed choices within a game. The teacher should be aware of whether he or she wishes to adopt deductive or inductive pedagogical strategies for linking a game with curricular aims.

- Challenge students' experience of specific game mechanics, game rules, or game outcomes as being monological truths. Games should be seen as contingent artifacts, where different choices can lead to many different consequences. Thus, it is important to foster students' critical thinking around the underlying model of learning or representations of a specific game.

- Identify different voices of specific games and among students-as-players to show different perspectives on a given subject matter. In this way, games can be used as a discussion tool to represent positions that are not necessarily present among students.

- Reflect on students' ability to collaborate through dialogue both within and around the game. It is important to set up guidelines for collaborative dialogue that match the specific game design being used. As an example, single-player games may require students to work in pairs, where they take turns at playing and engage in common dialogue around their game decisions. On the other hand, multi-player games allow all students to engage more directly in collaboration, which requires players to develop a set of shared ground rules on what characterize meaningful or valuable group dialogue.

OPENING UP SPACES OF POSSIBILITIES

In this chapter, we have tried to formulate a dialogic pedagogy for game- and play-based teaching. We want to put this model forward as a planning, teaching, and evaluation tool for teachers and educators interested in utilizing games for learning, but also as a model for design-based research. We do not believe that it is possible to formulate a generic and absolute model for game-based teaching. This would contrast with our dialogic approach to meaning-making. Still, we believe the model and the design principles can work as tools for making informed choices when introducing games into the classroom. As has become clear throughout our chapter, we do not believe that games and game-based learning will necessarily revolutionize education. On the contrary, we want to make the more modest claim that, given that games are informed by clearly formulated pedagogy, games can become interesting tools for and worlds in which not just to push students' understanding further, but also to change education and make it more relevant and interesting.

As the GTDT model suggest, there is no one-size-fits all solution when it comes to pedagogical principles for dialogical teaching with games. Digital worlds constitute interesting tools for dialogic teaching because they open up spaces of possibilities. They can support and afford the play of imagination.

NOTE

[1] "Glitching" is when a person uses flaws in a game to achieve something that was not originally designed by the game designers.

REFERENCES

Arnseth, H. C. (2006). Learning to play or playing to learn: A critical account of the models of communication informing educational research on computer gameplay. *Game Studies, 6*(1), 1–11. Retrieved from http://gamestudies.org/0601/articles/arnseth

Atkins, B. (2006). What are we really looking at? The future-orientation of video game play. *Games and Culture, 1*(2), 127–140.

Bakhtin, M. (1981). *The dialogic imagination: Four essays by M.M. Bakhtin.* Austin, TX: University of Texas Press.

Bakhtin, M. (1986). *Speech genres and other late essays.* Austin, TX: University of Texas Press.

Clark, D. B., Tanner-Smith, E. E., & Killingsworth, S. S. (2016). Digital games, design, and learning: A systematic review and meta-analysis. *Review of Educational Research, 86*(1), 79–122.

de Freitas, S., & Maharg, P. (2011). Digital games and learning: Modelling learning experiences in the digital age. In S. de Freitas & P. Maharg (Eds.), *Digital games and learning* (pp. 17–41). London: Continuum.

de Freitas, S., & Oliver, M. (2006). How can exploratory learning with games and simulations within the curriculum be most effectively evaluated? *Computers & Education, 46*(3), 249–264.

DeVane, B., & Squire, K. (2008). The meaning of race and violence in grand theft auto: San Andreas. *Games and Culture, 3*(3–4), 264–285.

Engle, R. (2006). Framing interactions to foster generative learning: A situative explanation of transfer in a community of learners classroom. *Journal of the Learning Sciences, 15*(4), 451–498.

Fields, D., & Enyedy, N. (2013). Picking up the mantle of "expert": Assigned roles, assertion of identity, and peer recognition within a programming class. *Mind, Culture, and Activity, 20*(2), 113–131.

Gee, J. P. (2004). *Situated language and learning: A critique of traditional schooling.* London: Routledge.

Gredler, M. E. (1996). Games and simulations and their relationships to learning. In D. H. Jonassen (Ed.), *Handbook of research for educational communications and technology* (pp. 571–581). New York, NY: Simon & Schuster Macmillan.

Gros, B. (2007). Digital games in education: The design of games-based learning environments. *Journal of Research on Technology in Education, 40*(1), 23–38.

Hanghøj, T. (2008). *Playful knowledge: An explorative study of educational gaming* (Doctoral dissertation). University of Southern Denmark, Copenhagen.

Hanghøj, T. (2011). Clashing and emerging genres: The interplay of knowledge forms in educational gaming. *Designs for Learning, 4*(1), 10–21.

Hanghøj, T. (2015). The school at play: Repositioning students through the educational use of digital games and game dynamics. In R. Munkvold & L. Kolås (Eds.), *Proceedings of the 9th European conference on games based learning* (pp. 227–236). Reading: Academic Conferences and Publishing International.

Hanghøj, T., & Hautopp, H. (2016). Teachers' pedagogical approaches to teaching with minecraft. In T. Connolly & L. Boyle (Eds.), *Proceedings of the 10th European conference on games based learning* (pp. 265–272). Sonning Common: Academic Conferences and Publishing International.

Hattie, J. (2009). *Visible learning: A synthesis of over 800 meta-analyses relating to achievement.* London: Routledge.

Hautopp, H., & Hanghøj, T. (2014). Game based language learning for bilingual adults. In C. Busch (Ed.), *Proceedings of the 8th European conference on games based learning* (pp. 191–198). Reading: Academic Conferences and Publishing International.

Hayes, E. (2007). Gendered identities at play. *Games and Culture, 2*(1), 23–48.

Hontvedt, M., Sandberg, M., & Silseth, K. (2013). På spill for læring: Om dataspill som læringsressurs i skolen. In S. V. Knudsen (Ed.), *Pedagogiske tekster og ressurser i praksis.* Oslo: Cappelen Damm Akademisk.

Huizinga, J. (1950). *Homo ludens: A study of the play element in culture.* Boston, MA: Beacon Press.

Hummel, H. G., Van Houcke, J., Nadolski, R. J., Van der Hiele, T., Kurvers, H., & Löhr, A. (2011). Scripted collaboration in serious gaming for complex learning: Effects of multiple perspectives when acquiring water management skills. *British Journal of Educational Technology, 42*(6), 1029–1041.

Linderoth, J. (2004). *Datorspelandets mening: Bortom idén om den interaktiva illusionen* [The meaning of gaming: Beyond the idea of the interactive illusion] (Doctoral dissertation). University of Gothenburg, Sweden.

Linell, P. (1998). *Approaching dialogue: Talk, interaction and contexts in dialogical perspectives.* Amsterdam, NL: John Benjamins.

Linell, P. (2009). *Rethinking language, mind, and world dialogically: Interactional and contextual theories of human sense-making.* Charlotte, NC: Information Age Publishing.

Marková, I. (1990). Introduction. In I. Markovà & K. Foppa (Eds.), *The dynamics of dialogue* (pp. 1–22). New York, NY: Springer-Verlag.

Nash, P., & Shaffer, D. W. (2011). Mentor modeling: The internalization of modeled professional thinking in an epistemic game. *Journal of Computer Assisted Learning, 27*(2), 173–189.

Sandford, R., Ulicsak, M., Facer, K., & Rudd, T. (2006). *Teaching with games: Using commercial off-the-shelf computer games in formal education.* Bristol: Futurelab.

Sawyer, R. K. (2006). *The Cambridge handbook of the learning sciences.* Cambridge: Cambridge University Press.

Shah, M., Foster, A., & Barany, A. (2017). Facilitating learning as identity change through game-based learning. In Y. Baek (Ed.), *Game-based learning: Theory, strategies and performance outcomes* (pp. 257–278). New York, NY: Nova Publishers.

Silseth, K. (2012). The multivoicedness of game play: Exploring the unfolding of a student's learning trajectory in a gaming context at school. *International Journal of Computer-Supported Collaborative Learning, 7*(1), 63–84.

Silseth, K. (2017). Students' everyday knowledge and experiences as resources in educational dialogues. *Instructional Science, 46*(2), 291–919. doi:10.1007/s11251-017-9429-x

Silseth, K., & Arnseth, H. C. (2011). Learning and identity construction across sites: A dialogical approach to analysing the construction of learning selves. *Culture & Psychology, 17*(1), 65–80.

Squire, K. (2005). Changing the game: What happens when video games enter the classroom? *Innovate: Journal of Online Education, 1*(6), Article 5. Retrieved from http://nsuworks.nova.edu/innovate/vol1/iss6/5

Squire, K., & Barab, S. (2004). *Replaying history: Engaging urban underserved students in learning world history through computer simulation games.* Paper presented at the 6th International Conference on Learning Sciences, Santa Monica, CA.

Thomas, D., & Brown, J. S. (2007). The play of imagination: Extending the literary mind. *Games and Culture, 2*(2), 149–172.

Valsiner, J., & van der Veer, R. (2000). *The social mind: Construction of the idea.* Cambridge: Cambridge University Press.

van der Meij, H., Albers, E., & Leemkuil, H. (2011). Learning from games: Does collaboration help? *British Journal of Educational Technology, 42*(4), 655–664.

Van Eck, R. (2009). A guide to integrating COTS games into your classroom. In R. E. Ferdig (Ed.), *Handbook of research on effective electronic gaming in education* (pp. 179–199). New York, NY: Information Science Reference.

Wegerif, R. (2006a). Dialogic education: What is it and why do we need it? *Education Review, 19*(2), 58–66.

Wegerif, R. (2006b). A dialogic understanding of the relationship between CSCL and teaching thinking skills. *International Journal of Computer-Supported Collaborative Learning, 1*(1), 143–157.

Wegerif, R. (2007). *Dialogic education and technology: Expanding the space of learning.* New York, NY: Springer-Verlag.

Wegerif, R. (2013). *Dialogic: Education for the internet age.* New York, NY: Routledge.

Weinberger, A., Ertl, B., Fischer, F., & Mandl, H. (2005). Epistemic and social scripts in computer-supported collaborative learning. *Instructional Science, 33*(1), 1–30.

Wertsch, J. (1991). *Voices of the mind: A sociocultural approach to mediated action.* Cambridge, MA: Harvard University Press.

Wouters, P., & van Oostendorp, H. (2013). A meta-analytic review of the role of instructional support in game-based learning. *Computers & Education, 60*(1), 412–425.

CHARLOTTE LÆRKE WEITZE

8. LEARNING AND DESIGN PROCESSES IN A GAMIFIED LEARNING DESIGN

Students Creating Curriculum-Based Digital Learning Games

ABSTRACT

This design-based research project investigated how a gamified learning design could enable adult learners to design digital games while implementing and thereby reaching learning goals from their curriculum. The aim was to develop a reusable learning design for upper secondary teachers and students who are game-design novices. The gamified learning design supported the innovative learning processes for the students, and the teacher participated as an inspirational guide for the students as they designed curriculum-based learning games. This chapter describes the learning design, how the teachers contributed to the students' cognitively complex learning processes, and how four parallel types of processes for designing and learning supported this gamified learning design. The study took place in a hybrid synchronous learning environment. The project revealed that the students experienced deep and motivating learning and that the teachers found this problem-based and activating learning design inspiring and easy to use as a variation to more traditional teaching approaches.

Keywords: learning-game design, teacher's role in gamified learning, gamifying education, game-design models, students as learning-game designers

INTRODUCTION

This introduction will describe the current need for motivating learning designs in Danish school contexts. This is followed by an introduction to the participants in the design-based research project and how the teachers at VUC Storstrøm decided to engage in the creation of innovative learning designs to motivate their students. Subsequently the introduction argues how constructionism and the use of learning through technology were chosen as pedagogical approaches to support the students learning process when learning through game design.

A Need for Motivation to Learn

According to researchers in motivation for learning Hutters, Sørensen, Katznelson, and Juul (2013), it is becoming increasingly difficult to motivate and engage young people in the Danish education system. Some researchers consider this a sign of a motivational crisis in the educational system (Hutters et al., 2013). The motivation to learn has an effect on the quality of students' results in school as well as on their ability to complete their education; this calls for new knowledge about what enables students' motivation to learn. This study therefore explores how it is possible to create innovative, effective, and motivating learning designs for students in formal learning environments.

Innovative Game-Based Learning Designs at VUC Storstrøm

The participants in this investigation were adult students studying at VUC Storstrøm (hereafter, VUC), an adult learning centre in Denmark. The students were participating in an upper-secondary general education programme, a full-time programme lasting two years. The group of VUC students was diverse, with a variety of academic levels and reasons for being in adult education as well as varying ages, life situations, and experiences. At VUC, many students (60%) attending the upper-secondary class have at least one instance of discontinued education in their past. This is often due to lack of motivation to learn (Pless & Hansen, 2010; Hutters et al., 2013). Certain students are at high risk of giving up when entering a new educational environment because of their previous negative experiences with the school system, which has led to low self-efficacy, and which, according to Liu, Hsieh, Cho, and Schallert (2006), is the belief in one's own capability to perform a task successfully at designated levels. Therefore, the teachers at VUC generally used a number of strategies as they strived to create a motivating and supportive learning environment for the students.

In 2014–2015 the teachers at VUC participated in innovative experiments and collaborated on creating new motivating learning designs for the students (Weitze, 2015c). The teachers suggested and worked with ways the students could be motivated to learn by (1) using subject-specific learning games as well as by (2) creating learning games with the purpose of learning about specific subject matter and, through this process, reach their learning goals. According to Takeuchi and Vaala (2014) teachers who use videogames as part of the class experience agree that videogames significantly increase students' motivation and engagement levels. Many adults, both men and women, spend time playing videogames in their spare time (ESA, 2014). In the current experiment 70% of the students played conventional games after school on a daily basis. This wide use of games invites continuing research into how the use of games or other playful elements can open up opportunities for merging motivational and engaging playful systems with the learning processes taking place in formal education. This design-based research project thus chose to go one step further than using prefabricated games for learning and, as an alternative, investigated whether the more active use of *learning-game design* as a means of learning could support the students in learning specific subject matter—that is, if the students would learn by creating learning games.

Learning through Creating

This learning through making games approach demanded that we found relevant tools and materials as well as pedagogical approaches for the teaching and learning process. But what materials may be useful in creating motivating gamified learning environments for students? One emerging trend within learning and technology is teaching students to create with technology. This movement was started by Seymour Papert at the MIT lab in the 1960s and has been evolving ever since. Papert took the constructionist approach: learning by creating (Harel & Papert, 1991; Kafai & Resnick, 1996; Papert, 1980). The learning by creating approach involving technology began with software tools such as Logo and Lego Mindstorms, recently introduced into the programming environment Scratch by the Lifelong Kindergarten Research group at the MIT Media Lab, launched in 2007 (Brennan, 2014). This learning-through-doing with technology approach is also called the 'maker movement' (Hatch, 2013). In the maker-spaces that often are used as informal learning environments, people work individually as well as collaboratively to solve technical problems and develop unique technology products. The positive experience of students working hard and being deeply engaged in learning processes in these maker-spaces has given teachers hope that this kind of engagement in active learning processes can contribute to new and more activity-creating learning designs for students in formal learning environments. The maker movement is undergoing a revival at the moment, perhaps because many of the technology-creation software products have reached more advanced levels; the newer software is web-based, with user-friendly, intuitive designs. An example of an intuitive creation tool can be experienced through the worldwide initiative The Hour of Code (http://hourofcode.com/dk/en). These technology-creation software products and other maker-tools assist students in the development of creative and innovative skills. As students learn to design with technological tools, they are also enabled to move from the role of technological consumer to the role of producer of digital content (Koh et al., 2015). According to Brennan and Resnick (2012) the development of computational thinking involves the ability to achieve an understanding of the logic of the technology behind the interface; and, as stated by Kafai (2006), the development of computational thinking may present new possibilities for creative and innovative expressions, empowering students to create their own ideas and worlds through these technological tools.

If we choose to use learning-game design as a means of learning specific formal subject matter, the question is this: How should a teacher, who is a novice in the creative and productive use of technology, approach a teaching situation if she or he wants to let students create and learn with and through technology? If he or she intends to implement cross-disciplinary subject matter into this learning process in order to use the technology as material for learning and conceptualisation, how should she or he create the learning design?

Creation of a Learning Design Supporting Learning through Game Design

Gamification is 'the use of game design elements in non-game contexts' (Deterding, Dixon, Khaled, & Nacke, 2011, p. 1). Seaborn and Fels (2015) have extended this definition as follows: 'The intentional use of game elements for a gameful experience of non-game tasks and contexts. Game elements are patterns, objects, principles, models and methods directly inspired by games'. In the current study the novice teacher and student game designers were supported in their learning process through gamifying the overall learning design. The intention of gamification and the use of game-like elements in education is to make educational situations more engaging, with a better learning outcome (Kapp, 2012). This has been done in many educational experiments, for example, by scaffolding the learning activities as missions and quests and by giving students experience points (EXP) as they move through the various levels of assignments in the gamified learning design for the course (Sheldon, 2012). The present study thus aimed to create an overall gamified learning design by facilitating the learning process for adult students by adding game elements (goals, action space, rules, choice, challenge, feedback) to the overall learning design for the class as well as letting the students be their own learning designers through designing their own digital learning games (small games) in cross-disciplinary subject matter.

The learning-through-game-design approach in the current investigation has its origins in a problem-based learning approach combined with a constructionist pedagogical methodology built upon the thesis that there is a strong connection between design and learning and that activity that involves making, building, or programming provides a rich context for learning (Papert, 1980; Kafai & Resnick, 1996). Since 80% of teachers that use games in class wish that it was easier to find curriculum-aligned games (Takeuchi & Vaala, 2014), the current study offers a new way to create game-based learning designs that are designed for and aligned to curricula.

THE GLOBAL CLASSROOM AS LEARNING ENVIRONMENT

An extended aspect of this investigation, one that this chapter will not have room to address, was that the learning took place in Global Classroom at VUC. The Global Classroom concept is a hybrid synchronous virtual and campus-based videoconference concept (Weitze, 2014a, 2014b). In this learning environment, students can choose, on a daily basis, whether they want to participate on campus or from home. This has forced many of the VUC teachers to alter their previous motivational pedagogical strategies to match the hybrid synchronous learning environment. Therefore, this study also aimed to develop new motivational pedagogical strategies for this type of learning environment. Along with an analysis of the game-based environment, the study additionally describes potentials of and barriers to conducting this kind of teaching in a hybrid synchronous learning environment. This is new research regarding the combination of the target group, the learning environment, the gamified learning-game design, and the students implementing curricular learning goals into digital games.

RESEARCH OBJECTIVE AND METHODOLOGY

This study was part of an iterative project that investigated how to create innovative and engaging learning designs for students. The investigation was conducted as a design-based research (DBR) study, in which the teachers and students are important co-designers in the development and test process. To investigate how the learning-game design experiments answer the research questions, the study used mixed methods. The data included field notes, audio- and videotaped actions and utterances, observations from the workshops, semi-structured interviews with teachers after each workshop, semi-structured interviews with students after the final workshop, informal meetings, evaluation documents written by the students, questionnaires, videos of students' games being discussed and play-tested, and the students' digital games themselves. The analysis was performed by coding the transcribed data with Thornberg's (2012) informed grounded theory approach. In informed grounded theory, the researcher is informed by the existing research literature combined with using a grounded theory approach to analyse the empirical data, with the premise that every code, concept, or theoretical idea the researcher constructs must be grounded in data using grounded theory methods (Charmaz, 2006). The analysis was thus carried out as concept-driven coding (using concepts from the theory and previous empirical data to find themes in the data) and as data-driven coding (reading the data and searching for new phenomena which are not known from previous preconceptions of the subject).

The questions for the research process were as follows: (1) Which elements, practices, and processes are essential when creating sustainable, innovative, and motivating learning designs for teachers and adult students engaged in learning by building games? (2) How does the gamified learning design contribute to enabling a cognitively complex and motivating learning process? (3) How can learning-game design be used as a means of learning by teachers and students who are game-design novices? (4) What are the potentials of and barriers to using the current learning design in a hybrid synchronous learning environment?

The investigation developed over three iterations, from spring 2014 to spring 2015. The empirical data from the research process involved the following: (1) observations of teaching practices in a Global Classroom; (2) questionnaire surveys of students and teachers from a Global Classroom; (3) one workshop and three meetings with the involved teachers: continuous interviews with the teacher team and debriefings, (4) three five-hour learning-game design workshops with students, and (5) material from student workshops, game concepts, play-test videos, the game homepage, play-test questionnaires, and learning-design documentation.

RESEARCH DESIGN

The research was a DBR study in three iterations, with two iterations at VUC taking place in spring 2014 and spring 2015. A shorter iteration in the autumn of 2014 experimented with a specific part of the learning design: the conceptualisation of *what a learning design is* and how to help students imagine *how to implement learning into a game beyond the quiz-level.*

In the third iteration, in spring 2015, two teachers and 19 students from a Global Classroom participated in an investigation on designing learning games that implemented specific subject matter: history and English as a second language. The learning goals focused on the American Civil War, human rights, and the emancipation of the slaves; the sources used and the game dialogue were expected to be in English.

The teachers initially participated in a workshop with the researcher. They were introduced to the overall learning design and tried some of the methods. Before the student workshops, the teachers briefly introduced the students to the subject matter, showed a film about the subject, and introduced a few relevant texts. The teachers and students then participated in three five-hour workshops. The researcher presented the initial ideas about learning by creating games for the students. The students conceptualised the learning games, built paper prototypes, and transformed them into digital learning games supported by the overall gamified learning environment. The students formed teams that collaborated and competed in a friendly way.

LEARNING AND MOTIVATION

In the first iteration (spring, 2014), the students worked with the game-design process as an evaluation of subject areas from prior lectures. This left the students with the feeling that they did not really learn anything new as they were only repeating and remembering the previously learned subject matter as they built their learning games. In the third iteration, the teachers agreed on a problem-based learning (PBL) approach. In PBL students engage in a learning process by being presented to a problem and are asked to apply reasoning, questioning, research, and critical thinking to find a solution for this problem (Savery, 2015). The PBL approach involved the students creating digital learning games while choosing specific learning goals for their games within the scope of the teacher's overall learning goals for the class. By taking a problem-based approach, one of the aims was that the students reached higher levels of cognitive complexity in relation to working with their learning goals. That is, that they moved beyond the cognitive complexity level of *remembering* their subject matter and additionally were able to work on *understanding, applying, analysing, evaluating,* and *creating* (Bloom & Krathwohl, 1956; Anderson & Krathwohl, 2001, pp. 67–68). The purpose of choosing the PBL approach was thus to deepen the learning process for the students.

As already stated it was crucial for the teachers to be able to motivate the students to learn. For us to learn something, it must ideally take place in an atmosphere we enjoy being in, and we must be interested in what we have to learn (Illeris, 2007). Therefore, the aim was to create interesting and motivating learning activities for the students. Motivation can be defined as 'the process whereby goal-directed activity is instigated and sustained' (Schunk, Meece, & Pintrich, 2010, p. 6), and motivation to learn is defined as 'the tendency to find learning activities meaningful and worthwhile and to benefit from them—to try to make sense of the information available, relate this information to prior knowledge and attempt to gain the knowledge and skills the activity develops' (Wlodkowski, 2011, p. 5).

But how can we acquire the motivation to learn? In their self-determination theory (SDT) Deci and Ryan (2000) describe how motivation can be regarded as a spectrum that goes from intrinsic motivation to extrinsic motivation. Intrinsic motivation can be characterised as the feeling that we are doing an activity for the inherent satisfaction of the activity itself and is regarded as highly autonomous. Extrinsic motivation, on the other hand, can feel more or less regulated; we may feel that we are invited—or 'forced'—to do something. According to Deci and Ryan (2000) the continuum of extrinsic motivation begins with the feeling of doing something we may not feel that motivated to do, but we understand the benefit we will have of doing it in the long run and therefore we decide to do it, that is, integrated regulation. At the other end of the extrinsic motivation continuum is external regulation; here there is very little motivation to do something, but we choose to do it because we are rewarded if we engage in doing it or perhaps punished if we do not. Though the educational system inherently uses extrinsic motivation in the form of rewarding grades, etc., the teachers always try to spark intrinsic motivation to learn in their students since we all prefer to do something because of the intrinsic satisfaction of engaging in the activity.

According to Bruner (1966) the three main underlying forces that drive our intrinsic motivation to learn are (1) curiosity: the desire and freedom to explore things and decide for yourself, (2) the feeling of achieving competence, and (3) reciprocity: the desire to be an indispensable part of the community. These three main motivations to a great extent resemble Deci and Ryan's SDT, as SDT argues that to achieve inner motivation, an individual should be reinforced in autonomy, competence, and relatedness and that these are vital for covering the essential psychological needs (Deci & Ryan, 2000). Bruner's (1966) and Deci and Ryan's (2000) principles for intrinsic motivation are represented in the lower part of the Smiley Model (Figure 8.2; Weitze, 2016). In applying these principles to the learning activities in this study, the intention was to build these motivational forces into the learning design of the game-based learning approach as a means for creating opportunities to spark the students' feelings of curiosity, autonomy, competence, and relatedness in order to spur the students' intrinsic motivation to learn. The intension was also to create and support the motivating learning processes by applying the game elements represented in the Smiley Model to the learning design (Figure 8.2).

LEARNING-DESIGN AND GAME-DESIGN APPROACHES

The big Game and the small games: In this study, the goal was to create a motivating learning experience for the students. The overall learning design was made into a game in which the students formed teams and created digital learning games that encompassed learning goals from the curriculum. The term *learning design* describes how a teacher shapes social processes and creates conditions for learning as well as the phenomenon of the individual student constantly recreating or redesigning information in his own meaning-creating processes (Selander & Kress, 2012, p. 2; Laurillard, 2012). In this investigation, the teacher was the learning designer, but the students were also their own learning designers as they discussed the subject matter, found content, and negotiated how to implement learning into the small digital games.

The literacy and learning-game theorist James Paul Gee (2011) uses the terms *little 'g' game* and *big 'G' Game*. By using these expressions, he distinguishes between the learning and play processes that takes place inside the little digital game versus 'outside', in the big Game, in all the interactions between the players/learners as they discuss and negotiate the content, intention, and meanings in the little game learning during this process (Gee, 2011). The purpose of gamifying the learning-game design process was to engage the students but also to structure and scaffold the students' creation of the small games (see Weitze, 2014a, 2014b for elaboration of this gamified scaffolding). This was necessary to be able to guide the game-design novices—both students and teachers—through the learning process.

The aim of the learning project was thus that students would discuss, negotiate, and finally master the intended learning goals while building and implementing these learning goals into the little game. In other words, *the student game designers are learning inside the big Game while designing the small games* (Figure 8.1). As in the first iteration of this investigation (spring, 2014), the goal was that the students afterward should be able to play each other's digital games while learning and being evaluated in the relevant subject matter in and around these learning games. In this third iteration (spring, 2015), three out of four teams reached this goal; it was possible to learn about the subject matter by playing the digital games. However, the learning process and experience of building the games—the big Game—was a more cognitively complex learning experience for the students (Weitze, 2015a).

In the first iteration (spring, 2014), the teachers were hesitant and left the teaching process to the scaffolded learning design document; they did not participate actively in the students' learning process. On the basis of these previous findings, one of the goals for this third iteration was to facilitate teachers' participation in the big Game (Figure 8.1) as a way to qualify and deepen students' learning processes.

The Smiley Model: To inspire and scaffold the gamified learning process in both the big Game and the small games, this research project used the Smiley Model (Figure 8.2; Weitze, 2016), a learning-game design model for creating engaging

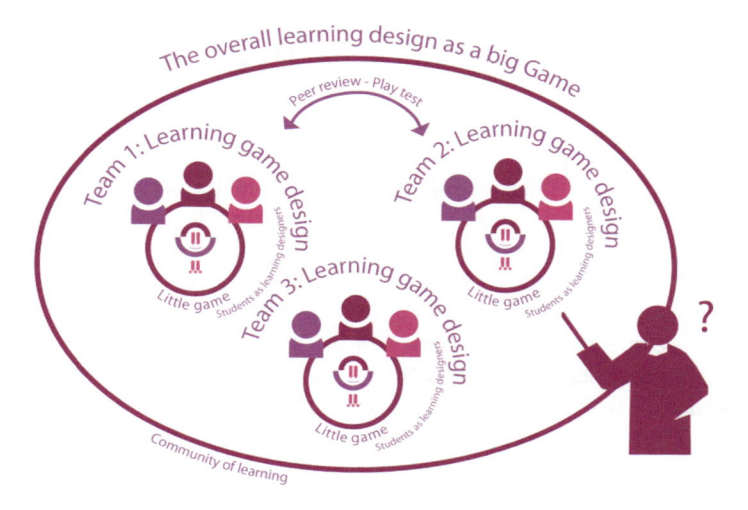

Figure 8.1. The gamified learning design and considerations about the teacher's role (Weitze, 2015a)

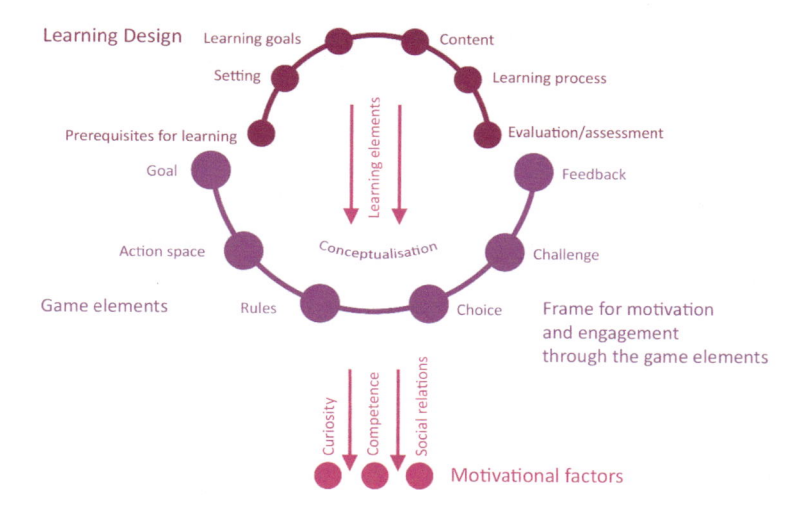

Figure 8.2. The Smiley Model (Weitze, 2016)

learning games (see Weitze, 2014a, 2014b, 2016 for a more elaborate explanation of this model and its implementation).

The Smiley Model starts out by describing the *learning design* of the game (Figure 8.2, top). Learning elements from the learning design are then set into play by using traditional game elements (goals, action space, rules, choice, challenge, feedback) (Figure 8.2) while also considering and designing for the previously

149

described motivational factors. The points in the model were used as inspirational guidelines for how to create the learning designs in the big Game and small games.

THEORETICAL AND GROUNDED ANALYSIS OF THE EMPIRICAL DATA

The empirical analysis of the overall learning design in this investigation found *four parallel types of processes for designing and learning* in the big Game (Figure 8.3): (1) the structured game-design process with carefully designed assignments for the students (with the Smiley Model as a frame); (2) concept-building processes: the use of prototype materials for conceptualisation and learning—learning by creating. These materials were changing through the learning process; (3) teaching processes: the teachers' involvement points and strategies as they supported, guided, and qualified the learning processes and provided formative assessment; and, most importantly, (4) according to Illeris (2007), student engagement in individual (acquisition), collaborative (social), and motivational (incentive) learning processes for learning to take place. As the students negotiated about and created the conceptual and physical/digital learning games they engaged in these three dimensions of learning.

Since the four areas (Figure 8.3) are interwoven this is an artificial division, but an elaboration of these four areas will increase knowledge about how the learning design works as well as how and where the teacher can support students' learning

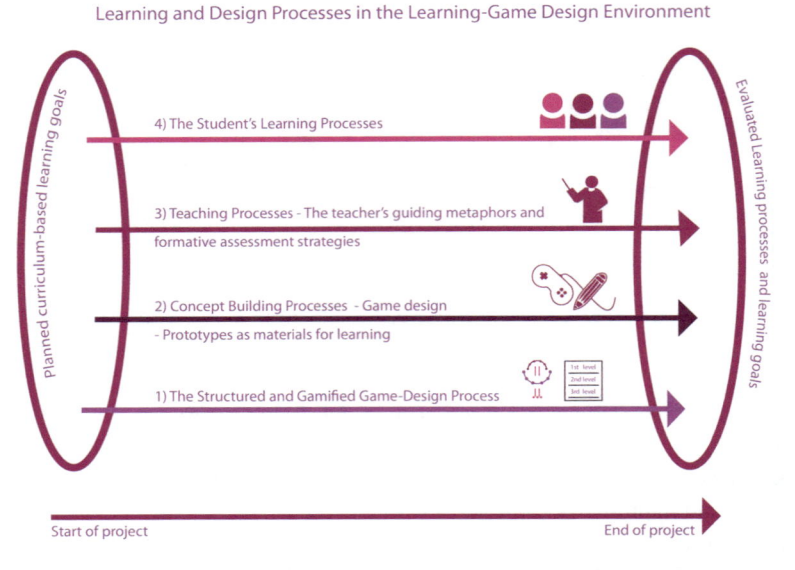

Figure 8.3. Various process types of learning and designing in the learning-game design environment

processes in this reusable learning-game design environment. The processes are explained below.

The Structured Game-Design Process

The goal was to create a sustainable learning design that could be used by both the students and the teacher—all novices in regard to learning-game design. But building a learning game can be a challenge for novices; therefore the learning design was scaffolded into a big Game with 25 levels/missions for the teams, with three to five questions or assignments at each level. This also involved the possibility for the students to gain EXP as they progressed through the levels. As the students worked through the assignments, they would create specific learning goals for their small games, make exercises in the game-design tool, build analogue prototypes of their games, gather information and discuss how to design specific learning goals and learning activities into their games, and finally transform their analogue prototypes into digital games. The levels and assignments for the big Game were presented in an online Google Document for each team, and here they could also write down the points they earned in the process. The overall scoreboard for the teams was presented on a webpage for the big Game. This offered equal access for the students in class and those at home. The levels were established to create a logical progression and to break the assignments down into easily understandable tasks to guide the students and lessen the level of difficulty, which otherwise could make them give up and lose self-esteem.

The overall inspirational framework for the big Game was, as noted earlier, the Smiley Model (Weitze, 2016). The big Game was designed to engage and motivate the students, inspired by Bruner's (1966) motivational forces. The intention was threefold:

1. *To spark curiosity* by introducing students to this new way of learning and by letting them choose how to design their own games and their own learning paths;
2. *To enable the feeling of achieving competence* by asking students to develop the small games and by having them move through the levels of the big Game, gaining EXP; and
3. *To enable the feeling of reciprocity* by letting students work together on a team and compete with other teams, gaining social experience points (SXP) for working together and for asking other teams for help.

In addition to the Smiley Model, the project used innovative methods from Design Thinking (Brown, 2009) and other interaction design methods in the assignments and invited students to sketch and prototype the small games. The teams were invited to play-test or peer-review each other's games in each workshop to deepen the learning process; this had been an engaging experience for the students in the first iteration, and by discussing and playing each other's games, the students learned what was taught about the subject matter through the other teams' small games. The students were also introduced to an example of a learning game in the chosen software

(Scratch, 2015), and from the beginning of the workshops the students carried out small tutorials for using the software as part of the assignments.

In the first workshop on day one, the individual teams worked diligently through the levels in the big Game. The students found it easy to understand and move through the levels. It worked well to introduce the teams to the game-design tool Scratch (2015) in some of the first assignments. This gave them a feeling for how this tool might prove helpful in the final learning-game version. As recommended from the first iteration (spring, 2014), the levels had both mandatory and voluntary tasks. The voluntary tasks gradually became more demanding to encourage teams to compete by going deeper into the learning process of each assignment instead of racing superficially through the levels in order to win. However, the finding in the third iteration was that the big Game still needed tweaking to find that delicate balance between keeping levels simple and challenging the teams to engage deeply in the process of learning-game design and provide good learning experiences to the teams themselves as well as to those who will eventually play their games.

In the second and third workshops, on days two and three of the third iteration, the teams took more differentiated and individual paths (the rules of the big Game allowed this). Two teams completed almost all the levels in the big Game, whereas the other two teams worked more freely on their learning games without collecting EXP. This independent way of working may have been caused by this second pair of teams working so well and intensely together. These teams worked with the concept development phases in a very effortless way and, according to the observations and the teachers' utterances, achieved a feeling of being on the right track, being competent, and heading toward their end goal: the finished digital learning game. These two teams thus solved the learning-game design assignments in a more self-driven manner. This movement from the rule-based big Game, solving every assignment, to a more sandbox-like big Game, where the teams were more self-directed and decided which task to solve next, can be seen as a movement between the two poles in the spectrum of human play: between Ludus and Paidia. The *Ludus* concept can be described as game-like structured activities with rule-based goals, whereas *Paidia* is the play-like, player-led activities with open goals (Caillois, 2001; Walz & Deterding, 2015). The Paidia end of the spectrum emphasises opportunities to let students decide their own learning goals, which harmonises well with constructionist pedagogies. The observed movement away from more structured assignments can also be interpreted as moving from extrinsic-motivated learning processes, with fixed assignments and points, to more intrinsic-motivated processes, with students taking responsibility for the progression of the project. That said, the learning situation still took place within a formal learning environment in which students had to attend to pass.

According to the teachers, the students working in the teams that remained at the Ludus (rule-based) end of the human play spectrum in the big Game were students who often found more traditional teaching situations difficult. Their choice of the more scaffolded and rule-based path in the big Game may indicate that they felt more comfortable solving assignments that were broken down into smaller tasks. The study therefore suggests that the big Game allowed flexibility for students to work according to their own preferences in regard to the Ludus or Paidia end of the human play spectrum, depending on the amount of support they required to have an experience of a successful learning process. The structure of the big Game worked well, especially in the first two workshops. But there were also findings that will inform further modifications—for example, limiting the number of assignments in the big Game design.

Concept-Building Processes: Prototypes as Materials for Learning and Learning by Creating

In the structure for the big Game, certain assignments were designed so students would use a variety of prototype materials. The use of paper and other materials for prototypes enables a fast iterative process, making the materials a visual and tangible language with which to discuss ideas and learn in this process (Buxton, 2007; Schøn, 1992). The teams chose many different types of materials: an old-fashioned blackboard, a whiteboard with sticky notes, and large prototype landscapes as means for discussing ideas for the learning games. Some students chose to begin working in the software parallel to the sketches they made (Figure 8.4). This was a fertile and useful process for all the teams. They had the opportunity to conceptualise and externalise their visions. This constructionist approach gave them a *concrete sensory language* that enabled them to project their ideas into the materials and discuss a variety of ideas for implementing the learning goals into the learning games in a way that integrated a learning process and an evaluation process for future players of their games. These processes enabled the students to use the materials as means for learning.

Figure 8.4. Prototypes: Materials for learning

The prototypes were also helpful as discussion facilitators or partners when conceptualising systems thinking for the games. For example, members of one team, with the help of the elements in the prototypes, discussed their game's storyline and game-mechanics by demonstrating and telling what should happen in the game. This gave the team an opportunity to discover blind spots and missing connections when developing the game. The use of prototypes as discussion facilitators helped them to learn about historical correlations, conditionality, and causalities. Systems thinking could thus be used and developed if there were contingent relations between things happening in the game (correlations), if a situation was conditioned by another situation (conditionality), or if one thing in the game produced a change in another part (causality). In this particular game, the actions of the northern U.S. states influenced the enemy in the southern states to take new actions, and the students learned a great deal from their thorough investigations into the actions and reactions between the northern and southern states when creating the concept for the game.

One important finding from the first iteration (spring, 2014) was that the game-design software was too difficult; for some students, this stopped the whole game-design process. In the third iteration (spring, 2015), we used Scratch (*Scratch, 2018*) and the built-in tutorials in the Scratch software. The learning community around Scratch and the opportunity to be inspired by and learn from other games made a significant positive difference. Scratch's training assignments were also tasks in the big Game, and all students were able to use the software. Some of the students looked for alternative software with more advanced game-design features or more aesthetically pleasing graphics. One team chose to use RGBMaker (a good but somewhat more difficult alternative; RPGMaker, 2018), but all other teams decided to create their games using Scratch.

In the first iteration (spring, 2014), some of the students in the cross-over groups (those that included both in-class and at-home students) collaborated by sharing the computer screen using TeamViewer (2018). This enabled all the students to watch and discuss the game development from their own devices as one student began to create the digital game. In the third iteration (spring, 2015), the teachers advised the classroom students in the cross-over groups to move into a room with a large video screen (Figure 8.5). This reduced noise distraction from other groups and enabled students to work on their laptop-screens instead of using them for the videoconference communication with other team members. In general, the classroom

Figure 8.5. Students collaborate over videoconference with additional larger screens

students handled the material development phase, and the at-home students took part in the collaborative discussions or participated in the group work by searching the Internet for information for the learning-game design. Though a variety of interactive collaborative tools were used throughout these iterations, it was found to be difficult to find tools that can replace the physical materials for students working remotely. There were, however, no limitations in working with the web-based Scratch game-design software for the at-home students.

Teaching Processes: The Teacher's Guiding Metaphors
and Formative Assessment Strategies

In this study, there was a strong focus on involving the teachers in the learning situation to enable a cognitively complex and motivating learning process for the students. In the first iteration, in spring 2014, many of the students produced quiz games. The learning process facilitated in these quiz games was shallow; the player would not learn inside the game but instead had to know the answers in advance to be able to solve and win the game. Therefore, the accomplished knowledge remained at the lowest level of cognitive complexity: *remembrance*. The learning processes that took place in the big Game as students designed the small games was limited to searching for questions and answers in the text. The teachers also found it difficult to identify their role in the process as students worked their way through the structured game-design process. In the spring 2015 iteration, however, the teachers were instructed by findings from the previous research and co-designed a new teaching approach. This resulted in the development and use of various concepts or metaphors to guide the students in their learning-game development process. The concepts or metaphors used by the teachers as they held discussions with the students can be divided into these four areas, as follows:

1. *Scratch software and mind map.* The teachers were introduced to (and later used) an example of a learning game in the Scratch software (see Weitze, 2015b for elaboration of this learning game example). This was supplemented with a mind map to illustrate how the learning goals were designed within the game. The game and the mind map conceptualised an example of how to enable a learning process as well as an evaluation process in a small game (equivalent to the learning design in the upper part of the Smiley Model, Figure 8.2). To create effective learning games there is a need to integrate the learning goals into the game mechanics (what you can do in the game; Weitze, 2014c). The teachers therefore also discussed how learning goals could be implemented within game mechanics as well as the game goals with the students.

2. *Narrative building and community of practice.* Communities of practice (CoP) can be characterised as a group of people that shares knowledge and learns together (Wenger, 2004). The teachers discussed with the students how to build a narrative inside the game, represented in the small games as a small CoP, to simulate real-life learning situations in the small games. In the small game, the

learner (through a game character) was able to learn about the learning goals in the 'real' (game) learning situations. This *narrative building and CoP* concept builds on findings from the first iteration (Weitze, 2014a), where this metaphor helped students create learning situations inside the small games.

3. *Discussions about systems thinking and game elements.* In the big Game, the teachers participated in discussions with the students about how to develop an understanding of systems thinking and cause and effects for the subject matter taught in their games (Meadows, 2008). In these discussions, the prototypes were used to discuss how various choices in the game would have various consequences; which goals, challenges, rules, and feedback would be relevant to create in the games; and how to evaluate inside the game (the game elements from the lower part of the Smiley Model, Figure 8.2).

4. *Meta-reflections about learning goals, formative assessment, and support of learning processes.* Throughout the process, the teachers continually returned to the stated learning goals. They discussed and made formative assessments in collaboration with the students. According to observations and the teachers' utterances, this facilitated a cognitively complex learning process, making the students more conscious of the learning goals and more meta-reflective about whether they were reaching them. It also gave the students an opportunity for self-assessment: How much were they actually learning while they were engaged in this innovative learning process, designing learning games as a means for learning? Did they achieve their learning goals? The observations showed that the teacher supported the students in all three dimensions of the learning process: (1) the inner psychological process of acquisition (content dimension), (2) the interpersonal interaction dimension (collaborative learning), and (3) the willingness and desire to deal with what should be learned (the motivational dimension). The teachers found it easy to guide the students. They used the same approach to guide and evaluate that they would have used in traditional PBL. Their experience and opinions were that the students had learned at least as much, and in most cases, more, as they would have learned with the more traditional learning approaches the teachers normally used. The teachers found it easy to teach with this game-based approach and went further by deciding on new subject matter and themes for similar game-based learning designs.

The Students' Learning Processes

The students were involved in both individual (acquisition) and collaborative learning processes. Cooperative work is when partners split the work, solve sub-tasks individually, and then assemble the partial results into the final output, whereas in collaborative work the partners do the work 'together'. They negotiate and share meanings relevant to the problem-solving task at hand (Dillenbourg, 1999). At times, the students worked cooperatively and divided the tasks among themselves; at other times, they discussed and carried out the steps in a process of collaboration.

According to the teachers' utterances and the observations, the work was divided among group members to a greater extent in the groups that included at-home students, whereas the in-class groups demonstrated higher levels of collaboration with more coordinated, synchronous group activity. However, according to the teachers, one notable advantage of this learning design was that the students had high levels of collaboration and discussion and were involved in social interaction and learning processes with each other to a much greater extent than they had previously demonstrated (the students had been in this class for five months). Normally, the students only conversed with a few other students in class, and during the breaks they frequently sat by their computers without talking. This social development was a positive gain that contributed to a deeper learning process, based on the observation that the students had previously been quiet and did not contribute during the lessons. This enhanced engagement in social interaction in other words gave the students new opportunities to engage in conversations and debates and thereby learn with and from each other. Since some of these students had motivational issues in formal learning situations, this was an important result and finding. This high level of collaboration was the same in all three iterations of the study (spring, 2014–2015).

Pedagogical approach: The PBL approach resulted in a more cognitively complex learning process for the students as they spent a great deal of time searching for reliable and relevant sources and thus learned about the subject in the process. The students also discussed how to implement their research in appropriate learning situations and trajectories inside the small games; this was, according to the teachers and the students themselves, a vital contribution to their deep learning process. In this process, the students became their own learning designers, and the analysis of the students' and teachers' utterances suggests that these meta-discussions about learning design contributed to their understanding of their own learning processes as self-directed learners.

CONCLUSION

This DBR study brings us one step closer toward creating a reusable gamified learning design for adult students working in teams to create curriculum-based digital learning games. The goals for this learning design were to provide the teams themselves with a cognitively complex and motivating learning experience by challenging them to design learning games as well as to challenge the teams to design games that provide relevant learning experiences to those who will eventually play them. Consequently, the maker-culture and its potential constructionist pedagogical approach—learning by creating—can also be used in formal learning situations with adult students, enabling motivating and cognitively complex learning processes.

The big Game—the gamified learning design—supported the students as well as the teachers through *four parallel types of processes for designing and learning*: (1) the structured game-design process; (2) concept-building processes in which prototypes served as materials for learning; (3) teaching processes in which the teacher's learning- and game-inspired metaphors were used to support the learning processes in the big and small gamified learning designs; and (4) the students' individual, collaborative, and motivational learning processes. The teachers found it easy to support and evaluate the students' learning processes with the help of concepts and metaphors guiding the students in their learning-game development process. The teachers observed an increase in socially engaged interactions among the students, a fact that contributed to more cognitive complexity and learning processes with more collaborative activity.

The students' movement through the big Game evolved from a rule-based approach (Ludus), sticking to the rules and levels, toward a more sandbox-like approach (Paidia), with some of the teams moving more freely and taking their own paths while creating the small games. This suggests a movement away from a more extrinsic motivation to participate in the gamified learning process among some of the students toward a more intrinsic motivation to design learning games. The learning design corresponds well with a constructionist and problem-based pedagogical approach.

Parts of the gamified learning design still need tweaking, and future studies could examine whether this design can be scaled up and reused with new students and teachers. This would be interesting to test in the future. Smaller investigations with younger children already indicate that they, too, can benefit from learning through designing curriculum-based digital learning games. This learning design can work in a hybrid synchronous learning environment, as the project has demonstrated. There have, however, been limitations in the work regarding access to physical materials for students participating from home; the classroom students primarily conducted the work requiring the use of physical prototypes. It is nevertheless equally possible for students in class and at home to work with the game design software. That said, though Scratch (2015) gives possibilities for sharing content and copying each other's projects in order to learn, the development of game-design software that afforded extended types of co-creation would have potential in this hybrid synchronous learning environment since this would give opportunities for more collaborative learning processes for students in class and students at home.

REFERENCES

Anderson, L. W., & Krathwohl, D. R. (Eds.). (2001). *A taxonomy for learning, teaching and assessing: A revision of bloom's taxonomy of educational objectives*. New York, NY: Longman.

Bloom, B. S., & Krathwohl, D. R. (1956). *Taxonomy of educational objectives: The classification of educational goals, by a committee of college and university examiners. Handbook 1: Cognitive domain*. New York, NY: Longman.

Brennan, K. (2014, January 8–9). *Social dimensions of computing education*. Presented at the Future Directions in Computing Education Summit, Orlando, FL.

Brennan, K., & Resnick, M. (2012, April 13–17). *New frameworks for studying and assessing the development of computational thinking*. Proceedings of the 2012 Annual Meeting of the American Educational Research Association, Vancouver, Canada.

Brown, T. (2009). *Change by design*. New York, NY: Harper Collins.

Bruner, J. S. (1966). *Toward a theory of instruction*. Cambridge, MA: Harvard University Press.

Buxton, B. (2007). *Sketching user experience: Getting design right and the right design* (pp. 102–143). San Francisco, CA: Morgan Kaufmann.

Caillois, R. (2001). *Man, play and games*. Chicago, IL: University of Illinois Press.

Charmaz, K. (2006). *Constructing grounded theory: A practical guide through qualitative research*. London: Sage Publications.

Deci, E. L., & Ryan, R. M. (2000). Self-determination theory and the facilitation of intrinsic motivation, social development, and well-being. *American Psychologist, 55*(1), 68–78.

Deterding, S., Dixon, D., Khaled, R., & Nacke, L. (2011, September 28–30). *From game design elements to gamefulness: Defining gamification* (pp. 9–15). Proceedings of the Academic MindTrek Conference, Tampere, Finland.

Dillenbourg, P. (1999). What do you mean by collaborative learning? In P. Dillenbourg (Ed.), *Collaborative learning: Cognitive and computational approaches* (pp. 1–19). Oxford: Elsevier.

ESA (Entertainment Software Association). (2014). *The 2014 essential facts about the computer and video game industry*. Retrieved from http://www.theesa.com/wp-content/uploads/2014/10/ESA_EF_2014.pdf

Gee, J. P. (2011). Reflections on empirical evidence on games and learning. In S. Tobias & J. D. Fletcher (Eds.), *Computer games and instruction* (pp. 223–232). Charlotte, NC: Information Age Publishing.

Harel, I. E., & Papert, S. E. (1991). *Constructionism*. New York, NY: Ablex Publishing.

Hatch, M. (2013). *The maker movement manifesto: Rules for innovation in the new world of crafters, hackers, and tinkerers*. New York, NY: McGraw-Hill.

Hutters, C., Katznelson, N., Sørensen, N. U., & Juul, T. M. (2013). *Unges motivation og læring: 12 eksperter om motivationskrisen i uddannelsessystemet*. Copenhagen: Hans Reitzels Forlag.

Illeris, K. (2007b). *How we learn: Learning and non-learning in school and beyond*. London: Routledge.

Kafai, Y. B. (2006). Playing and making games for learning instructionist and constructionist perspectives for game studies. *Games and Culture, 1*(1), 36–40.

Kafai, Y. B., & Resnick, M. (1996). *Constructionism in practice: Designing, thinking, and learning in a digital world*. New York, NY: Routledge.

Kapp, K. M. (2012). *The gamification of learning and instruction: Game-based methods and strategies for training and education*. San Francisco, CA: Pfeiffer.

Koh, J. H. L., Chai, C. S., Wong, B., & Hong, H. Y. (2015). *Design thinking for education: Conceptions and applications in teaching and learning*. Singapore: Springer.

Laurillard, D. (2012). *Teaching as a design science: Building pedagogical patterns for learning and technology*. New York, NY: Routledge.

Liu, M., Hsieh, P., Cho, Y., & Schallert, D. (2006). Middle school students' self-efficacy, attitudes, and achievement in a computer-enhanced problem-based learning environment. *Journal of Interactive Learning Research, 17*(3), 225–242.

Meadows, D. H., & Wright, D. (2008). *Thinking in systems: A primer*. London: Earthscan.

Papert, S. (1980). *Mindstorms: Children, computers, and powerful ideas*. New York, NY: Basic Books.

Pless, M., & Hansen, N. H. M. (2010). *Hf på VUC-et andet valg*. Center for Ungdomsforskning, Emdrup: DPU, Aarhus Universitet.

Santrock, J. (2006). Cognitive and language development. In J. W. Santrock (Ed.), *Educational psychology*. Boston, MA: McGraw Hill.

Savery, J. R. (2015). Overview of problem-based learning: Definitions and distinctions. In A. Walker, H. Leary, C. E. Hmelo-Silver, & P. Ertmer (Eds.), *Essential readings in problem-based learning: Exploring and extending the legacy of Howard S. Barrows* (pp. 5–15). Lafayette, IN: Purdue University Press.

Schön, D. A. (1992). Designing as reflective conversation with the materials of a design situation. *Knowledge-Based Systems, 5*(1), 3–14.

Schunk, D. H., Meece, J. R., & Pintrich, P. R. (2010). *Motivation in education: Theory, research, and applications* (3rd ed.). Upper Saddle River, NJ: Pearson.

Seaborn, K., & Fels, D. I. (2015). Gamification in theory and action: A survey. *International Journal of Human Computer Studies, 74*, 14–31.

Selander, S., & Kress, G. (2012). *Læringsdesign i et multimodalt perspektiv*. Copenhagen: Frydenlund.

Sheldon, L. (2012). *The multiplayer classroom: Designing coursework as a game*. Boston, MA: Cengage Learning.

Takeuchi, L. M., & Vaala, S. (2014). *Level up learning: A national survey on teaching with digital games*. New York, NY: The Joan Ganz Cooney Center at Sesame Workshop.

Thornberg, R. (2012). Informed grounded theory. *Scandinavian Journal of Educational Research, 56*(3), 243–259.

Walz, S. P., & Deterding, S. (2015). *The gameful world: Approaches, issues, applications*. Cambridge, MA: MIT Press.

Weitze, C. L. (2014a). *An experiment on how adult students can learn by designing engaging learning games*. Ann Arbor, MI: University of Michigan Press.

Weitze, C. L. (2014b). *Experimenting on how to create a sustainable gamified learning design that supports adult students when learning through designing learning games* (Vol. 2, pp. 594–603). Proceedings of the 8th European Conference on Games Based Learning, Berlin, Germany.

Weitze, C. L. (2014c). Developing goals and objectives for gameplay and learning. In K. Shrier (Ed.), *Learning, education and games* (pp. 225–249). Pittsburgh, PA: ETC Press.

Weitze, C. L. (2015a). *Learning and motivational processes when students design curriculum-based digital learning games* (pp. 579–588). Proceedings of the 9th European Conference on Games Based Learning, Steinkjer, Norway.

Weitze, C. L. (2015b). *Designing for learning and play: The smiley model as a framework*. Paper presented at Chitaly 2015, Rome, Italy. Retrieved from http://palx.inf.unibz.it/papers/Weitze.pdf

Weitze, C. L. (2015c). *Pedagogical innovation in teacher teams: An organisational learning design model for continuous competence development, ECEL 2015*. Hatfield: University of Hertfordshire.

Weitze, C. L. (2016). Designing for learning and play: The smiley model as framework. *Interaction Design and Architecture(s) Journal—IxD&A* (Special issue: Player and Learner eXperience).

Wenger, E. (2004). *Praksisfællesskaber: Læring, mening og identitet*. Copenhagen: Hans Reitzel.

Wlodkowski, R. J. (2011). *Enhancing adult motivation to learn: A comprehensive guide for teaching all adults*. Chichester: John Wiley & Sons.

Software

RPGMaker [Computer software]. (2018). Retrieved from http://www.rpgmakerweb.com

Scratch [Computer software]. (2018). Developed by the *Lifelong Kindergarten Group at the MIT Media Lab*. Retrieved from http://scratch.mit.edu

Teamviewer [Computer software]. (2018). Retrieved from https://www.teamviewer.com/da/index.aspx

CAROLINE CRUAUD

9. DESIGNING WITH TEACHERS

Contrasting Teachers' Experiences of the Implementation of a Gamified Application for Foreign Language Learners

ABSTRACT

Developing new gamified educational resources or educational games takes time, and it is natural to want to ensure the success of their integration in the classroom. For this reason, it is important to look at the role of the teacher before and during the implementation. However, research on gamification and game-based learning has been focused on students, and very little has been said about teachers (Kenny & McDaniel, 2011). This study contrasts two teachers' experiences of the implementation of a gamified app with regard to their participation in the design process. Interviews with teachers and video data from the classroom have been analysed to find out how the teachers experienced the implementation and in what ways their involvement in the project is reflected in their respective experiences and in the accounts of their experiences. The analysis reveals that the two teachers have had very different experiences of the implementation. Where the first teacher developed familiarity with and ownership over the application, the second teacher felt lost and stopped using it. Involving teachers through co-design or using flexible instructional designs has advantages, but other factors should be considered when implementing new resources (e.g., class context, teachers' previous experience, teacher training). This study opens up new questions on the teacher's role in the integration of games and gamified applications in the classroom but also raises the issue of their potential participation in the design of new resources.

Keywords: gamification, co-design, design-based research, teachers, game-based learning

INTRODUCTION

The research interest for gamification of education is quite recent (Kapp, 2012). Gamified practices are supposed to engage students in their learning by using game principles to promote playful and learner-centred class activities. Most studies have been focused on the student's side of the implementation of new applications or games (Berns, Palomo-Duarte, Dodero, & Cejas, 2014; Berns, Palomo-Duarte,

Dodero, & Valero-Franco, 2013; Chik, 2012; Perry, 2015; Reinders & Wattana, 2012). There has been very little focus on teachers, despite their importance to the success of the integration of modern technologies or new instructional designs (Ketelhut & Schifter, 2011). We need to know more about the role of the teacher in the implementation of games and gamified applications in the classroom, since creating additional resources is useless if teachers are not using them.

This chapter describes the design process of a web-based application for French as a foreign language in Norwegian high schools and focuses on the teachers' experiences with the implementation process. In this project, two teachers participated in the design of the application in collaboration with researchers and designers. It is interesting to look at their experience of the implementation of the application in regard to their involvement in its design. Interviews with the teachers and video data from the classroom are used to answer the following questions:

- How did the teachers experience the implementation of a gamified application in their classrooms?
- In what ways is the teachers' involvement in the design process reflected in their experiences and in the accounts of their experiences?

By contrasting the experiences of two teachers included in the project, this chapter illustrates the importance of taking the teacher's role into account when designing and introducing gamified tools into the classroom.

DESIGN-BASED RESEARCH WITH TEACHERS

A Design-Based Research Project

This project falls within the field of design-based research, which is 'concerned with using design in the service of developing broad models of how humans think, know, act and learn' (Barab & Squire, 2004, p. 5). Design-based research is an evolution from design experiments where the aim has been to 'engineer innovative educational environments and simultaneously conduct experimental studies of those innovations' (Brown, 1992, p. 141). It is an iterative process of design cycles and enactments where 'the design is constantly revised based on experience' (Collins, Joseph, & Bielaczyc, 2004, p. 18). However, design-based research is not only limited to designing and trying out new artefacts and learning environments. It also aims at testing, developing and generating new theoretical claims (The Design-Based Research Collective, 2003). Design-based studies take place in naturalistic contexts. The learning designs are implemented and tested in the 'real world' instead of the artificial settings of a laboratory (Barab & Squire, 2004). This call for natural contexts was described by Brown (1992) as the natural evolution from laboratory experiments in arbitrary contexts to the natural and social context of a functioning classroom. Following this principle, the project described in this chapter has developed and implemented a new digital resource in the natural context of two high school classrooms. A detailed account on the design process of the resource will be taken up in a following section. A last characteristic of design-based research is that the research process of the studies should be well documented, and its results must be shared with the research community, not only the design process of innovative learning environments but also theories that can have relevant implications for the research communities and practitioners (The Design-Based Research Collective, 2003).

Innovation at School and Teachers

Adoption and integration of new instructional design (e.g., modern technologies, new curricula) at school can be challenging (Kenny & McDaniel, 2011; Ottestad, Throndsen, Hatlevik, & Rohatgi, 2014; Squire, MaKinster, Barnett, Luehmann, & Barab, 2003). Success can depend on how well teachers perceive the innovation to fit their goals (Penuel, Roschelle, & Shechtman, 2007). In their study of teachers' use of computers in primary school, van Braak, Tondeur, and Valcke (2004) found that a favourable attitude towards computers and new technology is a predictor of supportive computer use. But their study also showed that teachers' past experience with computers had an even stronger effect on their computer use in the classroom. Similar findings have been discovered in the field of game-based learning: teachers need to see the connection between the game, or new technology, and their curriculum to integrate them in their teaching (Ketelhut & Schifter, 2011). Another study showed that teachers' beliefs and attitudes towards videogames influenced their decision to introduce them in the classroom (Kenny & McDaniel, 2011).

However, even when their attitude is positive, many teachers rarely use digital media in their classrooms (Kenny & McDaniel, 2011). Attitude is not the only reason why innovations can be difficult to integrate at school. Teachers need to be supported by the institution and the researchers to develop their familiarity with the innovation and 'their personal comfort with and ownership over the technological intervention' (Ketelhut & Schifter, 2011, p. 545). Ownership over and familiarity with a new tool is often cited as a main element of the successful integration of innovation (Hanghøj & Brund, 2010; Kenny & McDaniel, 2011; Ketelhut & Schifter, 2011; Penuel et al., 2007). In their analysis of the co-design process, Penuel et al. (2007) found that involving teachers in the design process increased their sense of ownership and agency, which led to a better integration of the tool and to teachers being advocates for its use. Indeed, in design-based research, involving practitioners and teachers in the production or analysis of the design is seen as a criterion for success (Barab & Squire, 2004; The Design-Based Research Collective, 2003).

Co-design also promotes teacher learning by giving teachers 'the opportunity to reflect on their teaching' (Penuel et al., 2007, p. 70). Professional development and teacher training, when properly adapted to the context and the new instructional design, are keys to a successful implementation of innovation at school (Ketelhut & Schifter, 2011; McLaughlin & Marsh, 1978).

In addition, several studies emphasise the importance of understanding and considering the local context (Ketelhut & Schifter, 2011; McLaughlin & Marsh, 1978; Penuel et al., 2007; Squire et al., 2003). Seeing the teacher as a re-designer (Squire et al., 2003) or using flexibly adaptive instructional designs (Schwartz, Lin, Brophy, & Bransford, 1999) gives more importance to the local context by offering teachers the possibility to contextualise the innovation to meet their local needs. Schwartz et al. (1999) recommended moving away from the extremes of leaving all the decisions either to the designers or to the teachers and finding a middle way where designers would provide flexible designs that teachers can adapt to the class context.

A GAMIFIED APPLICATION FOR FRENCH—DESIGNING WITH TEACHERS

Design Process

This project followed design-based research principles as presented above and had as a main goal the development and implementation of a gamified resource for French-as-a-foreign-language classes in Norway. The idea was to create an application that would follow gamification principles and at the same time address the competence aims for foreign language learning in the Norwegian curriculum.

A team of researchers, designers and developers from the University of Oslo with backgrounds from computer science and pedagogy (in particular, foreign language teaching) was formed. The first meetings focused on brainstorming ideas on the tool and the context of use. Three main themes were identified to be at the core of the new resource: collaboration, agency and differentiated learning. Paper mock-ups of the application were created.

An invitation to participate in the project, outlining the goals and conditions of participation, was sent to schools from the university research network. Two schools showed interest, but one had to drop out as their teacher was not available for the whole duration of the project. The participating school is situated in the Oslo region. The first teacher from this school (Mari) joined the project in January and started to work in close collaboration with the main researcher. They developed pedagogical content for the application and adapted it to the curriculum and learning plan. In addition, the teacher provided insights on the realities of her classroom and the school context and feedback from students on what ought to be changed in their learning situations. This feedback was used to inform the design process and adapt the application to its future pedagogical use. A second teacher (Emilie) joined the project in April (at that point of the year the researcher and Mari had completed three working sessions). Emilie heard about the project from her colleague and asked if she could also use the application in her class. She joined the following four working sessions and helped develop more pedagogical content for the application.

When Emilie joined the project, the application had already found its final form, and paper prototypes had been created and internally tested. A designer specialising in user experience (UX-designer) worked on the prototypes, and an alpha version was developed. This version was tested by a group of four teenagers. Further adjustments were made to the prototype according to the feedback from this pre-test group.

Description of the Application

The final prototype consisted of four main categories (see Figure 9.1): *quêtes*, *check-ins*, *activité* and *groupes*. The quests (*quêtes*) were group tasks meant to be solved by a team of three to four students. The *check-ins* were individual tasks that could be completed on a daily or weekly basis. *Activité* was a notification feed where students could write and read short messages and receive notifications from the application on individual and team progress (e.g., badges earned). In the group section (*groupes*), students could see information on each group's progress in the different quests and access the blogs created by each team at the beginning of the year outside of the application. Finally, an achievement system rewarded both the number of tasks completed and the quality of the students' work.

Figure 9.1. The different categories of the application

The resource was developed as a web-based application, so it would be accessible from a broad range of devices (e.g., computer, smartphone, tablet). The idea behind this choice was to avoid excluding students with limited access to specific technological equipment, such as new-generation smartphones, by making the application accessible through a web browser and ensuring that all students would be able to use it on their own devices. Developed as a research prototype, it was only available to the classes participating in the project.

The application was meant as an additional resource for the French-as-a-foreign-language course. During the working sessions with the researcher, the teachers decided that they would use it for around one school hour every week (out of four hours of French) to encourage autonomous and collaborative work. Once connected to the application, the teams of students could choose which tasks they wanted to work on and how they wanted to solve them. Most of the tasks were very open and could be solved using diverse types of media (e.g., written article, video, podcast). In addition, students could decide if they wanted to work together on one task or individually on several different tasks.

Implementation

The first step in the implementation at school consisted of an observation period during which the researcher attended several of Mari's classes and took fieldnotes on the class activities, the students' behaviour and the general mood of the class. Additional working sessions with the teachers were held to finalise the pedagogical content and answer the teachers' questions regarding the final prototype.

At the beginning of the implementation phase, the researcher introduced the new resource in both classes and shortly explained the different functions of the tool to the

Table 9.1. Timeline of the project

Dates	Description
January 2014–August 2014	Working sessions with the teachers
August 2014–September 2014	Observation in Mari's class Additional work sessions with the two teachers
15th September 2014	Introduction of the application in the two classes Presentation conducted by the researcher in Mari's and Emilie's classes
September 2014–June 2015	Period of use of the application in Mari's and Emilie's classes as projected in the design Collection of data: Video recording of 2 groups of students in Mari's class After-class interviews with Mari and Emilie Interviews with students at the end of the school year

students. Mari let the students decide on the groups' composition, only contributing when some students were undecided. Emilie chose to form the groups herself to pair students with differing levels of competency in French. Once the groups were formed and the application introduced, the researcher went back to her observer role and let the teachers decide when, and how much, they would use the gamified resource in their teaching.

The implementation phase in the teachers' classes started a few weeks after the start of school in September 2014. The two classes used the application until the end of the school year in June 2015. Video data were collected all along the testing period at school. Two groups of students in Mari's class were filmed while using the application and working on the tasks. In addition, both teachers regularly participated in after-class interviews where they were invited to share their thoughts and feelings about the intervention.

CONTRASTING TWO EXPERIENCES

Settings

The implementation of the new resource took place in a medium-sized school in a suburb of Oslo. The application was introduced in two second-year classes (VG2) of French taught by Mari and Emilie, respectively. Both teachers had been teaching French to the same students in the previous school year.

Mari has been a teacher for the last nine years. During this period, she has been teaching Norwegian for seven years and French for two years. She is Norwegian and has learned French as a second foreign language. Emilie has been teaching French for the last nine years. She is a native French speaker and has Norwegian as her second foreign language.

Methods

As mentioned previously, the teachers participated in recorded interviews after each fieldwork session. For the first semester, six after-class conversations with Mari were collected and five with Emilie. Regular after-class interviews with Mari were conducted during the second semester. No after-class interviews with Emilie were collected during the second semester at the time of the study, as she did not use the application in her classroom in that period. An additional and more general interview on her experience was conducted in March 2015. The after-class interviews were recorded right after the end of the class. During these brief interviews, the teachers were invited to share their thoughts and feelings on what had happened in their classrooms, on the project and on the use of the application in their teaching (Penuel et al., 2007). The interviewer used prompts to facilitate the teachers' narration when they did not know where to start (Brinkman & Kvale, 2015). These prompts were very general (e.g., How did it go today in the classroom? How did you feel today in the classroom?), and the teachers were free to bring up any topics they wanted to address. The conversations were conducted in French and were translated to English by the researcher for this study. The transcripts were analysed by marking recurring themes in the interviews (Brinkman & Kvale, 2015). The analysis revealed several main themes in the data related to the teacher's role in the classroom and students' motivation.

The researcher was present in 15 fieldwork sessions in Mari's class throughout the school year: three sessions before the introduction of the application and 12 sessions after the new resource had been implemented (including a session to introduce the application). During these last 12 sessions, video data of two groups of students using the application were collected.

The video data have been coded through a thematic analysis according to the students' interactions: what they are doing and what they are talking about. Sequences from the dataset have been extracted and used to deepen the analysis of Mari's implementation of the digital resource. The sequences for this chapter were selected due to Mari's participation in the interaction with the students.

To understand the teachers' positioning in the interview and video data, their utterances were analysed. Positioning is here understood in terms of alignment, footing and frame switch (Goffman, 1974, 1981). Footing could be seen as a reframing process. It is 'the alignment we take up to ourselves and the others present as expressed in the way we manage the production or reception of an utterance' (Goffman, 1981, p. 128). Over the course of a conversation we are constantly renegotiating our footing, our alignment: 'we change voice' (Goffman, 1981, p. 155). Through talk, 'the individual displays a self to others in social interaction' (Marinova, 2004, p. 211). The analysis of cues and markers in the utterances gives the researcher access to a speaker's alignment, in other words to the frame she is placing herself in, to her projected self (Goffman, 1981). Linguistic cues in the teachers' interviews and in the video data were integrated in the following analyses to understand their positioning.

The analysis of these two cases will help create narratives about each teacher and their experiences of their implementations of a new digital resource. The progression in the teachers' narratives can be studied in detail as the two teachers were followed for a whole school year and interviewed regularly. Although this limited dataset will not make possible a generalisation to a wider target population, it will bring to the foreground some issues crucial to the development of future design-based projects in the field of education. This research also raises important questions on the implementation of gamified resources in the classroom and how to facilitate this process for teachers.

Mari

During the fieldwork sessions in Mari's class, the researcher observed how she introduced the work on the application in each lesson. Mari usually started by announcing to the class that the rest of the lesson would be dedicated to the gamified tool and that they would start working in groups. She would then do a brief review of what had been posted both on the activity feed of the application and on the students' blogs in the previous session. Mari used the projector and the screen to show the whole class the different messages and blog posts. She would also point at the badges received and sometimes explain why the student had been awarded that badge. Once the briefing was over, she would ask the students to join their teammates and sit in groups to start working on the tasks. During the rest of the session, Mari walked around in the classroom from group to group to ask the students how they were doing and answer their questions.

The following sequence of video data presents a conversation between Mari and Jonas, a student from one of the groups filmed throughout the year. Names were changed for privacy reasons. The complete transcript of this sequence can be found in the appendices.

Mari, the teacher, is walking around in the classroom. The students are sitting in groups and working on the gamification tasks. Jonas asks her attention by calling her name, and she walks towards him. He wants some explanation on a specific task (task #3). Mari gets close to Jonas and sets herself behind him and looks at his laptop screen. Meanwhile, Jonas is pointing at the task on his screen.

| 3 | Jonas: | Is it like, *écris* an article, should we write down an article about |
| 4 | Mari: | Humhum ((affirmative)) but shouldn't you do it together? |

Mari is putting focus on collaboration by recommending Jonas work with a teammate on this task. She then navigates through the various levels and tasks of the quest to show him what he is supposed to do.

| 10 | Mari: | What is important, go back to *francophonie*, what is important is in the number 2, you're supposed to find information about the country and it's by using this information that you will write the article |

Jonas then tells her that he chose to write about Canada and explains to her that he decided on his own for the whole group. In the last part of the interaction, Mari gives Jonas some advice on strategies to work on the task and for a successful writing process.

| 24 | Mari: | But writing the article is a big task. I would recommend that you work together, that you decide, in a way, what should be in the article, and that you prepare a kind of skeleton-structure so it will be easier when you're writing. I would recommend that. |

She uses the word 'recommend' twice in this utterance. She doesn't directly order him to follow these writing strategies, but she gives him advice to use as he wishes.

In this extract, it is interesting to see how Mari is checking on Jonas' work strategies and how she is giving him advice on how to solve the task. We can also see her navigate through the application with ease.

In the interview data, Mari also described her role in the classroom as active, asking students questions and giving them advice on how to solve the tasks and with which resources.

Mari also often reflected on her practice, wondering how much guidance she should provide at times. She narrated an interesting episode in an interview when a student misunderstood a task direction and started creating a quiz about a topic completely unrelated to the task.

> Mari: One student completely misunderstood the blog quest, but I let him do. I don't know if I should have explained it to him but for now I let him do because he was working. He was having fun. It was creative so maybe misunderstandings are not always bad. If he is having fun, if he is learning something.

She chose to let the student complete the task in this unexpected way because she considered the work the student was doing more important than the task direction. Mari, in this example, did not hesitate to change the purpose of the task to serve the teaching purpose. She had taken ownership of the resource and felt free to modify it.

Another interesting point in the video data is that when she talked to the students, Mari often positioned herself as a designer. She often used the pronoun 'we' to include herself in the design team. The following quote is extracted from a video sequence where Mari is talking to the second group of students filmed. The students have written a text that makes no sense at all to solve a task, and Mari is discussing with them the purpose of the task and what they should be doing. The complete transcript of this sequence of interaction can be found in the appendices.

> 11 Mari: No but listen here. What do you really think is the purpose of this task? Why did we put it in the app? What do you think we wanted you to learn from it?

This positioning can also be found in the interview data. Mari used the pronoun 'we' (e.g., 'we created', 'we wanted') there as well. She expressed expected outcomes at the time of the design process, and she compared how she had thought the resource would work with its actual use in the classroom.

> Mari: I think it was my idea when we were making the quests. (…) While creating the quests I had in mind that they would work together but they aren't. (*November*)

These examples show that Mari was clearly involved not only in the implementation of the tool but also in how the tool was designed. She reflected on its use in contrast with the design goals and positioned herself as part of the design team.

Emilie

Emilie described her role in the classroom as one of a monitor, checking on students' behaviours and the amount of work completed. There are no video data showing how Emilie interacted with the students while they were using the application. However, she mentioned in her interviews that the students did not need her help as they were doing fine on their own. She used the word 'observer' to describe the passive role of the teacher.

March (when asked about her role when using the application):

Emilie: I would say it's more a monitor role. I didn't really have to give advice, maybe explaining some actions, some homework or tasks but I think that they get by pretty well on their own. So the teacher is more of an observer that checks the work.

Emilie mentioned several times that, even though the explanations of how to use the application were clear, she wished the researcher had been in her classroom to show her how to use the resource in a teaching situation.

Emilie: You gave me a good explanation. But I think it would have been good if you had come to my class to be in the situation. Being with me to do it in real time and see what was possible or not.

Unlike Mari, who altered some of the tasks to fit her students' progress, Emilie wanted to strictly follow the researcher's guidelines. She was not taking ownership of the new resource. She expressed in several interviews the need to be shown in detail how to use the application in her classroom and that she felt lost. She clearly explained it in the March interview:

Emilie: Because I hadn't integrated all the notions of this work in fact, all the possibilities. It was a bit difficult for me to understand in the beginning, so of course if I don't understand, it is a bit difficult to explain to my students all the things they can do.

In addition in the first four interviews, Emilie described the implementation of the new resource as a negative experience. She felt like she did not have a place in the classroom anymore and stayed in the background. She compared her role in the class when the students were using the application with when they were doing other class activities. She felt that she was doing less when the students were using the gamified application.

September (when asked about her feelings after the first class with the application):

Emilie: I would say a negative feeling, because I had almost nothing to do.

They don't really need my help, maybe yes, to translate some sentences, some things like that, words yes, but much less, they need my presence much less than usual. So I would stay in the background a lot, compared to all of the other activities we're usually doing.

I would say for now that I find it harder to find my place because I don't really need to help them.

After some weeks using the application, Emilie reported that she felt that the situation was getting better. She did not express clear negative feelings as in the first conversation, but she was not completely at ease with the tool yet. She said that she understood how the application was working. However, she still described her role as passive.

October (when asked if there were any changes in how she felt in the classroom):

Emilie: In fact, I understood how it works so I don't (.) I don't really need to intervene. Only looking, checking, seeing if they are really doing hum (.) It's mostly I would say a checking job so hum (.) because when, when I see them writing but they're writing mistakes I let them do. I say nothing. So that can motivate them more. So yes, we can say it's going better. I mostly had to (.) hum to understand how it worked yes.

It was a difficult and lengthy process for Emilie to reach the same familiarity with the tool as Mari. It could also be argued that she never quite reached the same level of understanding and confidence towards the application as Mari. Indeed, she mentioned several times in the interviews that the students knew how to use the application better than she did and that they did not need her help. She expressed several times not knowing all the functions of the application and how she wished the researcher had given her more precise guidelines on how to use the resource in the classroom situation.

Interview data correlated with the data log from the application showing that Emilie used the resource less than Mari in the first semester. Emilie also did not use the gamified application in her class in the first three months of the second semester, even though she still talked positively about it in the March interview:

Emilie: I think it's quite complete. They are working on the four competences in fact. So it's quite good. It's a different type of work and I think that they are interested. It stimulates them so it's good.

In her account of her implementation of the new resource, Emilie made it clear that the experience was a long and complicated process. She mentioned often how uneasy she felt with the digital tool and with its use in her classroom. Although she made some very positive comments on the application during the interviews, she used it very little throughout the school year.

DISCUSSION—TEACHERS' EXPERIENCES WITH THE IMPLEMENTATION

In the data presented in the previous section, the two teachers experienced the implementation of the application in different ways. The interview data describe the teachers' perceptions of the implementation of the resource and should not be taken as an evaluation of their teaching. The different elements presented in the section above can be summarised in three categories: (a) teachers' participation and training, (b) teachers' familiarity with the resource and (c) perception of the teachers' role.

Teachers' Participation and Training

The two teachers joined the design process at two separate times. Mari participated from the beginning of the design process, whereas Emilie joined from the fourth working session. Although being part of the process from the first working session might have influenced Mari's implementation of the application, it seems doubtful that this reason was the only source of Emilie's negative experience. When Emilie joined the design process, the application had already found its final form, and the working sessions were only dedicated to the development of pedagogical content. It could be argued that Emilie might have felt left out of the decision-making process concerning the application and its function in the classroom, which can be threatening for a project's success (McLaughlin & Marsh, 1978; Penuel et al., 2007). Participation in support activities provided by the researcher and teacher training can help improve the implementation of a new instructional design (McLaughlin & Marsh, 1978; Penuel et al., 2007). Both teachers participated in several work sessions at the end of the summer. But Emilie often expressed in the interviews her need for the researcher to come to her classroom to demonstrate the use of the application. Emilie's negative experience and her feeling lost in the classroom might be a sign that the format or content of these sessions needs to be improved. Ketelhut and Schifter (2011) suggest including models of successful implementation in the teacher training and providing just-in-time support at the beginning of the implementation.

Teachers' Familiarity with the Resource

Teachers' participation in the design process can also develop the teachers' sense of ownership of the new resource (Penuel et al., 2007; Squire et al., 2003). And, indeed, the confidence felt by the teachers in relation to the gamified application and the familiarity expressed with this tool are different. Whereas Mari took a clear ownership of the application and was at ease with the different functions of the tool, as seen in several of the excerpts presented above, Emilie expressed the need for clear and practical guidelines on the use of the new resource in her teaching. By adapting the new resource to her learning situation and the needs of her students, Mari acted as a re-designer and created opportunities for meaningful learning experiences (Squire et al., 2003).

Another difference between the two teachers' experiences expressed in the interview data and correlated by the data log of the application is the frequency and amount of time spent on the application by teachers. Data showed that Emilie used the resource less than Mari and stopped using it after the first semester for a period of almost three months. Several factors could explain this difference. Emilie explains it partly by the fact that it took a long time for her to understand the application and to feel confident enough to explain its different functions to the students. Ketelhut and Schifter (2011) emphasise that it takes time to develop familiarity with a new resource. Similar findings were found in the study on co-design by Penuel et al. (2007).

Emilie often expressed in the interviews positive feelings towards the project and positive expected outcomes in how the use of the application could help her students in their learning. It is worth noting that Emilie's positive comments on the application might have been influenced by the fact that the interviews were conducted by the same researcher who participated in the design process. However, she took the initiative to be a part of the project, so a lack of interest could probably be ruled out as an explanation for this difference in the amount and frequency of use of the new resource. Kenny and McDaniel (2011) show that, despite having a positive attitude towards them, many teachers are still not using modern technologies in their teaching, indicating that other reasons must explain this phenomenon.

Perception of Teachers' Role

The teachers also positioned themselves in different ways. In particular, Mari often spoke from the point of view of a designer. She used the pronoun 'we' and positioned herself as part of the team that developed the application.

Mari's and Emilie's perceptions of the teacher's role in the classroom were quite different. Mari perceived herself as a guide, helping the students and being very present in the classroom, whereas Emilie expressed her role as passive, an observer staying in the background of the classroom while the students worked on their own. The way Emilie described her role and how she felt in the classroom reflects a low sense of efficacy. She did not feel in control of the new resource and often mentioned that the students knew better than her how to use the application. McLaughlin and Marsh (1978) showed that the sense of efficacy positively influences the implementation of a new project in the classroom. Ketelhut and Schifter (2011, p. 545) recommended supporting teachers during the implementation to give them time to 'develop efficacy in using the innovation'. We can see a shift in how Emilie talked about her experience. In the fifth interview, in November, she said that she felt more at ease with the new resource. And indeed, from this point, she started using the application more regularly in her class for the rest of the first semester.

These elements show that the implementation of the resource was smoother in Mari's class, whereas the experience was more difficult, and at times perceived as negative, for Emilie. The experience of the teachers with Information and Communication Technology (ICT) might also have played a role in how the implementation went and how the teachers perceived it (van Braak et al., 2004). Before her participation in the project, Emilie rarely used ICT in her teaching. She also had more experience as a foreign language teacher, which might have made it more difficult to integrate a new instructional design into her teaching practice (McLaughlin & Marsh, 1978; Penuel et al., 2007).

The fact that Mari had participated in the development of the pedagogical content for the resource might have made the application more adapted to her students or her teaching style. She mentioned, for example, that when she participated in the development process of the application, she had her students in mind at all times. She always linked the resource with its use in her classroom. This might have made the resource more adapted to her class than to Emilie's class and might thus explain the difference in their implementation of the new resource.

It can then be argued that teachers' participation in the design process, when possible, can facilitate the implementation of new learning resources and help making the resource more relevant to the context of use. Teachers' participation in the design process should be encouraged and promoted when possible. However, it might not be the only factor that should be considered when preparing the integration of a new instructional design. As seen in Emilie's case, other reasons might influence the teacher's experience of the implementation and her use of the application.

There are many situations where teachers cannot participate in the development process of new resources, either because the resource has already been developed or for organisational reasons. In these cases, using flexible and open resources that would require teachers to add their own pedagogical content adapted to their context of use could be a way to facilitate the implementation process. The teachers would then act as re-designer of the new resource (Squire et al., 2003) and ensure a better link with the curriculum. Gamified applications like the one presented in this study could satisfy these criteria.

CONCLUSION

In the light of the analysis of the teachers' experiences, it can be argued that involving teachers in the design process has several interests, but should not be taken for granted. Teachers' previous experience, school context, and attitude towards ICT and innovation should be analysed before integrating a new resource. Teachers can give a project context-relevance by informing the design of the tool with feedback on the reality of their classrooms and of their learning plans. They can also gain a deep familiarity and ownership of the resource that will facilitate its implementation. The findings of this research study emphasise these advantages of involving teachers and practitioners in design processes. But they also show the importance of good teacher training, and of supporting the teacher along the way. Emilie's negative experience could maybe have been avoided, or minimised, if the researcher had been more present in her classroom or if the working sessions had given her a greater sense of ownership.

In the case of a learning game or a gamified resource, it is crucial to connect the game aspects and the pedagogical content to adapt the tool to its use in class (Johansson, Verhagen, Åkerfeldt, & Selander, 2014). To satisfy this point, designers and researchers should look at the context of use and could gain a lot by involving teachers in the design process. Another idea could be to create open and flexible learning resources easily adaptable by teachers to their own teaching contexts. Gamification could be a way of creating these type of resources. The application developed in the project presented above is very flexible and could be used in several different subjects, depending on what pedagogical content is added. Teachers can easily design it to fit their teaching context. Further research with this application could focus both on developing content within the same subject but for different student groups, or on developing content within other subjects. This research can also be used as a starting point for more design-based projects on the use of gamified applications in education and especially on the creation of flexible and easy-to-implement resources.

REFERENCES

Barab, S., & Squire, K. (2004). Design-based research: Putting a stake in the ground. *The Journal of the Learning Sciences, 13*(1), 1–14.

Berns, A., Palomo-Duarte, M., Dodero, J. M., & Cejas, A. (2014). Guess it! Using gamificated apps to support students foreign language learning by organic community-driven peer-assessment. In C. Rensing, S. de Freitas, T. Ley, & P. J. Muñoz-Merino (Eds.), *Open learning and teaching in educational communities* (pp. 482–485). Cham: Springer.

Berns, A., Palomo-Duarte, M., Dodero, J. M., & Valero-Franco, C. (2013). Using a 3D online game to assess students' foreign language acquisition and communicative competence. In D. Hernández-Leo, T. Ley, R. Klamma, & A. Harrer (Eds.), *Scaling up learning for sustained impact* (pp. 19–31). Berlin: Springer.

Brinkman, S., & Kvale, S. (2015). *InterViews: Learning the craft of qualitative research interviewing*. Thousand Oaks, CA: Sage Publications.

Brown, A. L. (1992). Design experiments: Theoretical and methodological challenges in creating complex interventions in classroom settings. *The Journal of the Learning Sciences, 2*(2), 141–178. doi:10.2307/1466837

Chik, A. (2012). Digital gameplay for autonomous foreign language learning: Gamers' and language teachers' perspectives. In H. Reinders (Ed.), *Digital games in language learning and teaching* (pp. 95–114). London: Palgrave Macmillan.

Collins, A., Joseph, D., & Bielaczyc, K. (2004). Design research: Theoretical and methodological issues. *The Journal of the Learning Sciences, 13*(1), 15–42. doi:10.2307/1466931

Goffman, E. (1974). *Frame analysis: An essay on the organization of experience*. Cambridge, MA: Harvard University Press.

Goffman, E. (1981). *Forms of talk*. Philadelphia, PA: University of Pennsylvania Press.

Hanghøj, T., & Brund, C. E. (2010). *Teacher roles and positionings in relation to educational games* (pp. 116–122). Paper presented at the Proceedings of the 4th European Conference on Games Based Learning, Reading.

Johansson, M., Verhagen, H., Åkerfeldt, A., & Selander, S. (2014). *How to design for meaningful learning: Finding the balance between learning and game components*. Paper presented at the 8th European Conference on Games Based Learning, ECGBL2014, Reading.

Kapp, K. M. (2012). *The gamification of learning and instruction: Game-based methods and strategies for training and education*. New York, NY: Pfieffer.

Kenny, R. F., & McDaniel, R. (2011). The role teachers' expectations and value assessments of video games play in their adopting and integrating them into their classrooms. *British Journal of Educational Technology, 42*(2), 197–213.

Ketelhut, D. J., & Schifter, C. C. (2011). Teachers and game-based learning: Improving understanding of how to increase efficacy of adoption. *Computers & Education, 56*(2), 539–546. Retrieved from http://dx.doi.org/10.1016/j.compedu.2010.10.002

Marinova, D. (2004). [Papers from the Special Session in Honor of Erving Goffman (Professor at the University of Pennsylvania 1968–1982)] Two approaches to negotiating positions in interaction: Goffman's (1981) footing and Davies and Harre's (1999) positioning theory. *University of Pennsylvania Working Papers in Linguistics, 10*(1), 17.

McLaughlin, M., & Marsh, D. (1978). Staff development and school change. *The Teachers College Record, 80*(1), 69–94.

Ottestad, G., Throndsen, I., Hatlevik, O., & Rohatgi, A. (2014). *Digitale ferdigheter for alle? Norske resultater fra ICILS 2013*. Retrieved May 4, 2018, from https://iktsenteret.no/sites/iktsenteret.no/files/attachments/icils-rapport.pdf

Penuel, W. R., Roschelle, J., & Shechtman, N. (2007). Designing formative assessment software with teachers: An analysis of the co-design process. *Research and Practice in Technology Enhanced Learning, 2*(1), 51–74.

Perry, B. (2015). Gamifying French language learning: A case study examining a quest-based, augmented reality mobile learning-tool. *Procedia-Social and Behavioral Sciences, 174*, 2310–2317.

Reinders, H., & Wattana, S. (2012). Talk to me! Games and students' willingness to communicate. In H. Reinders (Ed.), *Digital games in language learning and teaching* (pp. 156–188). Basingstoke: Palgrave Macmillan.

Schwartz, D. L., Lin, X., Brophy, S., & Bransford, J. D. (1999). Toward the development of flexibly adaptive instructional designs. *Instructional-Design Theories and Models: A New Paradigm of Instructional Theory, 2*, 183–213.

Squire, K. D., MaKinster, J. G., Barnett, M., Luehmann, A. L., & Barab, S. L. (2003). Designed curriculum and local culture: Acknowledging the primacy of classroom culture. *Science Education, 87*(4), 468–489.

The Design-Based Research Collective. (2003). Design-based research: An emerging paradigm for educational inquiry. *Educational Researcher, 32*(1), 5–8. doi:10.2307/3699927

van Braak, J., Tondeur, J., & Valcke, M. (2004). Explaining different types of computer use among primary school teachers. *European Journal of Psychology of Education, 19*(4), 407–422.

APPENDIX

Sequence #1

1	Jonas	Hey Mari when it says like that you have to make an article
2	Sara	It's a summary, isn't it?
3	Jonas	Is it like, *écris* an article, should we write down an article about
4	Mari	Humhum ((affirmative)) but shouldn't you do it together
5	Jonas	Ok
6	Mari	Because this one, let's see is it in *Quête* 2, could you click on this one
7	Jonas	Is it that one?
8	Mari	Yes precisely, yes it's in *francophonie*, yes indeed
9	Jonas	We shared the tasks a bit
10	Mari	What is important, go back to *francophonie*, what is important is in the number 2, you're supposed to find information about the country and it's by using this information that you will write the article

11	Jonas	Ok. I took Can I took Canada
12	Mari	Hum?
13	Jonas	I took Canada if it's in a way (.) a possibility
14	Mari	Yes but have you decided on a country together or have you taken a country each?
15	Jonas	Ah?
16	Mari	I mean did you choose a country together or a country each?
17	Jonas	I took the decision
18	Mari	Ah like that, yes it's fine, it's good to have some initiative
19	Jonas	Yes
20	Mari	Yes but then just do level 2 then *Cherchez de l'information*
21	Jonas	*Cherchez*? Oh that one, I found a page where there's everything
22	Mari	Yes. Then you can use it as a source when you're writing the article
23	Jonas	Yes
24	Mari	But writing the article is a big task. I would recommend that you work together, that you decide, in a way, what should be in the article, and that you prepare a kind of skeleton-structure so it will be easier when you're writing. I would recommend that. Sven multitasking even though it's not strictly forbidden it's not recommended either.

Sequence #2

1	Mari	So you're writing a text and you have to use these ((pointing at the screen))
2	Marianne	Yes (inaudible)
3	Mari	No, Benoît, he made me aware that
4	Marianne	That we wrote a lot
5	Mari	Yes, he said that it was very complicated and that it didn't necessarily give any sense ((laughs))
6	Sindre	No but it wasn't supposed to make sense
7	Mari	It has to make sense!
8	Sindre	[the meaning (inaudible)]
9	Marianne	[(inaudible)]
10	Sindre	The meaning was that there were many words
11	Mari	No but listen here. What do you really think is the purpose of this task? Why did we put it in the app? What do you think we wanted you to learn from it?
12	Marianne	Uh the words. And to be able to place them in a sentence
13	Mari	In a meaningful sentence!

THOMAS DUUS HENRIKSEN

10. GROUP PROCESSES IN LEARNING GAMES FOR ADULTS

ABSTRACT

This chapter examines how group processes unfold while playing a learning game for adults. Through the study of a Swedish deployment of 'The EIS Simulation', which is a collaborative learning game on change management and overcoming organisational resistance, it is shown how social processes emerge and affect the group's decision-making process. The chapter proposes an analytical distinction between two levels of interaction, which both affect decision-making, and consequently the learning process. The primary processes concern the direct interaction with the game, and governed by its mechanics. The secondary processes emerge among participants as a consequence of the game, but become governed by emergent social mechanics. From this distinction, the chapter finds that while secondary mechanics take up a significant proportion of the time spent playing, they offer an opportunity for a multitude of processes to unfold that are crucial to adult learning.

Keywords: learning game, adult learning, organisational development, business game, change management

INTRODUCTION

Since the 1950s, business games have been used for teaching and training organisational skills to employees and managers, thereby providing an operational approach to understanding particular organisational processes (Henriksen & Löfvall, 2012). When observing a group of adults playing a business game, they often appear highly involved in the process. While business games often portray their participants as highly engaged in the game, closer observation most likely reveals them to be engaged in discussions concerning the game, or with game-related issues, rather than with playing the game. In terms of Sørensen and Levinsen (2014), learning is designed as a composite of activities, which in case learning games involve the combination of lectures, presentations, reading materials, playing the game as well as various kinds of group processes. According to process psychology, game-based learning is a matter of making available and engaging participants in processes that contribute to learning (Henriksen, 2014), and business games often employ collaborative structures to stage reflective discussion among their participants.

Little research has been committed to better understanding how such group-based structuration affects learning. Despite this, adult participants in learning games are more often than not organised in a group structure, e.g. as small groups competing against each other (Graham & Gray, 1969; Henriksen & Löfvall, 2012; Lacruz, 2017; Ståhl, 1983). On several occasions, games have been structured as cooperative or semi-cooperative, thereby allowing the dynamics of mutual competition to be replaced, at least partly, by cooperative group mechanics. When played in groups, the sheer volume of activity bears witness to the level of engagement, but while the game and the group might serve as frame for this engagement, a multitude of other simultaneous activities are unfolding meanwhile. To better understand the game-based process, it is necessary to explore the various processes that emerge while playing a business game and how they affect the learning process.

To better understand how group emergent processes affect game-based learning, a case study of a French business game used in a Swedish setting is conducted. This study employs an analytical distinction between primary and secondary processes, which are elaborated below, from which the emergent processes are discussed in light of adult learning.

LITERATURE: BUSINESS GAMES, MECHANICS AND ADULT LEARNING

The Concept of Business Games

Games and simulations have long been used in business education to facilitate operational understandings of otherwise static theories, as well as to provide opportunities for practicing certain situations. The European tradition for using games in business education dates back to Vital Roux's Opérations de Commerce Simulées (Roux, 1800, in Touzet & Corbeil, 2015), who pioneered French business education. In 1812, the Prussian Army adopted the Kriegsspiegel as a management game for practicing battlefield tactics, causing their officers to outclass their opponents at that time. In 1912, Norman Angell published his Money Game as a saloon game for teaching small-scale business economics, and during the 1930s, a game called the Typewriter Factory was used in the USSR for leadership training (Marshev, 1983). The current tradition stems back to the 1950s when the US Army adopted Monopologs to train logistics management. Shortly after, learning games found their way into business schools and education (Andlinger, 1958), while being promoted as a dynamic approach to teaching and learning management (Greene & Sisson, 1959). Following this tradition, learning games and simulations have been used extensively as an educational tool at business schools and universities (Henriksen & Löfvall, 2012), as well as in non-formal education (see e.g. Faria, Hutchinson, Wellington, & Gold, 2009). Today, games are frequent in business education. Faria (1998) claims that most MBA programs require their participants to play one, and usage is even more extensive at undergraduate levels. According to Faria and Wellington (2004), business management games are frequently used in business education programmes.

A semantic debate on the wording has been ongoing, especially among the authors of the international journal of simulation and gaming (see also Åkerstrøm Andersen, 2008). This debate has emphasised the distinctions between simulations, which are often used to describe realistic representations, and games, which are often used to describe simplified presentations. This chapter employs business games as an umbrella term for the game-based activities aiming to teach business-, organisational- and management-related skills and competencies.

Adult Learning Processes

According to Knowles' andragogical assumptions, adult learners are distinct in several respects (Knowles, 1980; Knowles, Elwood, & Swanson, 1998), which must be taken into account when planning learning processes. Knowles claims adult learners are self-directed, influenced by experiences, oriented towards problem solving, motivated by current or future problems and process-driven by discussion among its participants. Illeris (2003) loosely defines learning as capacity changes not resulting from maturation, while emphasising its cognitive, emotional and contextual dimensions. Gagne (1965) distinguishes between eight types of learning and proposes a hierarchical model, in which more complex types of learning prerequisite the lower types. This distinction combines process and results. As his highest form of learning (problem solving) prerequisites principles, which again prerequisites concepts, the means for achieving higher types of learning is through the lower levels. At the bottom of the hierarchy are classical conditioning in terms of signal learning and stimulus-response learning, which are usually associated with behaviourism's operant conditioning and chaining, in which responses are combined.

According to Knowles, adult learners aim to become able to solve current, tangible problems, which according to Gagne prerequisites the understanding of principles and concepts, which ultimately prerequisites chains of associated stimuli and responses. To facilitate the development of a problem-solving capacity, the process must initially provide the basic building blocks on which to base the more complex understandings.

In addition, andragogy claims adult learners to have little patience when it comes to receiving instruction on how to solve problems. Instead, Knowles claims, they prefer to experiment, explore and discuss, and rather than accepting an instructor as a sole source for knowledge, they prefer to bring in their own knowledge. According to Ausubel (1968), a learner's existing knowledge plays key role in the process, and according to Mezirow (1991, 2000), adults tend to bring with them substantial knowledge, which is influential, but not always beneficial to the process. As adults seldom start from a clean slate, adult learning processes must take into account both the presence and importance of already existing participant knowledge. This understanding of learning as matters of refinement is apprehended by Kolb's (1984) elaboration of Lewin's circular model on learning, which describes learning as reflection from practical experiences, which are then elaborated in terms of abstract generalisations before being turned into plans on what to do when returning to the initial, practical experience. This model describes four qualitatively different processes, which in successive repetition provides an iterative exploration of a repeating, practical experience.

Primary and Secondary Game Mechanics

According to Salen and Zimmerman (2004), a game is defined as 'a system in which players engage in an artificial conflict, defined by rules, that results in a quantifiable outcome' (p. 80), which accentuates the mechanical rules and the quantifiable outcome, to which a set of legitimate acts are limited. From such understanding, playing a game constitutes interacting with its conflict through the actions made legitimate by its rules. This set of rules is referred to as primary mechanics in this chapter, and playing the game through these rules primary interaction with the game. This analytical distinction can be used to distinguish between primary interactions (with the game), and other kinds of interaction, in this chapter referred to as secondary interaction. A key example of secondary interaction are the processes taking place among participants playing a cooperative game, usually referred to as group processes. While these processes emerge from the game, they do not affect its conflict directly, only indirectly. In addition, this interaction is not governed by the primary mechanics, but by an emergent set of secondary mechanics that are interpellated from those of the game.

A group process refers to the situation in which the social interaction among participants consistently affects the individuals' participation (Henriksen, 2014). Tredgold (1950) makes a distinction between being together in terms of proximity, while being a group involves both interaction as well as the emergence of social structures that governs subsequent behaviour. Social psychology has continuously attempted to address this influence. Sherif and Sherif (1956) characterised groups as having a particular structure, a degree of role distribution, and a hierarchy of status, norms, standards and traditions, whose enactment affects its participants, which according to Merton (1957) contributes to a shared set of mutual expectations. Sjølund (1965) characterises a group as a combination of a shared purpose, objective and structure. In his early study of groups, Cooley (1909) established that connectivity, intimate collaboration and face-to-face interaction affected both group behaviour and performance.

Today, the impact and social mechanics of group dynamics is well understood (Henriksen, 2014), whereas authors like Trotter, Freud and Darwin attributed its effects to the metaphysical existence of a collective group-soul (Svedberg, 2008). Through the study of group behaviour, sociology describes how social structures govern agency through normative regulation (Rose, 1999) as well as how structures emerge from such agency (Giddens, 1984). Through the concept of role, social psychology has attempted to describe how social interaction was determined by individual characteristics (Mead, 1934); however, as described by Goffman (1961), not to a satisfactory degree. On basis of micro-sociology, Davies and Harré (1990) describe the processes involved in negotiating power, rights and duties through particular *illocutionary* speech acts, through which beneficiary social positions are established in a social interaction. This perspective emphasises the performative element of establishing social structures through participation.

While the primary interaction is governed by the game's rules, the secondary interaction might stem from, but is not determined by, those rules. Instead, the secondary interaction with the game is governed by a set of social structures that are established by participants, e.g. whether it is legitimate to talk out of turn or perform primary interactions without consulting the group, but may also include procedures for decision making, whether to follow some particular strategy, as well as what to discuss while playing.

For analytical purposes, this chapter makes a distinction between primary and secondary interaction. Primary interaction categorically refers to the direct interaction with the game, its messages, objects and otherwise provided by the game, whereas the secondary interaction categorically describes the interaction with other players beyond what may eventually be scripted by the game.

METHODS

This chapter uses a case study to explore the social interaction emerging from a business game. As a method, case studies rely on data from a limited site or sources (Peräkylä, 2004) to provide in-depth accounts of social interaction (Flyvbjerg, 2006), and in particular to examine the intricacies and complexities of the situation (Henn, Weinstein, & Foard, 2006). The data for this case study originates from an extensive study, which encompassed observations of several game deployments, extensive interviews with participants, facilitators and designers, as well as document and design-based studies (Henriksen, 2010). Parts of these data are used here in the form of a case study to address the group processes taking place during a business game, using one from one deployment as a key case on emergent institutional interaction, in this case interaction governed by the frames imposed upon the participants by the game.

The methodical reluctance on a single case is subject to much debate. Critics have disputed the external validity and generalisability of such studies, which has been dismissed by Flyvbjerg (2006). As pointed out by Peräkylä (2004), local or institutional particularities might cause blind spots in case studies. While this single case approach is viable for providing a description of the multitude of secondary processes taking place while playing a business game, this study of a particular group playing a particular game makes it is unviable for making subsequent generalisation. In this case, the approach is used to provide an illustration of how participants spent their time interacting with each other as part of playing the game.

An analytical strategy based on the distinction between primary and secondary interaction is used to explore group dynamics. According to Åkerstrøm Andersen

(1999), an analytical strategy is a composition of the perspective used for selecting and analysing data. According to Esmark, Laustsen and Åkerstrøm Andersen (2005), an analytical strategy makes explicit the position from which a phenomenon is observed, allowing both to be scrutinized, as well as acknowledging how other strategies would have yielded different results. While the analytical distinction between the group's primary and secondary interaction might appear forced, it provides a launch pad for addressing activities that stem from the game.

Case Study: The EIS Simulation

The EIS Simulation is a business game on change management from the French business university INSEAD. It combines a simple narrative with a complex set of game mechanics to provide a simulation of the challenges faced when change agents attempt to establish support for an organisational change project. In the sessions described for this chapter, the game was played in groups of five on a shared computer, and lasting 90–110 minutes. During that time, participants were to invest their resources in change management activities (referred to as decisions) while gradually convincing the game's 24 characters to adopt the project, but seldom managing to convince more than 0–6 characters to do so. When an initiative is decided upon, it is implemented into the game interface, which then generates and presents feedback. A brief overview of the initiatives in focus for this chapter are included in Table 10.1.

Table 10.1. Initiatives in data extracts

Initiative	Short description
Coffee breaks	Inquires about information on which directors and managers drink coffee with each other
Seek advice	A humble approach to meeting with a particular character
Staff discussion	A presentation for the managers below the director level
Memorandum	Writing and sending out a brief memo to five particular characters
External speaker	Hosting a presentation from an external expert
Internal magazine	Putting a generic article in the internal magazine
Covert lobbying	Without the approval of the directors, suggest that top managers meet with the CEO to lobby for the project
Face-to-face meeting	Setup a meeting with a particular character to influence him or her

On the basis of the game, its narrative and the initiatives available, the group discusses viable approaches and what initiatives might support these approaches. As can be seen in the extracts below, conversation is inconsecutive, as matters are only briefly touched upon before moving on.

FINDINGS

Identifying Secondary Processes

The game-deployment observed for this chapter took place in Sweden and included some 120 young managers from Scandinavia, the Balkans and Africa, who played the game in 24 mixed groups. During the game, the group in focus spent 110 minutes using 69% of their resources available while making 42 decisions, but without getting any of the 24 characters as adopters. In comparison, a controlled test shows that a winning game (getting the maximum amount of adopters) made in solitary, typically consists of 60–75 decisions while spending 80–100% of the resources and can be completed in less than five minutes. In the controlled test, time was spent interacting with the interface, making decisions and feedback assessment. For the group in the case study, the remainder of the time is obviously spent on discussions, hypothesising and in-group positioning, which are characterised as secondary interactions taking place among the participants rather than between the game and the participants. By making this distinction between the primary and secondary interaction, an analytical strategy is provided for understanding what is taking place in parallel to playing the game.

Data

Following the analytical distinction between primary and secondary interaction, the game is seen played as cycles between implemented decisions. As the game design is based on participant decision making, decision making and feedback assessment are considered primary interactions, while everything else is considered secondary. The data presented in this chapter includes descriptions of decisions 4–6, 18–20, 20–22 and 23–28 to describe the acts taking place in the group, as well as transcripts of decisions 20–22 and 23–28 to describe their conversation and other group processes. In the following extract, the group has been playing for 44 minutes and 44 seconds before making decision number four.

In this extract (Table 10.2), starting with the implementation of decision 6, the participants decide to inquire about information on what characters drink coffee with whom. Their aim is presumably to generate a map of influence to better target their efforts. They then assess the provided data, from which a suggestion is made to seek advice from a particular character. Having agreed upon this, the group types in an account for their decision and implements it (decision 5). The two decisions are qualitatively different, as the first provides information that can be exploited, while the second takes a humble approach to a character while seeking to influence her, generating both qualitative feedback and a quantitative shift in score. This latter feedback is quicker to assess. After having assessed the feedback from decision 5, a subsequent decision is suggested. However, a participant interrupts by reminding the group of their initial plan of first building awareness before moving on, using this as a platform proposing a plan, which is then discussed. On the basis of that plan, a new decision is suggested, which is then implemented (decision 6).

Table 10.2. Decisions 4–6

Time (vid 16)	Action
44:44	Decision 4 is implemented 'coffee breaks'
44:45	Reading game feedback on character networks
46:00	Suggesting new initiatives and deciding on 'seek advice' from a specific character
47:00	Typing an account for the decision (open the door to the CEO)
47:08	Decision 5 is implemented 'seek advice'
47:10	Reading feedback
47:35	New suggestion: Approach a particular character
47:50	Participant taking charge, proposing that first awareness should be built, and then proposing a plan, which is then discussed
48:20	New suggestion: Staff discussion
48:50	Collective navigation of the game's interface
48:57	Decision 6 is implemented 'staff discussion'

Table 10.3. Time spent on decisions 5 and 6

Decision	Primary processes	Secondary processes	Decision cycle total
5	84 seconds: 1:24 min Assessing feedback (76) sec Typing in an account (8 sec) Implementing the decision (0 sec)	60 seconds: 1:00 minute Suggesting decisions and discussing (60 sec)	144 seconds 2:24 min Primary 58% Secondary 42%
6	34 seconds: Assessing feedback 27 sec Interface navigation 7 sec	75 seconds: Making suggestions 45 sec Plan proposal and discussion 30 sec	109 sec 1:49 min Primary 31% Secondary 69%

When using the analytical distinction between primary and secondary processes to compare the two decisions, the following time distribution becomes apparent (Table 10.3).

As can be seen with both decisions illustrated in Table 10.3, secondary processes take up a substantial part of the participants' time. At a somewhat later point in the game, the group has picked up the pace and is churning out decisions at a faster rate (Table 10.4), thereby spending less time on secondary processes, such as discussing the game.

As indicated by the time intervals, sentences are short and are often provided as interruptions, and just as often interrupted before completion. Suggestions are

Table 10.4. Decisions 19 and 20

Time	Action
0213	Decision 18 is implemented 'memorandum'
0215	Assessing feedback
0233	Debate on the decision: 'I said that we shouldn't ...' 'But now [Character] is aware'
0245	Suggestions on decisions: Staff discussion External speaker
0255	Argument for suggestion
0325	Decision 19: External speaker is implemented
0327	Assessing feedback in silence
0337	Discussion
0355	Suggestion: 'Pilot test'
0400	Suggestion: 'Internal magazine'
0405	A suggestion is overheard due to an argument for doing the internal magazine
0415	The system prompts for an account
0440	An account is provided 'To follow up'
0443	Decision 20 is implemented (Internal magazine)

Table 10.5. Time spent on decisions 18 and 19

Decision	Primary processes	Secondary processes	Total/decision cycle
18	25 seconds Assessing feedback (20) sec Implementing the decision (5 sec)	58 seconds Debate the decision 13 Suggesting decisions 10 Argument for decision 25	83 seconds 1:23 min 30%/70%
19	38 seconds Assessing feedback in silence 10 System prompt for account 28	38 seconds Discussion 18 Suggesting decisions 10 Argument for decision 10	76 seconds 1:16 min 50%/50%

often presented as the name of the suggested action, without further argument or elaboration. Despite these shortened discussions, these secondary interactions take up as least as much time as the primary interactions with the game (see Table 10.5).

When making decisions that are unproblematic to the groups, these are conducted rather quickly. Unless much information is provided as feedback, the primary interaction is conducted in 25–40 seconds, and the secondary interaction in 38–75 seconds. This changes dramatically when the group resorts to covert lobbying (decision 21), which the game manual describes as a risky decision. As the group attempts covert lobbying, 95% of their achieved score is lost (see Table 10.6).

While decision 21 is made fairly quickly, its effects impacts the subsequent decision dramatically (see Table 10.7).

Clearly, the prompted effects were unforeseen by the participants, which became evident in their reactions. Until this point, decisions had been suggested as proposals in a trial-and-error-based approach to exploring the game, while gradually building support, but as they resorted to lobbying, they lost that support. This incident sparked a reflective discussion on the level of formality of the groups' decisions and general approach, thereby lifting the discussion from a tactical level and what decisions to make, to a strategic level on how to approach the organisation. At this point, the decision breaks with the participants' game flow that had been built up during the

Table 10.6. Decisions 20–22

0443	Decision 20 is implemented (internal magazine)
0443	Exclamation: 'See?'
0445	Suggestion: 'Covert lobbying' (overheard)
0450	Assessing feedback
0525	Suggestion: 'Covert lobbying' [This time directly to the participant who is dominating the game.]
0540	Accepted: 'Covert lobbying? Ok'
0550	Decision 21 is implemented (covert lobbying)
0555	Feedback reactions: [The decision removes 95% of the groups score] 'Oh my God!' 'Nervous laughter' 'Phew'. 'We were supposed to mention names'. 'Shit!'
0620	Discussion: 'We should now think of one thing. If we use formal thing, if we make any formal, we only make it worse'. 'No, this is not a formal action, because we did it without the approval of the directors [..]'[stands up] 'We have to be very formal and very polite'.
0730	Assessing feedback
0735	Mostly silent and passive
0800	A participant silently navigates the interface and makes a decision
0850	Decision 22 is implemented (electronic mail)

Table 10.7. Decisions 21 and 22

Decision	Primary processes	Secondary processes	Total time spent on the decision cycle
21	47 seconds Assessing feedback (37) sec Implementing the decision (10 sec)	20 seconds Suggesting decision 5 Repeating suggestion 15	67 seconds 1:07 min 70%/30%
22	85 seconds Feedback delay 5 Feedback reactions (assessment) 25 Assessing feedback 5 A participant autonomously makes a decision 50	95 seconds Discussion on the decision and how to handle its consequences 70 Silent and passive 25	180 seconds 3:00 min 47%/53%*

* A participant spends 50 seconds making an autonomous decision, which eschews the distribution

Table 10.8. Decisions 23–28

Vid17	
0950	Facilitator walks into the room, commenting 'Uhh .. what has happened? Too much action, eh?'
1000	Group discussion with facilitator
1130	*Decision 23 is implemented (face-to-face meeting)*
1135	Discussion: 'I would like [Character]' 'Why?' 'I have a good feeling about her' (rapid statements)
1200	*Decision 24 is implemented (face-to-face meeting)*
1232	*Decision 25 is implemented (face-to-face meeting)*
1235	Suggestion: 'And [Character], because she is the financer'
1255	*Decision 26 is implemented (face-to-face meeting)*
1257	Feedback read out aloud
1325	Several suggestions made in rapid succession
1345	*Decision 27 is implemented (face-to-face meeting)*
1347	Discussion: 'Now look at [Character], he is ready for a pilot test'. 'No'. 'Ok, let's do a staff meeting'. (counter argument)
1404	*Decision 28 is implemented (face-to-face meeting)*

prior decisions and their steady pace of generally positive feedback, and stages a brief, but reflective discussion. Moments after, a facilitator addresses the situation and provides the group with a recommendation. Following this recommendation, the group makes a rapid series of decisions (Table 10.8).

Following the facilitator intervention, the group makes five decisions in 2:30 minutes, which leaves little time for secondary interactions. In subsequent interviews with three of the five participants, much attention is paid to decision 21 and its consequences. In contrast, the interviews make no mention of decisions 23–28, indicating them to have had comparatively little impact on the group.

On the basis of the analytical distinction between primary and secondary processes, participant activity appears to be divided roughly equally between the two. When the game provides extensive feedback or when the group is determined on an approach, most of the time between decisions are spent on primary interaction. When the group is in disagreement, interrupted by facilitator input, or when confronted with unforeseen events, the scale tips towards secondary interaction.

Results: Secondary Processes Assessment

Having identified both primary and secondary processes to be present, the content of those processes and their effects are addressed. From the data, the following secondary processes are identified:

- Suggesting initiatives and making decisions
- Discussing possible options to pursue and providing arguments
- Performing analysis
- Debating already made decisions
- Facilitator intervention

Suggesting initiatives and making decisions. When playing the EIS, participants are provided with a handout that describes the different initiatives made available by the game's primary mechanics. In its most basic form, the game is played by selecting initiatives from that list and implementing them through the computer interface. When played as a group on a shared computer, this setup prompts its participants to agree upon what decision to make, thereby interpellating a secondary process. This process is exemplified in the becoming of decision 5: initiatives are suggested, and the group decides on making a particular decision, which is then implemented. In the decisions displayed in this chapter, the suggestions are most often met with an open mind, and disputes are short, which indicates as explorative, trial-based approach.

Discussing options to pursue and providing arguments. When deciding upon which of the initiatives to implement, the group performs small discussions and short arguments are provided. The specificities of these discussions provide insight into why participants suggest and groups decide upon particular lines of action. This

Table 10.9. Decision 20 (expanded)

Video 17	
0325	*Decision 19: External speaker is implemented*
0327	Assessing feedback in silence
0337	Discussion 'These two are more and more interested (2x [Character])'
0355	Suggestion: Pilot test (A) 'Maybe we can make this pilot test with [character]. I don't know'.
0400	Suggestion: Internal magazine (B) 'Let's do the internal magazine again. Just try it one more time. And then ...'
0405	A suggestion is overheard due to an argument for doing the internal magazine (C) 'Maybe we should do this questionnaire?' 'Yes, but the internal magazine, we can do that, like once a month or so'. 'Ok'.
0415	The system prompts for an account 'Create awareness' 'To follow up. You do it to follow up. You did it once, this is a follow up move'.
0440	An account is provided 'To follow up'
0443	*Decision 20 is implemented (internal magazine)*

is exemplified in the development of decision 20, which is provided in expanded view below (Table 10.9).

In the development of decision 20, three different initiatives are suggested. Suggestion A is put forward with little assurance and the 'I don't know' addition indicates the participant to be guessing. Suggestion B is linked to previous action (and implicitly success), but with similar confidence 'just to try it'. Suggestion C is largely overheard due to an argument to support the previous suggestion, but with a similar degree of uncertainty through the use of maybe. Neither of the three suggestions indicate a deeper understanding of what to do other than to make a decision. Whether it is the connection to previous experiences with the initiative, its presentation as explorative or the indication of having a plan that causes it to be decided upon is unknown, but the subsequent account on awareness indicates some level of understanding or hypothesis regarding the relationship between the AITA model and how the game's mechanics interpreters the initiative.

Performing analysis. Making analysis is an important, but often opaque part of the group's decision making. To navigate the primary mechanics of the EIS, the group must correctly assess the situation in terms of AITA and select an initiative that is effective in that part of the model. When reading the game's manual, the initiatives are clearly listed in terms of the AITA categories, and initiatives effective in more than one category are listed in all those categories. A category of 'risky actions' is provided as a separate list, which includes the covert lobbying initiative used in decision 21. The internal magazine initiative is categorised as an 'awareness building action'. As the group account for their decision 20, 'to create awareness' is mentioned, but is displaced by another account, despite indicating a correct understanding of the game's mechanical model. In terms of situational analysis, only 14 of the games' characters are either in the aware or interested phase, whereas the remaining 10 characters are completely unaware. As the group's initial strategy was to first generate awareness, the choice of using an awareness-building initiative at this point indicates a sound analysis of the situation, although in terms of score, it only managed to make aware one additional character. The participants' analysis seems to be the cardinal point in a game-based process. Not only will decisions based on sound analysis improve the group's quantifiable outcome, they also offer an opportunity to apply a theoretical model to a practical situation. In case of the EIS, the game provides a situation and frames it in terms of Roger's AITA model, and playing it means to handle that situation in terms of the model. One such analysis is made in the becoming of decision 6 as a participant takes charge of the process by making references to the group's initial strategy, and presents her analysis:

> Maybe ... we said that we had to do the awareness for all?

> (broad acceptance from other participants)

> Because the first thing was to approach [character], say, "Hello, we are just here to be polite" [...] now we should do the staff meeting, and then pick people. (vid16, 47:50–48:20)

On basis of this analysis, the group decides upon an initiative that addresses the issue of building support. However, as indicated in the decisions displayed, the decisions do not always appear to be based on analysis, but also on (a) intuitive guesswork or (b) secondary mechanics, which are addressed below.

Intuitive guesswork appears when no argument is provided for a suggested approach, or when emotional accounts are provided (see decision 24). Three suggestions were offered when making decision 20, all using connotations that indicate guesswork before an argument was provided for one of them. As the group made decision 24 as part of their recovery, a particular character is targeted because 'I have a good feeling about her'. Here, the decision is made in 30 seconds, presumably based on a combination of the character's name, picture and recollection of a short profile description. Instead, the group might have used the information already available to them, including the character profile and their assessment of informal coffee break networks from decision 4. Instead, the group resorts to an explorative trial-and-error approach. In subsequent interviews, which are not presented here, participants refer to the effects of the internal magazine and covert lobbying, but make little mention of the initiatives that were decided upon without discussion.

The use of decision making through secondary mechanics appears when making decision 21. As a participant in vain tries to propose a suggestion, but is overheard, he approaches the dominant participant directly without involving the group. This participant has positioned herself favourably throughout the game, and her approval causes the decision to be implemented without further discussion. As the decision turns out to have catastrophic consequences, his attempt to defend his suggestion is overheard.

Despite being staged and played as a collaborative game, group dynamics begin to affect this process as soon as the group has been formed. Though the use of *illocutionary* speech acts to frame problems or situations in particular manner, participants will position themselves and others in more or less favourable positions in terms of influencing the groups process (Davies & Harré, 1990). The occupation of a favourable position provides better opportunity for influencing the group's process, whereas a more exposed position will make it harder. Even seating and facial exposure will affect the individual opportunity for influencing the group's decision making.

Having failed in positioning himself favourably in the group, he uses another member to put forward his suggestion. While other participants had managed to put forward equally unsubstantiated suggestions, their position in the group provided them with the speaking rights to make them heard, indicating that the secondary mechanics have a determinate effect on which suggestions are implemented, and which are overheard.

Ideally, decision making should be based on the sound analysis of the game's feedback, its mechanical model and underlying theory, but it can also be seen as made based on intuitive guesswork and group hierarchy. This shift can be seen as a displacement of the game process, away from the game's intention.

Debating already made decisions. When making suggestions, participants commit themselves in various degrees to the process as they hypothesise on its positive effect. If the decision is made, the game provides feedback on whether it was a sound approach, or not, which sometimes triggers debate on the decision.

Following decision 18 on sending out a memorandum, one participant debates the decision as being problematic, whereas the one who suggested it defensively points out its positive, however minimal effect. Following decision 20 on putting an article in the internal magazine, the participant who both suggested it and provided an argument for trying, exclaimed 'See?' as the positive result became apparent. However, as mentioned earlier, in the three suggestions leading up to decision 20, more caution is taken not to commit to promising a desirable outcome. Evidently, the debate becomes more explicit following the effects of decision 21. One participant, who has continuously pushed for adopting an informal approach, uses it as leverage for arguing his case once again, but fails in doing so as the downfall was triggered by an informal approach, and consequently ends up strengthening the opposite position.

In terms of understanding the group process, debating decisions play an important role in establishing a social structure and a hierarchy of statuses. According to positioning theory (Davies & Harré, 1990), debating someone else's proposal is a means of attacking that person's opportunity for them for making future proposals, hence strengthening one's own. Caution is often made when proposing suggestions to make oneself less vulnerable, and successful suggestions are celebrated. Though this secondary game of interactions, the social hierarchy of the group is continuously negotiated, and with it, the opportunity to suggest and decide on what to do in the game. As a consequence, the one who suggested to commence in covert lobbying in decision 21 virtually lost his influence for the remainder of the game.

Facilitator intervention. In terms of primary and secondary interaction, facilitator interaction is considered secondary. Facilitation might affect game outcome indirectly, but the conversations involving game facilitators do not have direct consequences in the game. When mainframes were introduced in business gaming during the 1960, the facilitator role was supplemented with a game administrator (Henriksen & Löfvall, 2012), who were tasked with managing the game, typing participant decisions into the mainframe, conveying feedback, etc. As PCs became commonly available, participants could interact with the game directly, making game administrators superfluous. Today's facilitators are tasked with governing the processes surrounding the game, e.g. in terms of presenting, staging and facilitating the process.

With only two facilitators for 120 participants, the 24 groups are only visited occasionally, and by large left to play the game on their own. During some visits, the facilitator observes in silence, while at others, he/she intervenes directly in the process through commenting, reflective questioning or situational framing. Just after the downfall of decision 21 and 22, a facilitator walks into the room and comments. In a 90-second discussion, the facilitator asks a series of reflective questions, explains the situation and illustrates how it would appear in a real organisation as well as how to proceed from there by meeting with the relevant people. The group picks up on this recommendation and initiates a series of face-to-face decisions, which are illustrated as decision 23–28.

As the group has gotten stuck in the process staged by the game, the facilitator steps in to reshape that process. Through reflective questions, an understanding of what has happened is established, through illustration, the importance of knowing and being able to handle that situation is established, and finally by showing the next step, motivation for proceeding is established. In this sense, the facilitator intervenes in the group's secondary process, and thereby indirectly in the game's primary processes as both subsequently gain momentum.

DISCUSSION OF INTERACTIONS IN LIGHT OF LEARNING

As can be seen from the data, participants spend a significant proportion of their time engaged in secondary interaction, during which they perform a multitude of activities relevant to learning. From the data extracts, four kinds of learning can be identified from the secondary processes: exploration, hypothesising, analysis and reflection.

Exploration is apparent when the group retorts to rely on trial-and-error and other kinds of guesswork for their decision-making. When exploring, the group palpate the game's causal model to reveal its primary mechanics, trying out various initiatives to see their effect. Compared to Gagne's (1965) hierarchy, this resembles a behaviouristic approach to learning, by which certain behaviour is established by using a game-score as a conditioner, eventually establishing chaining, in which responses are combined. To Gagne, such basic blocks are the foundation for higher-order learning. Exploration also complies with Knowles' assumption that adults prefer to learn through self-directed activities, rather than through instruction, but when viewed in light of Kirkpatrick's taxonomy for training evaluation, exploration seemingly has a more motivational than educative contribution.

Hypothesising is apparent when participants propose an initiative to a certain effect. While all suggestions presume to have some kind of effect, some hypothesise particular effects to occur. Whenever a decision is made, those hypotheses are tested through the game's primary mechanics.

Kolb (1984) adopts Piaget's conception of hypothetico-deductive learning to describe the process of translating an abstract understanding into an experiment for testing. In decision 6, participants hypothesised that a staff discussion would heighten awareness, which the primary mechanics would have disproven, had it allowed the group to test it. Presuming the group to still follow their strategy of establishing awareness before moving on, the group hypothesised in decision 20 internal magazine as a means to this end. While the initiative is listed in the manual as an awareness building initiative, it mainly helped the group in building interest and only very little awareness, thereby dismissing an otherwise correct assumption. According to Gagne's hierarchy, complex understandings are based on the building blocks of simpler understandings. These building blocks are established by testing causal assumptions while gradually establishing a conceptual understanding of awareness building.

Analysis becomes apparent when participants makes a situational assessment on the basis of a theoretical model and adopt a line of action accordingly. The game already performs key parts of the analysis by presenting the individual character's degree of adoption in terms of AITA, which greatly reduces the challenge, but the participants still have to correctly identify who to approach with what initiative. As could be seen in the data, the analysis is less apparent, and decision making is often informed by intuitive guesswork and group processes, which displace analysis when informing decision making.

Decision making in games is a much-debated topic, and especially whether high scores are indicative of sound decision making. Knotts Jr. and Keys (1997) claim that high scores can be achieved through lucky guesses, and grade points are also seen awarded on the basis of game performance (Henriksen & Löfvall, 2012). As primary mechanics, game scores are indicative of whether participants exhibit behaviour in accordance to the game's underlying model, while secondary processes might complicate this understanding.

Reflection, and in particular reflective discussion, becomes apparent when participants debate their decisions on the basis of the game's feedback. As could be seen following decision 20, personal investment in a suggested line of action appears to trigger reflections on the viability of the process, regardless of whether it was based on analysis or guesswork. As could be seen following decision 21, the impact of the effect is also likely to trigger reflection. In addition to decision 21, other data support the idea that inconsistencies between expectations and effects also trigger reflective comments (Henriksen, 2010).

Reflective processes play a key role in adult learning theory as discussions (Knowles et al., 1998), means for addressing assumptions (Mezirow, 1991) and to develop generalised understandings (Kolb, 1984). As participants get caught up in the action (decisions 23–26), little or no reflection seems to be taking place as participants fail to take that step back, which according to Høyrup (2006) is a prerequisite for reflection. Only when prompted by expectancies, or when imposed by a facilitator, does the group pause to reflect. In addition, data shows little indication of non-formal discussion. According to Henriksen and Børgesen (2016), formal discussion concerns playing the game, and non-formal discussion concerns game-related topics, e.g. sharing war stories from practice or understandings that contradict the game's model. The only non-formal discussion taking place is initiated by a facilitator, who explains decision 21 through a practical example.

CONCLUSION: LEARNING FROM PRIMARY AND SECONDARY INTERACTION

To better understand game-based learning, the analytical distinction between primary and secondary interaction provides two distinct approaches to learning. The primary interaction, which is based on the game's underlying model, provides an opportunity for interactive exploration of that model, using behaviouristic models for imposing a particular behaviour onto its participants. The secondary interaction, which unfolds among the participants, provides both an opportunity for collaborative learning and an obstacle. As the secondary interaction unfolds on the basis of the primary, they are seen as compliments rather than contrasts. Together, the group explores the primary mechanics, but only the roads upon which they can agree. On the basis of individualised hypotheses on the game's model, disagreements arise, which prompt arguments and further analysis, and, if the results are significant, a debate in which participants reflectively revisit the original argument. At some points, facilitators intervene, either to qualify the participants' understanding of the game, to bring in a perspective from practice, or to dampen some effect and hurl the group back into the primary interaction.

In terms of making game-based learning more efficient, the question emerges of how to strengthen those processes through mutual integration. While the primary and secondary processes both contribute to learning, they do so in different manners, and while a group process might impede explorative learning processes, they make available processes beneficial to higher learning. If analysis is to play centre stage, secondary mechanics must be provided to make secondary processes beneficial to that aim by promoting analysis rather than other means for making in-game decisions. Likewise, primary mechanics must provide input for relevant, secondary processes to emerge.

The analytical distinction between primary and secondary interactions provided a fruitful insight into the processes taking place during a game. They do also point out that game-based learning is not happing in one particular activity, but rather is a multitude of processes dispersed in a network of activities. Group processes might appear to draw away attention from the game, but at the same time provide the process with valuable contributions. Therefore, learning game design should not be considered solely a matter of designing specific processes, but rather to design learning that spans across different micro activities while taking into account how primary and secondary processes should contribute to this process. More knowledge is needed to understand this interplay between primary and secondary processes and should be explored further in future studies of game-based learning processes.

REFERENCES

Åkerstrøm Andersen, N. (1999). *Diskursive Analysestrategier*. København: Nyt fra Samfundsvidenskaberne.
Åkerstrøm Andersen, N. (2008). *Legende magt*. København: Hans Reitzels Forlag.
Andlinger, G. R. (1958). Business games—Play one. *Harvard Business Review, 36*(2), 115.
Ausubel, D. P. (1968). *Educational psychology: A cognitive view*. New York, NY: Holt, Rinehart & Winston.
Cooley, C. (1909). *Social organization: A study of the larger mind*. New York, NY: Charles Scribner's Sons.
Davies, B., & Harré, R. (1990). Positioning: The discursive production of selves. *Journal for the Theory of Social Behaviour, 20*(1), 43–63.
Esmark, A., Laustsen, C. B., & Åkerstrøm Andersen, N. (2005). *Poststrukturalistiske Analysestrategier*. Frederiksberg: Roskilde Universitetsforlag.
Faria, A. J. (1998). Business simulation games: Current usage levels—An update. *Simulation & Gaming, 29*(3), 295–308.
Faria, A. J., Hutchinson, D., Wellington, W. J., & Gold, S. (2009). Developments in business gaming: A review of the past 40 years. *Simulation & Gaming, 40*, 464–487.
Faria, A. J., & Wellington, W. J. (2004). A survey of simulation game users, former-users, and never-users. *Simulation & Gaming, 35*, 178–207.
Flyvbjerg, B. (2006). Five misunderstandings about case-study research. *Qualitative Inquiry, 12*(2), 219–245.
Gagne, R. (1965). *The conditions of learning*. New York, NY: Holt, Rinehart and Winston.
Giddens, A. (1984). *The constitution of society: Outline of the theory of structuration*. Cambridge: Polity Press.
Goffman, E. (1961). *The presentation of self in everyday life*. New York, NY: Garden City.
Graham, R. G., & Gray, C. F. (1969). *Business games handbook*. New York, NY: American Management Association.
Greene, J. R., & Sisson, R. L. (1959). *Dynamic management decision games*. New York, NY: John Wiley & Sons, Inc.
Henn, M., Weinstein, M., & Foard, N. (2006). *A critical introduction to social research* (2nd ed.). London: Sage Publications.
Henriksen, T. D. (2010). *A little more conversation, a little less action, please*. Saarbrücken: Lambert Academic Publishing.

197

Henriksen, T. D. (2014). *Procespsykologi. Facilitering af øvelser i grupper og teams*. København: Akademisk Forlag.

Henriksen, T. D., & Børgesen, K. (2016). Can good leadership be learned through business games? *Human Resources Development International, 19(5), 388-405*. doi:10.1080/13678868.2016.1203638

Henriksen, T. D., & Löfvall, S. (2012). Experiences and opportunities for enhancing business education with games. A review on current and past experiences with learning games at business schools. In C. Nygaard, N. Courtney, & E. Leigh (Eds.), *Simulations, games and role play in university education* (pp. 151–170). Oxfordshire: Libri Publishing.

Høyrup, S. (2006). Reflection in learning at work. In E. Antonacoloulou, P. Jarvis, V. Andersen, B. Elkjaer, & S. Høyrup (Eds.), *Learning, working and living: Mapping the terrain of working life learning* (pp. 85–101). New York, NY: Palgrave Macmillan.

Illeris, K. (2003). Towards a contemporary and comprehensive theory of learning. *International Journal of Lifelong Education, 22*(4), 396–406.

Knotts Jr., U. S., & Keys, J. B. (1997). Teaching strategic management with a business game. *Simulation & Gaming, 28*(4), 377–394. doi:10.1177/1046878197284004

Knowles, M. S. (1980). *The modern practice of adult education: From pedagogy to andragogy*. Englewood Cliffs, NJ: Prentice-Hall.

Knowles, M. S., Elwood, F. H., & Swanson, R. A. (1998). *The adult learner. The definitive classic in adult education and human resource development* (5th ed.). Houston: Gulf Publishing Company.

Kolb, D. (1984). *Experiential learning: Experience as the source of learning and development*. Englewood Cliffs, NJ: Prentice-Hall.

Lacruz, A. J. (2017). Simulation and learning dynamics in business games. *Mackenzie Management Review, 18*(2), 49–79.

Marshev, V. (1983). Gaming in the USSR. In I. Ståhl (Ed.), *Oprational gaming: An international approach* (pp. 83–96). Oxford: Pergamon Press.

Mead, G. H. (1934). *Mind, self and society from the standpoint of a social behaviourist*. Chicago, IL: University of Chicago Press.

Merton, R. (1957). *Social theory and social structure*. Glencoe, IL: Free Press.

Mezirow, J. (1991). *Transformative dimensions of adult learning*. San Francisco, CA: Jossey-Bass.

Mezirow, J. (2000). Learning to think like an adult: Core concepts of transformation theory. In J. Mezirow & Associates (Eds.), *Learning as transformation: Critical perspectives on a theory in progress* (pp. 3–33). San Francisco, CA: Jossey-Bass.

Peräkylä, A. (2004). Reliability and validity in research based on naturally occurring social interaction. In D. Silverman (Ed.), *Qualitative research: Theory, method and practice* (pp. 283–304). London: Sage Publications.

Salen, K., & Zimmerman, E. (2004). *Rules of play—Game design fundamentals*. Cambridge, MA: Massachusetts Institute of Technology.

Sherif, M., & Sherif, C. W. (1956). *An outline of social psychology*. New York, NY: Harper.

Sjølund, A. (1965). *Gruppepsykologi*. København: Gyldendal.

Sørensen, B. H., & Levinsen, K. (2014). *Didaktisk design & digitale processer*. København: Akademisk Forlag.

Ståhl, I. (Ed.). (1983). *Operational gaming. An international approach*. Oxford: Pergamon Press.

Svedberg, L. (2008). *Gruppepsykologi. Om grupper, organisationer og lederskab*. København: Dafolo.

Touzet, L., & Corbeil, P. (2015). Vital Roux, forgotten forerunner of modern business games. *Simulation & Gaming, 46*(1), 19–39.

Tredgold, R. F. (1950). *Human relations in modern industry*. New York, NY: International University.

HENRIK SCHOENAU-FOG, LISE BUSK KOFOED,
LARS RENG AND OLGA TIMCENKO

11. MOTIVATED LEARNING THROUGH PRODUCTION-ORIENTED GAME DEVELOPMENT

ABSTRACT

Game-oriented learning has proven to have many possibilities for supporting better learning outcomes. Using the right educational or commercial games in the classroom has shown to be a great learning motivator. Now new development tools and supporting software have made it easier to build games. When students work with game development, they often end up in activities that are very similar or even identical to those done by professionals in the industry. Setting up a learning environment where education can simulate a real production of meaningful games, can give students experience and knowledge about all aspects connected to producing a purposeful game and might give students a new motivational support. This chapter is based on two experiments of Purposive Game Productions (PGP), conducted in 2014 and 2016. The learning environment was designed as a virtual game production team. The pedagogical approach is Problem-Based Learning (PBL) combined with a design-based learning strategy founded on a production-oriented game development, which did show successful results. The students have increased their motivation as well as developed special knowledge and experiences about game development, while getting an experience very close to a real professional production process. The PGP learning strategy seems both sufficient and demanding for the students. The chapter is finalized with a best practice framework including a list of requirements to consider when running a problem-based and production oriented project work based on game oriented learning.

Keywords: game-oriented learning, game development, purposive game, problem based learning, production-oriented learning

INTRODUCTION

The concept of game-oriented learning, when using educational or commercial games in the classroom, has been proven to have many possibilities for supporting the motivation to learn and ensuring better learning outcomes (Sitzmann, 2011;

Crocco et al., 2016). There might also be a great potential in using game *development* as a motivator in several areas (Star et al., 2017). The skills and efforts needed to produce even simple games have, for decades, been a barrier for many educators. However, in the last few years, new and simpler development tools and supporting software have made it significantly easier to build amazing artefacts and interactions (e.g. Game Engines such as Unity 3D (Unity, 2017)), as also stated in Chapter 9 (Weitze, 2018). Recent developments in media hardware, such as virtual and augmented reality devices, wearables, tablets and smartphones, have additionally created rapid growth in possibilities, impacts and future careers for those who learn to master the development of games and other interactive media solutions. Software development jobs alone are projected to grow by 24% in the U.S. from 2016 to 2026 (US Bureau of Labour Statistics, 2017), while Europe is facing an ICT employee shortage, exemplified by the fact that 41% of all companies that tried to hire an ICT employee in 2015 had trouble finding a suitable candidate (Eurostat, 2016). Many young people are aware of this trend, but many more need to have technical competence. Based on this notion, we began to study how we could motivate students further and encourage their interests in gaining ICT competence. This chapter thus addresses the following question: what kind of learning environment supports ICT students' engagement, interest and learning?

When students work with game development, they often end up in activities that are very similar or even identical to those done by highly paid professionals in the industry. Setting up a framework where education can simulate the *real* production of meaningful artefacts with a purpose allows for educating and investigating a series of important areas, which are often very hard to fabricate in an educational environment. The following will thus explore and compare the approaches of these design-based experiments, which the authors conducted through game production activities at Aalborg University in the fall semesters of 2014, 2015 and 2016, in order to investigate if the format works with different procedures and students.

This chapter is based on earlier work on game fabrication in an educational context (Schoenau-Fog et al., 2015), and the current study focuses on the investigation of results from the 2014 and 2016 experiments, to investigate whether the initial results could be confirmed. In this chapter, we thus describe the production process during purposive game production (PGP) as well examine students' learning and motivational processes while working in a production-oriented environment to develop purposive games. Furthermore, we shall investigate, compare and analyse the learning outcomes and motivational factors present during the project process, before we conclude with an updated best practice framework for running purposive game production when planning game-oriented learning activities within problem-based production-oriented project work (PPP). The results and experiences show that the PPP concept can be applied not only in our Medialogy curriculum but also in Humanistic and Engineering studies as well as in other educational curricula (Reng & Busk Kofoed, 2016; Weitze, 2018).

BACKGROUND

Games as learning tools have been utilised and studied for several years in higher education, and learning outcomes are often reported as being relatively successful (Wang, 2010; Yang, 2012). The prevalence of digital game-oriented learning has furthermore been proven within higher education settings (Hwang, 2012), with motivational factors behind using games being a major part of the learning success (Woo, 2014). At the same time, the general lack of student motivation and engagement is still a big problem within universities (Armstrong et al., 2013), and we have found that a major challenge is establishing a teaching and learning environment that utilises features from digital game-oriented learning and simultaneously focuses on motivational and engaging factors. One of our main questions was and still is: how can a learning environment be established based on digital game-oriented learning, promote the integration of learning-specific topics and allow students to acquire practical and academic skills while maintaining their motivation and interests through an existing curriculum? We find that the highest quality of learning occurs when it is active, goal-oriented, practice-based, contextualised and interesting, in which case the teaching/learning environment should be interactive, provide ongoing feedback, maintain attention and promulgate appropriate levels of challenge (Woo, 2014). This learning approach is reflected in the "Aalborg problem-based learning (PBL) model (Barge, 2010; Arnseth et al., 2018), which also builds on democratic processes in students' learning groups (Arnseth et al., 2018). Furthermore, using the Aalborg PBL approach, which focuses on a critical and reflective pedagogical approach, could help shift current understanding of game-oriented learning away from linear, solid and content-driven models of learning towards more creative approaches (Savin-Baden, 2014). Aalborg University applies PBL pedagogy in all of its programmes, and an important and fundamental feature of this model is motivational factors (Zhon et al., 2012). However, we have found that even when using the PBL model, students can lack a certain degree of motivation (Reng & Kofoed, 2012). We have also discovered that students in Media Technology education can be highly motivated when developing or using games in their studies (Reng & Schoenau-Fog, 2010). Against this backdrop, we decided to introduce a learning environment that would enhance students' motivation and at the same time give them the competences and skills required in the study regulation (SICT, 2014).

Currently, all technical programmes at Aalborg University are based on PBL, whereby each semester is divided between courses (15 European Credit Transfer System (ECTS) points) and problem-based projects (15 ECTS points). This is also the case for Media Technology, where 100+ students study at each semester. However, in the later stages of Bachelor studies, many students begin to show fatigue and ask for more opportunities to hone their practical skills as opposed to working on standard "academic" reports. They also wonder if their competences are good enough for future employment, particularly as many of them hope to get a job within games industry or interactive media experience companies after graduation. Therefore, the need to design a new and fresh learning environment which reflects the "real world" better has led to rethinking project work for fifth semester Media Technology students. To meet these challenges, some of this chapter's authors interviewed leaders from several successful European game companies about the structure and workflows of their best development teams. Based on these interviews, a new educational format was proposed, namely a game-oriented learning environment, i.e. the purposive game production, which is founded on problem-based production-oriented project work and was intended to let students develop a game in a virtual game company while working as part of a real production team. Three experiments were carried out with this format in 2014 (described in Schoenau-Fog et al., 2015), 2015 and 2016. In the following, we describe the pedagogical approach and background, with a particular focus on motivation and the learning process during purposive game production when working with different procedures and students.

PEDAGOGICAL APPROACH

The purposive game production experiments were based on various pedagogical approaches and theories. We used experience taken from the pedagogical ideas used during all three experiments, and in the following we describe these further.

The pedagogical background is based on Aalborg University's PBL approach. The Medialogy is project- and group-based, and students can gain 15 ECTS points. In order to heighten student motivation and engagement during problem-based project work, as well as to provide them with new knowledge and ability in game production, project planning and project management, the new format contributes a design-based learning approach founded on production-oriented game development, through which they create educational computer games. In other settings, the design-based approach has shown that giving learners an active designer role enables learning and eases knowledge transfer that closely mirrors a future work environment (Savin Baden, 2014; Ke, 2013; Wang & Hannafin, 2005). A design-based approach has furthermore shown good results relating to the development of skills and understanding, helping them formulate solutions to complex and sometimes ill-structured problems (Ke, 2013). According to problem-based and situated learning theories, the design process creates contextualised and authentic learning, because design tasks force students to understand and work in an environment that demands skills and domain knowledge close to a real-work environment (Savin-Baden, 2014). Knowledge and skills required in such situation are also more transferable to future work situations (De Vries, 2006). Design-based learning using "enactivism" is a framework that argues for a close connection between the provision of a learning environment and a learner's capacity for action and perception in knowledge development (Lo, 2012), which seems to fit to our PBL pedagogical approach. Digital game development has been considered and examined as a "powerful learning environment" to stimulate active, autonomous learning via rich contexts and authentic tasks of composition and construction (Robertson, 2008). Moreover, educational game fabrication, which requires content application, can be applied as a "micro-world", akin to a compressed part of a natural universe observed at the microscopic level, where designers or learners get to explore, represent and test their domain knowledge and skills, and to integrate them into the designed game (Mitchell & Saundry, 2007). Furthermore, the knowledge focus in purposive game production exceeds disciplines and is produced in and validated through project work, which is supported by cooperation within the group. We find that design-based learning in general, and purposive game production in particular, is well connected with PBL and project work, which is the pedagogical approach to experiments conducted in the fifth semester of Media Technology studies. The approach holds the potential to use game production as a strong motivational factor, thereby enabling students to gain knowledge from all aspects of this genre. According to self-determination theories, there are strong links between intrinsic motivation and satisfying the need for autonomy, competence development and relatedness; however, people will only be intrinsically motivated to carry out activities that are interesting to them and have the appeal of novelty and a challenge (Ryan & Deci, 2000). Throughout the game production process, the students will gain competence, relatedness, autonomy, experience and time management (Abeysekera & Dawson, 2015) (see Figure 11.1).

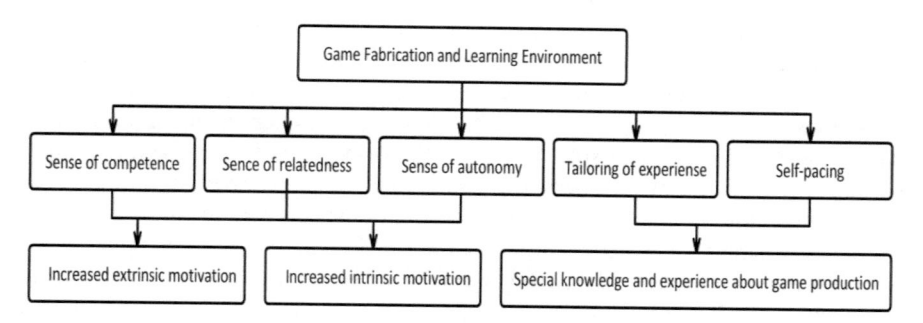

Figure 11.1. Pedagogical elements in the fabrication of games and learning production environment inspired by Abeyseker and Dawson (2015) (from Schoenau-Fog et al., 2015)

Concepts in relation to the development and understanding of game fabrication and learning environments also include theories concentrating on learning in communities of practice and collaborative learning (Lave & Wenger, 1991). Here, the focus is on the potential of situated learning and understanding purposive game production, where knowledge of a topic is mediated through game development (Reng & Schoenau-Fog, 2016).

PURPOSIVE GAME PRODUCTION—A DESIGN-BASED EXPERIMENT

In order to improve the quality of Media Technology education, in recent years we have greatly increased collaboration with both neighbouring universities and industry. During the project work in 2014–2016, as a pedagogical approach to Media Technology studies, we experimented with purposive game production, whereby students in their fifth semester developed games with a meaningful purpose. Through a close partnership with many national and international media companies, we learned about the structure and procedures of many successful development teams. The idea behind these PPG experiments was inspired by these companies, but it was mainly motivated by students' uncertainty about the usefulness and application of their qualifications. Students reaching the end of their Bachelor education seemed to have a growing concern about transitioning from the skills and abilities they had learned during education to the needs and requirements of industry. In essence, they believed they needed more in-depth practical knowledge about an individual skill or discipline, in order to understand what is required to master it fully. Furthermore, and perhaps more tellingly, they were uncertain and not easily convinced that our candidate educations would offer this depth of practical knowledge while still holding a strong academic focus, although many went on to run successful projects at both Bachelor and Master levels, a good number of which have resulted in published peer-reviewed papers presented at international conferences.

In order to create a format that would: (a) give full production control to the teacher, (b) give students an experience as close as possible to being in a company; (c) stay within the requirements and rules of current study plans and (d) be feasible to execute within a very limited time frame of 15 ECTS points for one semester, we settled on the format described below (Figure 11.2). Consequently, the students would have their semester split into two. First, they would have a three-month period in which they would be part of a 'virtual' company working in purposive game production. Second, a one-month academic project would involve students splitting into smaller 4–6-person project groups and running a semester theme-based project using their product (the purposive game) from game production. This second part would develop further by adding an academic and theoretical framework to the production process, which would include performing a user test following the methods and requirements of fifth semester learning goals.

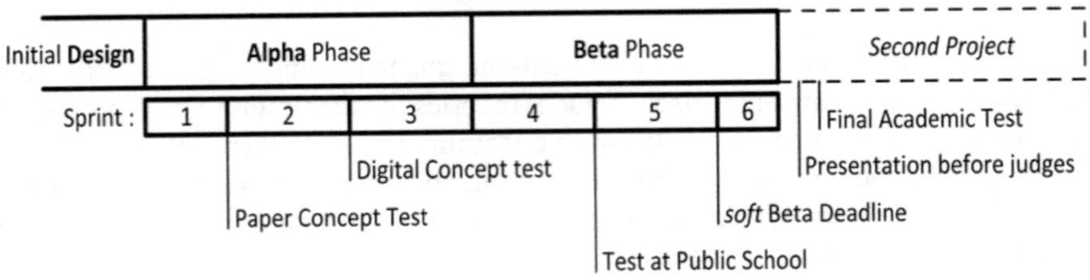

Initial **Design**	**Alpha** Phase	**Beta** Phase	*Second Project*

Sprint :	1	2	3	4	5	6	Final Academic Test

Digital Concept test

Paper Concept Test

Presentation before judges

soft Beta Deadline

Test at Public School

Figure 11.2. The purposive game production timetable (2014)

Caused directly by the short timeframe, we had to give the students a simplified timetable with only a few of the traditional phases used in game production. Since we knew the students were in an unfamiliar environment in so many aspects compared to their traditional semester projects, we decided to keep a fairly high amount of regularly spaced deadlines, to ensure that mismanaged activities were detected early (see Figure 11.2).

In order to assist the management of the production, we chose to use some form of flexible method, such as SCRUM, which is used to manage and control production development (Schwaber, 2004). Most SCRUM models function through a project owner role, which is part of a company but not part of the development team. The project owner is placed between the development team and the customer and sets up the requirements for the product. By giving ourselves (the supervisors) these roles, we would have full control over production but none of the daily management tasks, which should be done by the students.

The most important requirements for the games developed in 2014–2016 were:

- The game must be meaningful and purposive, built to enhance the teaching of a real, critical and important topic or theme.
- The game should be based on valid information and reflect the latest research in the field. However, fictional elements could be used to make the game more engaging.
- The game must give players an experience that would facilitate a fact-based discussion about the topic and its possible solutions.
- The game had to meet professional standards that would allow students to use this example when applying for future jobs.
- The game had to be of a quality and integrity that would allow it to be used in our game-researchers' future work.

The 2014 Experiment

The procedure for the first experiment in 2014 was that students should not be selected based on skill level or previous grades. All interested students could apply for the positions in a mode of game production about which they felt the most passionate. Before they went on their summer holiday, we informed them that they would receive an email with a job offer from our new virtual game development company. A few weeks later, we distributed an email, giving them the chance to apply for one of the positions in the game development team. We required that they send a portfolio, relevant to the role for which they were applying, and, additionally, accept the terms and conditions of a 'contract', saying that they would work full-time, including attending all semester lessons and fulfilling their course duties.

A few weeks before the end of the summer holiday, we started to receive a series of unusual emails. The students were highly motivated and asked if they could be informed about the requirements of purposive game production, because they wanted to skip the last few weeks of their holiday, if we allowed them to start early. Based on the fact that they had to do a unique project in comparison to other students on the same semester, we agreed to give them a kick-off meeting 10 days before the official semester start.

The number of students who fulfilled the requirements from the application process was 25, and the distribution of roles was also almost exactly as desired, so every applicant was given the position of their choice. Later, more students from other (more experienced) semesters joined as well. The theme for the game in 2014 was 'Global Warming'—an educational game for eighth-grade school children (Schoenau-Fog et al., 2015).

To provide another incentive to perform their best and meet the final production deadline, we called in a group of seven game company CEOs to judge the quality of the final product. Even though the quality of this finished product was not nearly as high as required for a professional company, some of the students were offered jobs by these CEOs in the weeks following the final presentation.

In order to continue the development of the concept and framework, we also ran a similar experiment by organising the students in the purposive game production group in 2015, where the theme was 'The Challenges of Virtual Reality Technology'. We did not collect any survey data for this year; however, observations from supervision meetings support the findings of the 2014 and 2016 experiments, as it was apparent that the students were highly motivated, as they worked a lot of extra hours to make their games and projects as good as possible. The major challenge of the 2015 production was the technical complexity of networking in the game, which needed the simultaneous presence of three persons in virtual reality (Timcenko et al., 2017).

The 2016 Experiment

In 2016, we followed up with the third experiment, based on the experiences from the previous two experiments. Instead of the successful application process used in the first experiment, we decided to see what would happen if we left the formation of the team entirely to the students, which is the standard procedure at Aalborg University, whereby, each semester, they form their own project groups of approximately six persons. The purpose of this third experiment was to see if the students were able to form a 20-person production team on their own—as in their traditional group-forming process.

Group-forming can be very complex and difficult for students, since it could be a high-risk strategy for them to leave their 'old' group in the hope of a position in the production team, especially because if they wanted to change their mind and work in a traditional project group, they would have to go back and either find a group that would take them in or form a new six-person group with those students not yet in a group.

Students interested in joining the production team were given a list, describing the profile of each of the 20 positions they needed to fill to form the team, and then they were asked to isolate themselves from the rest of the students. A group of approximately 30 dared to join the team-forming process, and very quickly, they ended up with two 15-person groups. After a long debate, a few left to join one of the traditional six-person groups, and 12 of the best-qualified students suddenly formed two six-person groups and left the process to join in with traditional project work. The remaining group of students was now forced to take in anybody they could find. The final production team ended up five positions short and consisted of only 15 students, along with a very mixed set of skills. This group also included several persons who had not been accepted into any other project group, as their peers viewed them as weak candidates. However, the production group was instructed to accept everybody who showed interest.

The roles of the students in the 2016 team were as follows: producer/production manager, lead programmer, assistant programmer, lead sound designer, assistant sound designer, 2D art lead, 2D artist, 3D art lead, 3D artist, 3D models, 3D animator and creative designer.

The theme of the 2016 PGP was "The Internet of Things", and the resulting game became an experience which let the player encounter various challenges when all appliances are connected. The game was aimed at public schools and colleges, where teachers, pupils and students could use it to initiate discussions about the topic and the challenges of using new technology.

The two experiments had a different starting process and also differed in numbers of students, but the procedure and aim of the game production, as well as the curricula, were the same.

METHODS

We used an exploratory case study approach (Stebbins, 2001; Remenyi, 2013), in combination with a descriptive, mixed-methods case study (e.g. Stake, 1995; Yin, 2008), to investigate the students' results and experiences. The parameters of the study are reflected in the survey questions and elaborated in the interviews.

This examination explored the process of learning by design within the context of purposive game development, project management, planning and production. In particular, it compared the experiences gathered from the 2014 and 2016 experiments and addressed the following research questions:

1. Did participating in game development enhance the motivation to learn and study further in general, and in particular within Media Technology?
2. How did the differences in the group-forming process influence students' attitudes to working in big groups?
3. How did the different aspects in the game production process provide knowledge and understanding of various tasks and other valuable skills (mentioned in Figure 11.1)?

Even though the two experiments differed in several ways (the pre-procedure and the number of students), we looked for results regarding motivation, learning and production experience, and to determine if the game production concept based on problem-based product-oriented project work is sufficiently strong when applied in different situations, and is able to show the same results.

Data Collection

In order to acquire data from the two experiments, we conducted a number of supervision meetings with the students during the semester, in which we enquired about their experiences (2014, 2015 and 2016). Furthermore, we distributed a survey at the end of the game production phases in 2014 and 2016, in which we asked them about their motivation levels before, during and after production, as well as learning outcomes and questions related to their experiences. In order to verify the results of the survey, we conducted an interview with the whole team at the end of the production periods. The data were analysed according to motivation, learning outcome, new skills and generic competences related to game production experience.

RESULTS

In the following, the results from the survey, as well as observations and interviews from 2014 and 2016, are presented.

Survey Results

In 2014, 25 students participated in the survey, four of which were female and 21 male. In 2016, all 15 students in the group participated, four of which were female and 11 male.

Motivation

The survey included a series of questions asking the students to rate their motivation or learning outcome compared to previous semesters on an 11-point scale (0 = much less/none, 5 = same, 10 = much more/very high). Questions in the form of Likert items are summarised in Table 11.1. In the survey, there were eight additional open-ended questions, which we used to triangulate the numerical results and make better sense of them.

It is clear from question Que1 in Table 11.1 (*"How high would you rate your motivation at the beginning of the project?"*) that the students' anticipation was very high in 2014 (median=9, lower quartile Q1=7, upper quartile Q3=10), and almost the same in 2016 (median=9, Q1=8, Q3=10), which was expected for a newly hyped, production-oriented style of project work in 2014. The results for 2016 were also as expected, as the students either fulfilled their wish to work on a bigger product or were accepted into a project group (weak students). The challenge was to see if, when using "standard-procedure" group-forming, the students would maintain their motivation throughout the project period. More importantly, we were curious to see if the PGP format would also increase their motivation in relation to their next project and education as a whole in 2016. The questions used to check these aspects were: (*Que2*): "*How high would you rate your motivation at the end of the Alpha phase of project?*" (median=7, Q1=5, Q2=8 for 2014 and median=5, Q1=3, Q3=7 for 2016) and (*Que3*) "*How high would you rate your motivation right now (end of Beta)?*" (median=6, Q1=4, Q3=7 for 2014 and median=5, Q1=5, Q3=8.5 for 2016). Although the results are quite similar, there is a subtle difference. Motivation for project work in 2014 was the lowest at the end of the Beta phase, i.e. it was constantly falling during the process, while in 2016, it was lowest after the Alpha phase and then increased as the game fabrication came to an end. In fact, students from the 2016 team were much less motivated during the middle of the production (Q2) than the 2014 team (see Figure 11.3).

From the interviews in both 2014 and 2016, it is clear that many of the students had worked harder than on any other previous projects. There is no doubt that they paced themselves to reach their own production goals, which were supported by being a member of a team with a common goal. The SCRUM system, with task lists, internal self-monitoring and the weekly presentation of work-effort graphs for all, made it impossible to 'free-ride' unnoticed. With the newly enlarged team, communication and management became much bigger issues than in traditional project work allocated in previous semesters. From both the weekly status presentations to the project owners and the interviews, the students clearly stated that they were surprised and somewhat demotivated by the effort it requires to manage such large teams. An additional explanation could be that in 2014, the students felt somehow frustrated when the quality of the game they produced did not meet the initial hype, while in 2016, the students were just very happy to put together a playable version of their game.

The changes in motivation throughout the phases also clearly depict the onset of fatigue towards the end, as shown in Figure 11.3 (Que1-Que3) for 2014, though we also see a novel level of enthusiasm when the Beta phase was successfully finalised for 2016.

In addition, when the students were asked about their motivation to join another similar project in the future (Que4), the cohort from 2014 was almost as motivated as at the beginning of the project. This is a significant answer, because the survey was conducted when they were most fatigued (at the end of the production process). Students from PGP 2016 were much less motivated to work on a product again—most likely as a consequence of working in an under-staffed team with several weak participants. The very 'high' boxplot for Question 4 in 2016 (lower quartile 3, upper quartile 9, on 11-level scale) indicates various opinions, which could be explained by the already mentioned fact that the students in 2016 were of very mixed abilities and working cultures.

As stated earlier, one of the main goals of the PGP format was to investigate whether the flexibilities and production-oriented possibilities of the PBL-based semester projects would increase students' desire to continue studying. Questions (Que9 + Que10), in combination with the interviews, aimed to clarify this point:

Table 11.1. Results from the survey questions
(0 = much less/none, 5 = same/middle, 10 = much more/very high)

Question No.	Question text	2014 Median	2014 Lower quartile Q1	2014 Upper Quartile Q3	2016 Median	2016 Lower Quartile Q1	2016 Upper Quartile Q3
Que1	How high would you rate your motivation at the beginning of the project?	9	7	10	9	8	10
Que2	How high would you rate your motivation at the end of the Alpha phase of project?	7	5	8	5	3	7
Que3	How high would you rate your motivation right NOW?	6	4	7	5	5	8.5
Que4	What is the possibility that you would join a production semester project in the future?	9	7	10	7	3	9
Que5	How much do you feel you have improved your skills/crafts in this project, compared to earlier semester projects?	7	6	9	8	7	8
Que6	How much do you feel you have learned about the challenges of managing a large production group in this project, compared to earlier projects?	9	8	10	9	8	10
Que7	How would you rate your skills in your role before the project launch?	5	3	6	5	3	6
Que8	How would you rate your skills in your role right now?	7	6	8	8	7	8
Que9	How high would you rate your motivation to continue studying Media Technology at the end of the final semester?	6	5	8	6	4	6.5
Que10	How high would you rate your motivation to continue studying Media Technology right now?	8	7	9.5	6	5	8

2014

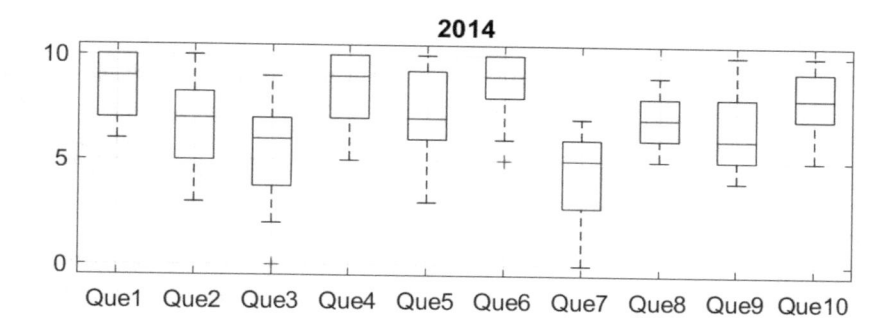

2016

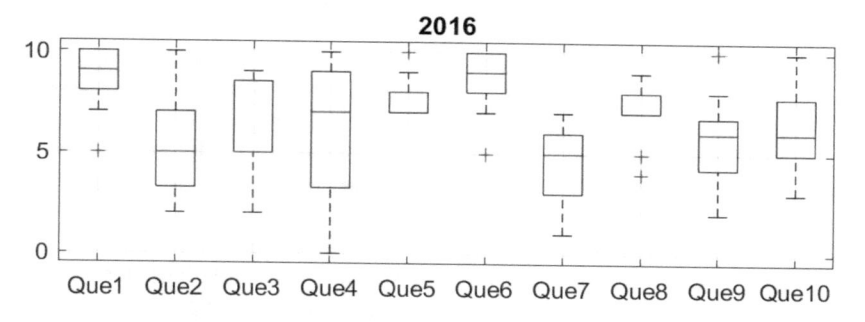

Figure 11.3. Motivation and learning outcome. Questions Que1-Que10 are described in Table 11.1

(*Que9*): "*How high would you rate your motivation to continue studying Media Technology at the end of the final semester?*" (median=6, Q1=5, Q3=8 in 2014, and median=6, Q1=4, Q3=6.5 in 2016).

(*Que10*): "*How high would you rate your motivation to continue studying Media Technology right now?*" (median=8, Q1=7, Q3=9.7 in 2014, and median=6, Q1=5, Q3=8 in 2016).

As shown in Figure 11.3, there is an indication that the motivation to continue the study indeed increased from Que9 to Que10 in 2014. In 2016, though, the increase is very subtle. However, both results indicate that students may become more motivated to study after a PGP production-oriented activity. Again, the 2016 team members were less motivated than the 2014 team to continue their studies in Media Technology, which may the result of problems with weaker students joining the team in 2016.

When looking at the above results, it can thus also be concluded that the results indicate that students had greater motivation to continue their studies after the PGP production, although the difference was less among the 2016 group with weaker group members.

Learning and Skills

One of the clear benefits of a production-oriented project format with clear roles is that it allows students to gain a much deeper understanding of a single craft/skillset. Naturally, there is also the negative effect that they do not get any practice in the areas they do not select. We specifically selected the fifth semester for this experiment, since it is so close to the candidate studies, where students select a discipline to focus on and master, before applying for their first job.

The students rated Question 6, *"How much do you feel you have learned about the challenges of managing a large production group in this project, compared to earlier projects?"*, as very important and relevant to their learning outcomes for the semester. In spite of many difficulties in communication and management, caused mostly by inexperience, this question scored very positive answers for both years. This was even more important for the 2016 cohort, since, due to the group-forming process, many students who had not wanted to work together and did not appreciate each other due to previous year's experiences and conflicts still needed to make a team. The process was very rough, which can be confirmed by answers to open-ended questions, and yet the students graded the experience as an important learning curve and not a disturbance.

While supervising both years, it became clear that the increased team size forced the students to abandon their usual simple management technique and search for a more stable and professional solution. The learning outcome in this area of the production was also much higher than expected during the planning stage. Students in both years rated their learning outcome in the management field much higher than in earlier projects (2014: median=9, Q1=8, Q3=10 and 2016: median=9, Q1=8, Q3=10).

When questioned on their perceived skill levels, before and after the production, students from both years, on average, felt they had increased their skills in their chosen role (see Que7-Que8 and Figure 11.4). Furthermore, Figure 11.4 shows a progression for acquired skills from Que7 and Que8, in that there is a significant difference between perceived skills before and after production. This can be seen in Que7: *"How would you rate your skills in your role before the project launch (0–10)?"* (median=5, Q1=3, Q3=6 in both 2014 and 2016) when compared with Que8: *"How would you rate your skills in your role at the end of the production?"* (median=7, Q1=6, Q3=8 in 2014 and median=8, Q1=7, Q3=8 in 2016).

It is interesting to note that although both yearly groups rated very differently according to supervisors' opinions (reflected also by grades), the students subjectively evaluated their skills at the beginning and the end of the project with almost identical answers!

In addition, when directly comparing increased skill level to the increase of earlier semesters, there is a clear tendency that both sets of students felt they had increased their skills/crafts significantly as a result of the new format: (Que5): *"How much do you feel you have improved your skills/crafts in this project, compared to*

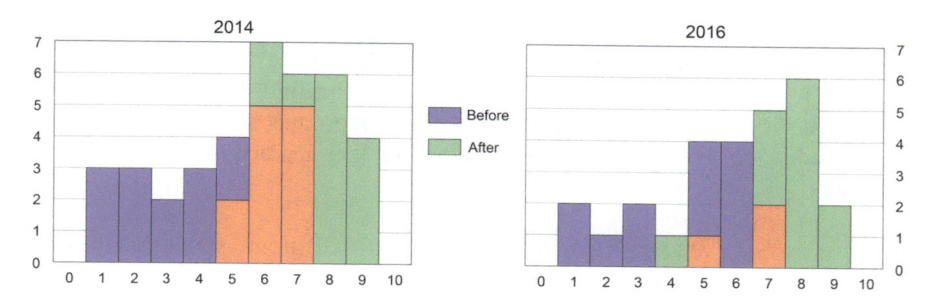

Figure 11.4. Self-reported skills before (Que7) and after production (Que8) for 2014 and 2016

earlier semester projects?" (median=7, Q1=6, Q3=9 and 2016: median=8, Q1=7, Q3=8).

The results presented above show that the PGP production format clearly gives the students a significantly higher perceived learning outcome than the traditional, smaller PBL-based semester projects.

Focus Group Results

In November 2014, we conducted an interview with the first group of students who participated in the purposive game production. Twenty-five participated in the focus-group discussion, which was led by the authors. Four of them were female and 21 male. The focus group interview was semi-structured based on the interest we had to verify the survey results and to get more detailed explanations for students' responses. When the participants were asked to provide one word that summarised their experience, they discussed the matter among themselves and replied with the following: a good learning experience, hectic (in a positive way), hard, confusing/chaotic, frustrating, awesome, fun and "a different, good concept".

In addition to the interviews conducted in 2014, the authors conducted a similar focus group interview in December 2016. All 15 students participated in the interview (four female, 11 male) and the resulting themes at that session were: skills, experience in the production pipeline, opportunities, focus, challenge, motivation, fun, confusing/chaotic, scale of production, stressful, tiredness, management, many meetings and communication issues, collaboration, a positive experience and frustration.

The statements used in 2014 and 2016, when describing the choice of themes, are presented in detail in the following subsections.

A good learning experience/skills/experience: Students stated that they learned a lot from the project, especially in relation to new tools, skills, communication, collaboration, production management, resource management, working in a company, defining a target group, working with a production process and following a professional production pipeline, SCRUM, using each other, having the freedom to learn and doing everything by themselves. Likewise, they learned how to focus on a specific problem, see it as a challenge and find solutions. Everybody stated that they were motivated to work again on a product such as the purposive game production. Half of the students stated that they learned more than in other semesters.

Hectic/stressful: Students from the 2014 and 2016 PGP groups stated that they had been overly ambitious with the scale of the game, as their skills were not at a level to match their vision. Deadlines were not communicated clearly and there were many communication problems between the different sub-teams, while the production lacked structure due to management challenges. Furthermore, they did a lot of 'all-nighters' on the project, i.e. they kept working through the night. The leads also stated that managing the team had been very time-consuming. Finally, on a positive note, they mentioned that they had learned to listen to each other and to solve problems by themselves when problems arose, which also relates to Figure 11.1, where self-pacing and relatedness are important for continued motivation.

Hard: 'Tough but good'. Most students thought that the project was 'Awesome, but hard'. They faced some challenges in understanding how some of the different roles fitted in to the process, and the leaders faced challenges in dealing with such a large amount of responsibility, as exemplified in this response: 'To give and to take responsibility'. On the other hand, assistants often did not always have an overarching view of what to do, and so the leads would have to take over and manage their study colleagues' work load. Moreover, it was not possible to curtail the projects' lofty ambitions before it was too late, and for some it was too much responsibility to be a lead and a scrum-master at the same time. It was also hard to follow the semester courses whilst involved in the project.

Confusing: Organisation could have been better, with students in both 2014 and 2016 feeling the project had been somewhat chaotic and resembling "management hell". The structure was not set up from the start, and SCRUM should have been learned beforehand, but there were also communication problems at the beginning of the projects and there were too many tasks to complete simultaneously. It was hard to take design decisions initially, and the production pipeline did not work at the start, with people changing roles throughout. Having a production team with more than twenty members were also considered too many, students reported in 2014. In 2016, there were only 15 students, who stated that there had not been enough group members. Based on this particular finding, we would recommend a group size of around 20 in future.

Frustration: For most students, it was frustrating that the final game did not end up as they wanted, due to setting the bar too high and the low technical skill level of most team members. In the programming team, for instance, four were experienced programmers, while the other four were new to programming. Nonetheless, the students were also very proud of what they produced in both year groups when showing them to their respective jury, and even though they were frustrated, they kept working hard and dedicated themselves to solving problems.

Awesome, new opportunities, fun and a different, good concept: students stated in 2014 that it was a good initiative, due to the possibility of working with other semesters (Master students). Additionally, they enjoyed a more personal relationship with other students on other semesters and gained new friends with other interests, because within the large group, smaller teams formed based on their roles in the production. It was also good to learn to work together, and they felt that they networked more and had a common goal to make something bigger, to finish something. While learning from other students, team members gained a lot of experience, which they thought would be valuable in the future. They also stated that they really enjoyed ownership of the project and that it was good that they were in charge themselves. In 2016, the students also stated that they appreciated the concept, albeit they were more challenged, due to the weaker students in the group.

Other Comments from the 2016 Interview

During the 2016 interview, the students also provided other comments. For example, all participants should have some basic knowledge in their field before they are involved (in 2016, there was no application process, so supervisors had no chance to make sure that those signing up for the production actually had the required skills). They also felt that each department was short of one or two people as well as an overall game designer who could work on how to create game mechanics etc. This is in line with the suggested size of the group, which is 20, while in 2016, the group only consisted of 15 people.

Initially, there was sparse communication between the design and programming teams, so it is important to encourage programmers to talk with level designers in the early phases. If there had been more people on the team (as suggested, around 20) it would be beneficial to have a game director, who could lead the team in an overall artistic direction. Students also remarked that it would help to have a bit more knowledge about game design/development before endeavouring to make the project a success.

As the students are still doing traditional semester courses at the same time, it is very important to coordinate with other course hand-ins (which requires a lot of work on certain times), and if the production is delayed, there should be consequences and the supervisors should "boss up more" during short. constructive feedback meetings with every department. Finally, with the short time span of the production run, no code was reusable and there was no time for UML diagrams, so next time, the team should be given time for the latter task and to clean up the code.

Feedback from the Jury

In 2016, the "Internet of Things" team received feedback from game designers from the game industry, among which were some from IO Interactive (e.g. "Hitman"). All students expressed that they learned a lot from this professional feedback. The main message for the team was to always ask: "What is the player experience? And how is that experience going to be designed? In other words, design is key!" Another valuable piece of feedback was that the game in development should be played by members of different departments every day, and that all team members should be able to work in the game engine (e.g. Unity). Finally, even in a professional production setting it is hard to plan everything from the outset, because "When we are done, we know how it should have been done".

CONCLUSION

It can be concluded that the group-organized purposive game production does have the flexibility and framework to establish a game-oriented learning/teaching environment which could enhance students' motivation for further studies and at the same time enable them to gain knowledge and experience of larger projects, especially from a management point of view. The PGP is an example of a problem-based production-oriented project work learning activity, and this approach furthermore supports students' different interests within the semester study regulations and provides experiences very close to a real production setting.

The main findings of the two experiments, the surveys, observations and interviews are that students learned a lot and a game development-based learning strategy seems equally efficient and yet demanding. Their motivation to continue working fell during the process, but it increased towards the end. Many students furthermore still wanted to work on another similar production, and their motivations to continue their studies were indicated as being higher in both 2014 and 2016. They also experienced a lot of frustration, due to the overwhelming challenges involved in managing a team of more than the usual five or six team members, causing them to understand truly the importance of good project management. The students learned through experience that sufficient communication, collaboration and the planning and coordination of the game production as a whole are very important, and that they have to be better equipped regarding these aspects. These reflections might be the best starting point for new learning processes—a notion emphasised further by the fact that members of the jury committees offered jobs to some of the students. In answer to the claim that it requires an extensive amount of knowledge to build a knowledge-mediating purposive game, we witnessed that the students—on their own initiative—found it necessary to build their own wiki and knowledge databases, in order to structure the large amount of research gathered on the themes of the games, i.e. climate change and the internet of things.

Based on the pedagogical approach illustrated in Figure 11.1, we can conclude that the students' sense of learning new competences, their sense of relatedness through cooperation and teamwork and the sense of being an important part of game production strengthened their extrinsic as well as their intrinsic motivation. Furthermore, the specific knowledge and experience related to the production process, as well as their wish to work very hard to accomplish the different tasks, gave them a very special experience and knowledge about game development. They also praised the format, for giving them the chance to focus on the craft/skill they were planning to focus on in their candidate studies.

In summary, we can conclude that the new PGP learning environment format, together with the elements in our PPP pedagogical model, gave the cohort in our study the impetus to continue their education as well as special knowledge and experience about specific game development elements and in general about professional production pipelines.

The findings from the supervision, survey and interviews can be used to summarise ideas on how future purposive projects may be organised even better.

Best Practice Framework

To sum up the findings and the experience taken from the purposive game production, the following best-practice framework includes a list of requirements to consider. The framework may be used as inspiration for similar problem-based production-oriented project work learning activities based on game-oriented learning and design.

- It is advisable to let students go through some kind of application process, in order to recruit those who are motivated and ready to work harder in the group.
- Maximum 20 students per group, during their first experience of problem-based production-oriented project work.
- Important roles: manager (head of the production team and link to supervisors. Also, given the power to fire any team-member not following the rules) and art director (directs the overall creative production of the game).
- Introduction course to overall game production as well as production management tools and SCRUM, so that the team knows what it is, before the production starts.
- The game design should be decided on and fixed at an early stage. This can be done by making all non-leads into game designers in the first week or two, following which a dedicated game designer (manages the design of game mechanics, challenges, balance, etc.) takes over a little later.
- Roles and responsibilities in different departments should be clear.
- Students may be able to choose their own teams based on portfolios and early discussions.
- A good management tool is essential.
- Develop ideas across the different roles.
- The leads should have the power to decide (democracy is not always the solution).

- Project owners (supervisors) may help a lot by supervising the group closely and by setting clear goals, requirements and demands. It is essential that they make sure they give feedback often, and it is okay to be "bossy".
- Latest versions of the game ('builds') should be available all the time, so team members can test the game continuously.
- The group-forming process could have a major impact on work, learning outcomes and motivation, during and after the semester.
- The group should meticulously evaluate each member's skills before setting arbitrary targets.

In conclusion, the purposive game production experiment illustrates that there is a lot of potential in using purposive game production and problem-based production-oriented project work as a learning environment.

Future work will focus even more on improving the context of the productions and the procedure, in order to make it even more beneficial for students and their ongoing education. Another step will be to apply the PPP/PGP concept in other study areas within Humanities, Engineering and other educational systems outside universities (Reng & Kofoed, 2016; Weitze, 2018) and bring it into the framework of the Scandinavian tradition (Arnseth et al., 2018).

ACKNOWLEDGEMENTS

We would like to thank the students involved in the purposive game production projects between 2014 and 2016 for their energy, engagement and valuable feedback during game fabrication.

REFERENCES

Abeysekera, L., & Dawson, P. (2015). Motivation and cognitive load in the flipped classroom: Definition, rationale and a call for research. *Higher Education Research & Development, 34*(1), 1–14.

Amseth, H. C., Hanghøj, T., Henriksen, T. D., Misfeldt, M., Ramberg, R., & Selander, S. (2018). *Introduction to games and education: Designs in and for learning* (NORDGOLD forthcoming).

Armstrong, S., Brown, S., & Thompson, G. (2013). *Motivating students: Staff and educational series.* London: Routledge.

Barge, S. (2010). *Principles of problem and project-based learning: The Aalborg PBL model* (Online). Retrieved from http://www.aau.dk/digitalAssets/62/62747_pbl_aalborg_modellen.pdf

Crocco, F., Offenholley, K., & Hernandez, C. (2016). A proof-of-concept study of game-based learning in higher education. *Simulation & Gaming, 47*(4), 403–422.

De Vries, E. (2006). Students' construction of external representations in design-based learning situations. *Learning and Instruction, 16*, 213–222.

Eurostat. (2016). Retrieved from http://ec.europa.eu/eurostat/statistics-explained/index.php/ICT_specialists_-_statistics_on_hard-to-fill_vacancies_in_enterprises

Hwang, G. J., & Wu, P. H. (2012). Advancement and trends in digital game-based learning research: A review of publications in selected journals from 2001 to 2010. *British Journal of Educational Technology, 43*(1), e6–e10.

Ke, F. (2013). An implementation of design-based learning through creating educational computer games: A case study on mathematics learning during design and computing. *Computers & Education, 73*, 26–39.

Lave, J., & Wenger, E. (1991). *Situated learning: Legitimate peripheral participation.* Cambridge: Cambridge University Press.

Lo, Q. (2012). Understanding enactivism: A study of affordances and constraints of engaging practicing teachers as digital game designers. *Educational Technology Research & Development, 60,* 785–806.

Mitchell, J., Kelleher, H., & Saundry, C. (2007). A multimedia mathematics project in a teacher education program. In L. F. Darling, G. Erickson, & A. Clarke (Eds.), *Collective improvisation in a teacher education community* (pp. 101–118). Dordrecht: Springer Science Business Media.

Remenyi, D. (2013). *Case study research.* Reading: Academic Conferences and Publishing International Limited.

Reng, L., & Kofoed, L. B. (2012). *Enhance students' motivation to learn programming: The development process of course design.* Proceedings from CDIO 2012 Conference, Brisbane, Australia.

Reng, L., & Kofoed, L. B. (2016, October). Game production: Teachers' challenges in a Danish Public School. In T. Connolly & L. Boyle (Eds.), *European conference on games-based learning* (p. 552). Reading: Academic Conferences International Limited.

Reng, L., & Schoenau-Fog, H. (2010). Using problem-based learning and game design to motivate non-technical students to engage in technical learning. In C. Swertz & M. Wagner (Eds.), *GAME PLAY SOCIETY: Contributions to contemporary computer game studies* (pp. 27–39). München: Kopaed VerlagsGmbH.

Reng, L., & Schoenau-Fog, H. (2016). The game enhanced learning model. In T. Connolly & L. Boyle (Eds.), *Proceedings of the 10th European conference on games based learning.* Reading: Academic Conferences and Publishing International Limited.

Robertson, J., & Howells, C. (2008). Computer game design: Opportunities for successful learning. *Computers & Education, 50*(2), 559–578.

Ryan, M. R., & Deci, L. E. (2000). Self-determination theory and the facilitation of intrinsic motivation, social development and well-being. *American Psychologist, 55*(1), 68–78.

Savin-Barden, M. (2014). Using problem-based learning: New constellations for the 21st century. *Journal of Excellence in College Teaching, 25,* 197–219.

Schoenau-Fog, H., Reng, L., & Kofoed, L. B. (2015, October). Fabrication of games and learning: A purposive game production. In T. Connolly & L. Boyle (Eds.), *European Conference on games based learning* (p. 480). Reading: Academic Conferences International Limited.

Schwaber, K. (2004). *Agile project management with scrum.* Redmond: Microsoft Press.

Sitzmann, T. (2011). A meta-analytic examination of the instructional effectiveness of computer-based simulation games. *Personnel Psychology, 64*(2), 489–528.

Stake, R. (1995). *The art of case research.* Thousand Oaks, CA: Sage Publications.

Star, J. R., Chen, J., & Dede, C. (2015). Applying motivation theory to the design of game-based learning environments. In J. Torbeyns, E. Lehtinen, & J. Elen (Eds.), *Describing and studying domain-specific serious games* (pp. 83–91). Cham: Springer International Publishing.

Stebbins, R. A. (2001). *Exploratory research in the social sciences.* Thousand Oaks, CA: Sage Publications.

SICT. (2014). *Study regulation* (online). Retrieved from http://www.en.sict.aau.dk/digitalAssets/91/91650_ bsc-medialogi-2014.pdf

Timcenko, O., Kofoed, L. B., Schoenau-Fog, H., & Reng, L. (2017, July). *Purposive game production in educational setup: Investigating team collaboration in virtual reality* (pp. 184–191). International Conference on Human-Computer Interaction, Springer, Cham.

Unity. (2017). *Game engine.* Retrieved from https://unity3d.com/

US Bureau of Labour Statistics. (2017). Retrieved from https://www.bls.gov/ooh/computer-and-information-technology/software-developers.htm#tab-6

Wang, F., & Hannafin, M. J. (2005). Design-based research and technology-enhanced learning environment. *Educational Technology Research and Development, 53*(4), 5–23.

Wang, L. C., & Chen, M. P. (2010). The effects of game strategy and preference-matching on flow experience and programming performance in game-based learning. *Innovation and Teaching International, 47*(1), 39–52.

Weitze, C. L. (2018). Learning and design processes in a gamified learning design: Students creating curriculum based digital learning games. In H. C. Arnseth, T. Hanghøj, T. D. Henriksen, M. Misfeldt, S. Selander, & R. Ramberg (Eds.), *Games and education: Designs in and for learning* (NORDGOLD forthcoming).

Woo, J.-C. (2014). Digital game-based learning supports students motivation, cognitive success, and performance outcomes. *Educational Technology & Society, 17*(3), 291–307.

Yang, Y.-T. C. (2012). Building virtual cities, inspiring intelligent citizens: Digital games for developing students' problem solving and learning motivation. *Computers & Education, 59*(2), 365–377.

Yin, V. K. (2008). *Case study research: Design and methods.* Thousand Oaks, CA: Sage Publications.

Zhon, C., Kolmos, A., & Dalsgaard Nielsen, J. F. (2012). A problem and Project-Based Learning (PBL) approach to motivate group creativity in engineering educations. *International Journal of Engineering Education, 28*(1), 3–16.

INDEX